Nearer

Nearer

Essays

Arthur Saltzman

Parlor Press
West Lafayette, Indiana
www.parlorpress.com

Parlor Press LLC, West Lafayette, Indiana 47906

Library of Congress Cataloging-in-Publication Data

Saltzman, Arthur M. (Arthur Michael), 1953-
  Nearer : essays / Arthur Saltzman.
    p. cm.
  ISBN 1-932559-73-6 (acid-free paper) -- ISBN 1-932559-72-8
(pbk. : acid-free paper) -- ISBN 1-932559-74-4 (Adobe eBook)
  I. Title.
  AC8.S225 2006
  081--dc22
                                        2006002762

Printed on acid-free paper.
Cover and book design by David Blakesley
Cover photograph: "Hubble's Sharpest View of the Orion Nebula."
NASA,ESA, M. Robberto (Space Telescope Science Institute/ESA)
and the Hubble Space Telescope Orion Treasury Project Team

Parlor Press, LLC is an independent publisher of scholarly and
trade titles in print and multimedia formats. This book is available
in paperback, cloth and Adobe eBook formats from Parlor Press
on the WWW at http://www.parlorpress.com. For submission information or to find out about Parlor Press publications, write to
Parlor Press, 816 Robinson St., West Lafayette, Indiana, 47906, or
e-mail editor@parlorpress.com.

For Joy
and the search for the third thing

Contents

Contents

Nearer

Sure, he thought, back on the highway, the manageable ordinary. And where was it to be found?

Under the unicorn fast asleep.

—from *The Franchiser*, by Stanley Elkin

Standing on Fishes

Before we knew better, before we knew worse, before we knew there was worse to know, we roamed all over the city, unattended, self-possessed, charmed. We were probably no more ingeniously self-destructive in our derring-do than today's kids, but a relative absence of adult supervision allowed us to do more daring than they do now. Contemporary children are virtually encysted in care, their time mortgaged and their activities cultivated in wholesome programs and parent-patrolled clubs, where mischief, like bacteria, is pretty much neutralized. But we were blessedly abandoned to our own devices. Back then we did not worry about the traffic turning against us as we pedaled into its teeth. There was nothing on the news about abduction to worry anyone's parents. In fact, you could ride past the grocery store and see a line of buggies parked outside, all filled with unsponsored babies, dazed and writhing, while their oblivious mothers shopped in peace. Vigilance in those days was reserved for casseroles. "Be home by dinner" was the only caution that accompanied us, eager and incognito, out the door.

Occasionally, someone was late getting back home, so vexed and sundry mothers brought out the remote controls. Mrs. Green went to the porch with a policeman's whistle taken from Mr. Green, who was a cop. (But he did not bother to lend her a nightstick or issue her a sidearm to deter intrusion, not in our neighborhood, not in the youth we knew.) Mrs. Teitelbaum blared the hour from the megaphone Mr. Teitelbaum used for coaching his Little League team. Mrs. Deutsch resorted to the air horn her husband took to Bear games. One by one, the dispersed children came back to their keeping. Mostly we returned without prompting, just in time to wash up, and not one mom on the block was curious about the intervening hours we had spent away—an indifference we reciprocated. There was no confusion of realms: during meals and sleep, parents and children occupied the same general air spaces but seldom one another's attention. It was common, natural, and, in the urban America that preceded televised child psychologists and *Parents* magazine, good enough.

One of the places we'd target was Variety Fair, a dime store whose distance—a good mile and a half from any address of ours—was further inducement to go there. The stock at Variety Fair defied all organizational and fiscal logic—indeed, the business has not survived, retail's evolutionary forces having transformed the site several times since I was young—but for explorers with nothing but afternoon to do in, there were treasures to be had. Variety Fair held the cut-rate spoils of immature dreams. Tempting our interests and our allowances were comic books, disguises, and confections of every conceivable hybrid of chocolate, caramel, nougat, and nut. There were water pistols and cardboard puzzles, keychains and tempera paints. There were baseball cards and bags of army soldiers. Rank upon rank of the deliciously useless—everywhere the lure of waste. In this penny-ante nirvana, every novelty imaginable, every variation on petty plastic manufacture already halfway to crap, could be had.

Best of all, best because they promised most and therefore disappointed hardest, were the ramshackle magic tricks. A couple of bucks could buy all sorts of "professional-style" bluffs. We examined rigged decks and ropes whose knots bit and slid away with a flick. Egg cups that gobbled green balls then opened to reveal red ones. Seemingly solid rings (clack) that somehow (clack) intersected then (clack) separated, solid once more. Loaded dice, trick handcuffs, vanishing coins, spring-loaded wands and fans, counterfeit, nested, and false-bottomed boxes: the store was a veritable cradle of deception.

In retrospect, of course, the magic on hand was tinny, transparent. We could wear our fingers raw practicing legerdemain, but the enchantment we could accomplish was as cheap and meager as the cheap, meager items we brought home. Mothers might have pretended to be amazed by their earnest children, and fathers might have put down their papers for two minutes to play along, but not even loving condescension could convince any kid older than eight that anyone was truly taken in.

Then our parents returned to parental matters, and, caught up in the throes of instinct, we went on our adolescent prowl again, spilling over the city like ants over the rim of a picnic, looking for other ways to risk ourselves and stronger magic.

༺

Bryan is explaining his need for the new version of his video game to a man who cannot fathom the obsolete one in front of him. "SYNTHECITY is okay, I guess, but it's still pretty lame. I mean, the simulations, they don't hold up after a while. And it's slow. I mean, *really*. You do get to build parks and streets and office buildings and stuff, and you get to decide how to spend your budget. Which is pretty cool, but still."

Bryan is eleven, which means that he has another five years before he can drive—seven, actually, if the new state law passes. He's chafing constantly, my nephew, impatient for the upgrade. Or, to turn his own expression on him, he's pretty cool, but still. The mayor, chief civil engineer, city planner, sole shareholder, and demiurge of SYNTHECITY, Bryan orchestrates the seasons, deems the yield of every fruit tree and utility, contrives the virtual firmament and configures the presumptive beasts and creatures, including man, extrapolating from him his glittering dominion.

And Bryan saw everything that he had made, and, behold, it was, considering the limits of his system, for the time being, okay.

But barely. "See, once your water and electricity are running and your houses are built, you pretty much wait around watching your money. After a while, it's no big deal. But SYNTHECITY II has fires and hurricanes that come in off your coast, plus a working airport with an air traffic control tower you have to stay on top of or else, plus crime, so you sometimes get to chase and apprehend criminals. You can program the game to increase the chances of getting disasters to happen if you want. But you still have to keep track of your money, you know? I mean, what if you want to send your police after a serial killer but you've blown your budget on something like food for a homeless shelter or a fireworks display?"

It's hard on my back, leaning over him to see, leaning in. The power grid steadily pulses color and light. From what I can tell, all is well in SYNTHECITY on this digital night. The supposed population is sleeping in, but it is possible to imagine that in the blinking trellises that represent SYNTHECITY's office complexes a few people are working late, concentrating as best they can in the pixilated confines. In the green smear that is the SYNTHECITY supermarket, hypothetical shoppers sound the sweet pocked hearts of uniform melons. All around them the impalpable, compounding plenty. The flashing dashes are railways, where in some unenvisioned distance trains are lowing, obeying some vague, industrial estrus. Then there are the rows of glittering suburban smithereens: the equal signs stand for townhouses containing stable marriages. And beneath the scene, in the metropolitan bowels, some semblance of mind is curled and brightly seamed like the Sunday *Times* in the fireplace, I suppose, but I suppose alone because Bryan is on to other business.

He doesn't wait for me any longer. "You're screwed, is what. That's the whole game, see? It's up to you to make it work, and if you don't stay with it, the whole thing destroys itself. My friend Josh left his game on one night while he was sleeping, and when he woke up the next morning, it was ruined. Crashed ambulances, starving people. A blackout. He couldn't do anything with it. He couldn't delete his way out or invent his way out. Nothing. Two months he'd spent on his city, and all he could do was pull the plug." Bryan lets this sink in for a second, then he gives me a significant look, as if we're in on something together. "Maybe for my birthday I'll get it."

Being only so computer savvy, I can't make out the deficiencies in SYNTHECITY that are so obvious to Bryan. "While towers threatened, / while the city surrounded me, its aims still a secret," I wonder if there is anything incidental in that scintillating grid. Going by Bryan's sober management of the game, I guess not. He is the single artificer of the world he fusses over, "majestically indifferent and composed," like Rilke's swan, glaring at the glaring terminal, sliding over that wakeless surface. He betrays no marvel, no surprise.

Does the government there have a budget line for poetry? Unlikely. So the boy wouldn't know Rilke's roses, either. "Living in silence, endlessly unfolding, / using space without space being taken." The city synapses fire: blue, yellow, orange, red. Bryan is intent, more or less serene before the softly rippling imagery, while my eyes ricochet among competing blinks (not a decent independent bookstore among them, I'd wager). "They are so utterly in, so strangely delicate / and self-lit—to the very edge: / is it possible we know anything like this?"

The headlines in the SYNTHECITY GAZETTE must be the same every day: Semaphore and Entropy. I cruise off on one vectored avenue until it disappears over the curvature of the screen.

Bryan continues to diddle with the controls, then sours. I could tell him that "your simply gazed-over world / wants to grow greater through love," but SYN-THECITY is already a stagnant empire in his eyes, the capitol of a dying venture and unredeemable. Despite the fervent, italicized testimony on the back of the CD box—from Columbus, Ohio, to Richmond, Virginia, to Beaumont, Texas, to Fayetteville, Arkansas, they weigh in, adoring—the ur-city is outmoded even as he operates it. Like ancient Troy trumped and driven underground by less ancient Troy, only to succumb to each more recent Troy in turn, SYNTHECITY has been built to be buried by its sequel, as its sequel will be. No federal bailout has been scheduled to save this community. Every unseen current resident will be purged, invisible employee outplaced, and on-screen ethnic shimmer cleansed through the most ruthless sort of urban renewal imaginable, and my nephew can't wait. Rilke's Fifth Elegy has him down: "this informing spirit, master of all that's earthly, / loves nothing more than the moment of turning."

And when obsolescence descends over the unsuspecting city, is there an unjaded child who dreams free of the coming holocaust, with a cache of comics beneath his bed or with decals of fantasy creatures stuck to his window so that their eyes, when headlights scour the alley and discover them, shine? An absurdity I think better of and keep to myself. Meanwhile, for Bryan, there is only the cold glow and dapple without shadow.

ॐ

The Magic House was neither.

"Delights, surprises, and hands-on fun for children of every age!" the highway billboard read. It showed a clutch of children, equally fascinated and racially diverse, looking up at a spangled whoosh coming from a floating wand; their beaming parents shared in their rapture from behind. Something in the color coming from the wand always caught the sun. We saw the billboard each time we drove through St. Louis, and although Elizabeth never reacted to the advertisement, we made a point for once of giving ourselves enough time on this visit to take advantage, for her sake.

What we discovered was that the Magic House was basically a daycare center writ large. In reality, because it combined safe play with demystification, it was doubly discouraging. Each thickly carpeted "learning station" featured either harmless toys or "wonders of science." In the former areas, kids crawled through intestinal tubes, swam through seas of whiffle balls, flung Nerf darts against Velcro targets, dueled with oversized balloons, or joined a gridlock of Big Wheel cars too tightly jammed together to allow for any impact at all. The adults watched from a raised track. Some of us talked on cell phones, some directed their kids to look up at video cameras, and once in a while someone would swoop down to separate stubborn Legos when the whining started or to rescue an ankle from protective nylon netting. In the lesson-oriented areas, the older children could witness or activate a variety of phenomena: a perpetual motion apparatus, a bubble that enveloped you and contoured itself to your gestures and shrieks, a soundboard whose pitch rose and fell as you passed your hands over it, and so on. Each was explained by a posted legend; or the kids were shepherded through by a Magic House Helper (I'm Melissa—Just ASK Me!); or, in the case of the massive static electricity ball that lifted the hair of anyone who touched it, a timed voice recording emanated from the far wall.

The Magic House was a harbor of reliable hygiene and perfect sense. Don't bother. We went for ice cream afterwards and, thanks to the fact that they had the kind Elizabeth liked best (with the pink bits of gum tucked inside), salvaged the trip for her.

Doubtless it is deprivation to be doubtless, I have no doubt. There are times I want to be taken in, not so much in the sense of a patsy who cannot keep his money safe in his pockets as in the sense of a stranger caught out in the cold. Once in a while I want the world to be more possible than it is, instead of always sniffing at the magician's deck to see if it's salted with extra aces or waving away the fist that dribbles endless change.

One night we tucked the baby away with a sitter to give us an evening of grown-up entertainment, and I chose to stop at the New York Lounge, a Chicago bar whose bartenders were all moonlighting magicians and where "It's Fun to Be Fooled." It was mostly sleights of hand and coarse patter. A half-dollar dropped in your beer would manifest dry beneath the glass, or your drink would dissolve into a sponge and wring out red. Then there were the requisite jokes about your "drinking problems." Close-up, throwaway stuff—nothing to interrupt purchase and consumption. There was also a miniature speaker hidden beneath the toilet tank in the women's restroom, which was connected to a microphone behind the bar. A customer would excuse herself, and, after a calculated delay, one of the magician-bartenders would take up the mike and whisper a scurrilous suggestion up her dress. She would eventually slink back to the bar, receive general teasing and congratulations, then wait with the rest for an uninitiated patron to fall for the same ploy.

The evening was less than successful, clearly beyond what ice cream might save. I should have known, just as I should have known even as a child that any magic stashed in a dime store would betray, just as I know now that every conjurer is really a complex of hidden pockets where a hundred colored kerchiefs secretly bloom. Is growing up growing immune to wonder, like getting over measles?

Even Bryan, only eleven, for all the vigor of his commitment to his visionary, gleaming city, does not believe.

I remember climbing cellar stairs in the dark and miscounting the steps. Anticipating one more, I lifted my leg to take it, only to find myself stamping away at empty air and, for a few seconds' feeling for an absence, until my equilibrium returned, amazed. In another, nobler context, Rilke refers to that sensation as "standing on fishes." Poetry can cause it, too, just as love, loss, or any instability can—that feeling that familiar ground is giving way, that solids are sheer and things can manifest in a word. Then "every fortune-favored space you wander through, astonished," whether it is the street you frequented as a boy or the magician's glass box that suddenly flutters with doves, is rich with presentiment. Anything might live in all we cannot see. Until—all too soon, I'd say—we turn the lights on and realize our mistake. We catch the magic in the act, and we find our usual footing again, and we are left knowing, and we know, and we know, and we know, and we know, and we know.

Impostors

The art is in the execution. Three or four players are optimal, but in a pinch, two are sufficient to perpetrate the game. The key here, as in so many things, is to play swiftly and assuredly, for expertise is its own enchantment and disguise. Cards should be snapped confidently down and winning tricks, finesses, and all other methods of swelling the progress announced with appropriate emphasis. As the players act and react, weigh and inveigle, they must remember that they are scheming centrifugally, that their apparent competition with one another is in fact a tacit collaboration. In other words, the players are engaged in a consensual ruse. They are playing to the house.

This is TEGWAR, The Exciting Game Without Any Rules. In truth, it is not so much a game as a staged performance, whose fantastical strategies are only show and whose complex flourishes matter only insofar as they inspire bystanders to try to comprehend and, later, to participate. For it is one of humanity's irrepressible tendencies to compel a chaos to come to order. Since none of us can bear a wilderness for long, we assume an etiology. Which is what stalwart TEG-WARRIORS rely on.

TEGWAR requires that its players heed Jimmy Cagney's warning about acting: "Don't get caught at it." Unless every seam of your sham stays sealed, even the most gullible will hang back. (In sports, they call this "selling the fake." The halfback charges hardest into the line when he doesn't have the ball, while the quarterback steals around the end for six. With a hard jab step or a series of epileptic feints, the basketball player sheds his defender and opens a path to the hoop.) Emily Dickinson, that most estimable hustler, summed up the method rather neatly: "Success in circuit lies." Nevertheless, if the game must not be too obvious, neither should it be too obscure. Like those dreamy nymphs who bathe away eternity, the players want to seduce and elude at the same time.

Properly primed, the pigeons will be mesmerized by the crusts that fall nearby. They'll see a club trump a heart or a pair of twos earn an extra turn; they'll note the surrender of everyone else's aces to the player who flashes the first black queen; with fascination they'll watch the strange, random mutations of the game, trying to grab a handle, or at least to figure out where the handles are located. Admittedly, many witnesses, unable to grasp the calibrated excesses on display or follow the phony reasoning behind any lead, may recall their Thomas DeQuincey, who in his *Confessions of an English Opium Eater* predicted their confusion: "In parts and fractions eternal creations are carried on, but the nexus is wanting, and life and the central principles which should bind together all the parts at the center with all its radiations to the circumference, are wanting." Absent enlightenment, they will stay intrigued only so long.

But there may be one, the one who has been steadily edging in from the periphery, who thinks he might be getting the hang of it (so eager are we to believe that there is a hang to be gotten). That's the guy who will be invited to sit in. He'll even begin to win a bit, hardly sensing why. He'll be congratulated on being such a quick study. He'll be encouraged to play for higher stakes. And as soon as he gets sucked into a sizeable pot, the trap will be sprung. Perhaps someone will scuttle his flush by flaunting the suddenly fatal five of spades. Perhaps someone will advise him that his diamonds are disqualified—didn't he see the dealer flip a black seven after the last raise? It's irrelevant why his hand is deemed irrelevant. What matters is that the other players sell him assiduously on the fact that he was in over his head, that, in the end, he was the real impostor at the table.

⚮

Because the talk shows say that there is no past tense for "love," not as far as she is concerned, your concern must go further. Because the only given is that nothing can be taken for granted, in any working relationship, the work goes on. So you take your resolve from Hollywood and glamour magazines. Mutt-clumsy as you are, you make an effort anyway. In your office, under the fluorescent hum of the spastic fixture that never gets fixed, you dream up a bit of wistful mischief. For once, you might think, you might think outside the cubicle, as it were, as you are, in your duty to her try to be something more than dutiful, something other. Someone preferable. Someone else.

Because your usual avowals have in recent years been sloppy, too few, and, well, usual. "I'm here for you" has never been more assuring than a modest savings account—a pittance you can hardly bank a future on. As for sex, well, lately it seems as though you've been entering her like a burglar, if at all (on this point the talk shows are merciless), and even at your most devoted, you are predictable and, frankly, unlovely, to her or any mirror. So you deliberate, turning over each idea like a dripping chicken on a spit, hoping to create something satisfactorily tender between you. Romance may loom like boot camp, but you prepare, for her sake and (on this point the talk shows are adamant) yours, the daffy extrapolations of the heart.

You decide to sneak back on an evening you know she'll be out and salvage as many of the Christmas lights as you can from their tangle on the floor of the front closet. (The unknotting alone takes an hour, a practice she'd have to appreciate, although—on this point the talk shows are cautionary—not as much as she would your restraint in not calling attention to this.) You string the rooftop with blinking braids to make for a more intimate, more manageable heaven than the unpremeditated heavens provide. (Didn't some diligent lover in a film she misted over do that? That the notion stuck somewhere in your memory must count for something.) You wrap yourself in the rented tux that only James Bond or Fred Astaire could keep from feeling silly in. (The gleaming trousers bind up on you in a way that Bond never betrayed in any adventure; wearing the same kind of cummerbund as Bond barely connects you. And even after taking dance lessons on the sly, you cannot choreograph a single step, much less imply Astaire. Press on anyway.) Having never once in your life discriminated among grapes, you complete the scene by setting out the unpronounceable wine you asked the clerk to choose. In short, you prepare to wow her with all that isn't you.

And when she takes it all in, including your puppy-hoping-to-go-for-a-walk expression, what she compliments is your exertion, not your transformation. The problem is that it takes more than a coat of paint to make a paragon, and no one can subsist on a confected essence for very long. Contrivance isn't metamorphosis, a word that recalls Kafka, of course, in the wake of whose extraordinary fiction the paltry changes you've played ring false.

Speaking of Kafka, keep in mind that when his Gregor Samsa becomes a bug, everyone in the family recognizes the inherent Gregor in him anyway. No one shouts, "My God, it's a gigantic insect! He must have eaten our boy!" On the contrary, they wonder why he's gone to such selfish lengths. They fret about what to feed him, whether or not to clear out his room, and how to conceal him from the houseguests. They never question who he is. The creature confirms the Gregor they know. Gregor in costume is Gregor revealed, and Gregor nonetheless.

Doesn't your beloved have as much sense as a Samsa? Do you really believe that she grieves for the health of the dashing actor when the character he plays takes a bullet on-screen? Are you shocked that she is not shocked to see him beaming at the Oscars months later?

Because you did not fall for a fool, you must take care not to fall over your own footing. Remember that suicides use rooftops, too. Even at this unaccustomed height, she does not get dizzy. You can't afford to, either.

☙

In this age of cyborgs and clones, when movies and rumors scarcely stay abreast of what's being concocted in laboratories every day, we don't know how to refer to "normal" anymore. How many people do I know who, physiologically speaking, stand as miracles of interior decoration—who are, for that matter, standing solely because of it? Thanks to the precise violations of surgical engineers, some of my closest friends have all sorts of technology sewn up inside them. An alarming percentage of them have replaced an alarming percentage of themselves with hardware. Just a month ago, Jack's chest was the site of an impromptu medical conference. Half a dozen doctors prodded about in there the way that, back in the 1960s, we used to fish for errant crusts in the fondue pot. They inserted a pacemaker to thrum alongside his discreetly metered heart, and then they restrung him like a tennis racket. He's up and walking already, feeling more or less like his old self, he says, and in some ways better than ever, or at least other than ever. I am perforce pleasant about it with him, and I know that the doctors are optimistic about a full recovery of what remains of him to be recovered. Nevertheless, I have to admit that when I encountered him outside the hospital, putting my arms around his retrofitted body gave me a sensation similar to bumping into a refrigerator.

And this is only the most recent example. Somewhere below and behind the belt, Bill is held together by a special mesh; although the reality is far more elegant and complex, I can't help but picture his renegade innards being caught in the webbing of an infielder's glove. Definitely I am at the age when I am surrounded by friends who because of sports injuries sport joints alloyed with polymers or bend plastic knees, who, having worn away shoulder sockets and gnawed sugars for fifty years, now lick, speak, and kiss through silver and shoulder steel. You could count enough pins in the ankles and wrists at the gym to practice voodoo against half of Congress if you wanted to. In all of us still going around, there isn't all that much of us still going around.

You may have heard about the prospective medical student who had a computer chip installed in the side of his head as a kind of upgrade of his natural RAM. It's a cognition switch of sorts. During a test, he might scratch above his ear to access relevant binomial equations, wince to trigger an annotated display of the human skeletal system for private viewing by his mind's eye, or blink on keywords flashing against his cortex to download crucial histories. Both university officials and board exam manufacturers have tried to prohibit these tactics, just as they once outlawed the use of calculators during SAT tests when I was taking them and the way they still police casinos to detect and remove blackjack players who illegally count cards. The student himself maintains that he is not cheating at all since the answers are, quite literally, in his head. Furthermore, he suggests that as a practicing surgeon someday he'll be all the more effective if he can review thousands of procedures on the spot simply by having a nurse deliver a couple of well-aimed pokes along his hairline. He goes so far as to predict that some day these chips will become mandatory accessories—a day he eagerly awaits. Thus may we eventually become multiple: fastidious, aswarm, and perpetually involved in consultation.

Paradoxically, there is no more reliable source of credibility than the fear that one is a fraud. My friend John, who, like me, teaches college English, is particularly and quite vocally committed to this argument. Unless someone occasionally wonders whether or not the professional jig he dances, however deftly, is up, he is simply not to be trusted with his station. In fact, John maintains, we are all of us impostors; integrity is a matter of not succumbing to one's own pose. (Heed the warning label on the package: Be advised—swelling is common.) Even as we accept the prize, the promotion, the appreciative batter of glad hands, we must not neglect our daily dose of chagrin. However much worth is urged upon us, we should always be subdued by the prospect of exposure and if we rise, rise with our heads held low.

Actually, I am rather fond of the word "impostor," from which I detect the scent of dinner theatre. You know the sort of play I mean: one of those conventional whodunnits whose doer's undone by the timely revelation of the detective-hero. "That man, the man who calls himself 'Uncle Basil' . . . is an *impostor!*" he booms accusingly, setting off gasps from the rest of the bewildered cast. Just enough artifice to seem quaint, but not so much as to put you off your feed, as dinner theatre by definition demands. Somehow, in retrospect, we realize that the clues were right in front of us all the time, apparent as the silverware. An impostor? Obviously. We knew it all along.

Unfortunately, certain literature leads us astray when it tells us that we may be remade entirely each day like the disheveled beds we dream in and desert the memory of ourselves altogether. George Orwell's narrator in "Shooting an Elephant" pondered how one "wears a mask, and his face grows to fit it." But notwithstanding the metaphor, there is no denying that the next morning would find Orwell's sahib shaving the same stubble from the same chin. Similarly, when Kurt Vonnegut opened *Mother Night* with what he asserted to be the moral of the novel—"We are what we pretend to be, so we must be careful what we pretend to be"—he was only half right. While we must take pains to resist our own prevarications, it is because they are likelier to deceive than determine us.

To correct the impression that one's intrinsic self may be burked or buried without a trace, consider *The Wizard of Oz*. "Pay no attention to that man behind the curtain," thundered the bloated, floating head, through which subterfuge the wizard hoped to keep his littleness hidden. Had Orwell and Vonnegut been accurate, Toto would have nosed out nothing more than a distracting flounce of drapery, for there would have been no disappointing center to refute that imposing circumference. Yet even in the absence of an undisciplined dog, there will be some inevitable slip, some peeking through the seams of our seeming so. Ultimately, the fumbler will emerge from the appurtenances he crouches behind.

No one over five is really surprised that the wizard's wizardry is solely a product of public relations. Outside of expensive special effects, authentic magic has always been hard to come by and accomplishment an occasion to inspect the deck. Maybe it began when as children we saw Mom post our latest drawings on the kitchen cabinets, drawings whose quality came from mother-love alone; and as she proclaimed our giftedness to dinner guests, we came to question her taste in everything from then on. Even as they guarantee our advancement, we sense that letters of recommendation are formulaic—their authors merely tweak the templates in their hard drives to suit the institution we're after and leave all the old adjectives intact. We doubt the positive reviews in the *Times,* thinking them more advantageous than true, while the real proof of us is in the pan. Downing the heady wine of success, we know that everyone else does not get drunk when we do. For the sake of the sober, we sober up; and if we do occasionally gush, we gush on guard.

To his credit, John does not exempt himself from his own philosophy. A successful college professor by most standards—he has earned promotion at a university prestigious enough that its name does not contain a compass direction—John regularly effaces himself with the diligence of a teenager treating his acne. He asks his students to refer to him by his first name, feathers his office door with cartoons that playfully denigrate his profession, and often quotes his most humbling student evaluations. At times, his humility is so extreme as to seem a sort of hubris all its own. "Look," he says, "I never kid myself," and in saying so, he implies that you, too, would do well to be consistently in on your own joke.

If commencement ceremonies teach us anything, it must be that our allotment of pomp far outstrips our circumstance.

The cardinal sin is swagger. For we know deep down that we are getting better mention than better but unmentioned men. Sir Edmund Hillary may have planted the flag and the fable in the British papers, but his virtue came by virtue of Tenzing Norgay, the inconspicuous Nepalese guide who helped to make Everest surmountable in the first place. The videotape report on ESPN proves that the winner of the Iditarod actually finished twelfth, only after his pack of forgotten dogs had crossed the line; afterwards, heaped in a drafty kennel, the dogs did the only valid gasping there was to do. Research shows just how seldom renown is founded or vanity fair. Modesty must stay the best of us—it is what makes the best of us the best of us—who in our guilt-ridden, sleepless nights secretly count ourselves among the sheep we count.

Now I am not counseling legal counsel to abandon his clients in the throes of Latinate courtroom debate because he has suddenly come down with an inconvenient case of shame. Having binged on improper fractions, irrational numbers, and empty sets, a given mathematician may be prone to prune, but not, I trust, to cut all sums permanently from his diet. Let the surgeon who wonders mid-bypass if, career-wise, he has taken a wrong turn, who plunges his hand up to the wrist in an open bowel and, following W. H. Auden's instruction, stares, stares, in that corporeal basin and wonders what he's missed, delay his contemplation for later, when he's washing off the blood. John is quite right when he says that hesitation marks the exemplary professional. But that does not mean he should cancel his appointments or fail to meet his office hours. He should not let his clients, patients, or students founder without him in the hall.

☙

Conspiracy theories will prosper in any field. A tasty one that has recently sprouted in mine is that modernist literature may have been composed as military code. Wouldn't that to some extent explain its inexplicability? We might forgive Wallace Stevens his sludgy verse if it turns out that *An Ordinary Evening in New Haven* was devised to convey troop movements or that James Joyce was really working in Zurich to transmit information to the Allies under cover of *Finnegans Wake*. What if Patton's Third Army was sustained during its dash across Europe by pentameter alone? Perhaps 'twas well-aimed assonance sank the Bismarck. (Indeed, every schoolchild can recite the legend that our country came into being because the British marched in strict quatrains, while plucky colonists, taking their cue from free verse. . . .) Had the literary canon proven as crucial behind the lines as cannons at the front—imagine Eliot ensuring through irregular stresses as many victories as superior artillery did, or Faulkner, via *The Sound and the Fury*, laying successful siege to the Siegfried Line—then it would all make sense. So to speak.

As it happens, I have discovered no foundation for these suspicions, so there must be another reason behind the pleonasms and opacities perpetrated by the most elevated members of my syllabus. Nor are they the worst culprits. For truly repellant specimens of style, browbeaten readers would have us look to recent critical theory. "Poststructuralism" is the brush we typically use to tar such untouchable prose. Writing smothered in austerity, writing stripped clean of felicity—it would be painful to rehearse the symptoms further. "Language most shews a man; Speak, that I may see thee," wrote Ben Jonson. Centuries ago, he never dreamed we would one day have to look through lead.

How dismaying or gratifying—depending on one's mood—to learn about the Sokal Hoax. In that infamous coup of 1994, a theoretical physicist from New York University, Alan Sokal, submitted to *Social Text* a Trojan Horse of an article, a work so sublimely impenetrable that infiltration of that journal was assured. He had milked and mingled the vaguest vocabularies, combined "hermeneutics" and "hegemonies" like a tenure-driven witch out of *Macbeth,* and the plausible, intimidating haze that rose from that vile broth sufficiently impressed the noses of the editorial board that they published it.

The surprise is not that impostors pass through customs but that we have grown so accustomed to it. We are pretty much convinced that barbarians bar the gates that were established to keep the barbarians out. Pundits and apologists are still stumbling over the rubble left after the academic tempest Alan Sokal caused. Incidentally, this parodic impulse continues to thrive on a website called The Postmodernism Generator, whose randomizer program enables anyone to construct instantly his own venerable gibberish. He may then set loose his subaltern, neo-narrativized, postcritical, nickel-and-paradigmed Frankenstein monster of jargon upon submissions editors and seminar leaders, as his conscience dictates.

⌖

When things get too dense to endure, I have found that the best respites are found in the dark.

For me, the most satisfying moment in *Invasion of the Body Snatchers* comes when we discover that Leonard Nimoy, who plays a psychiatrist in the film, has already been supplanted by a soulless, pod-spawned double. I get a kick out of the idea that in this case the alien replica is more or less impossible to differentiate from its human counterpart. I am not sure whether this is meant as a comment on psychiatrists or on Leonard Nimoy, but the ambiguity does not dampen my pleasure.

I do not mean to minimize the political implications or the more notorious horrors in this film. As Kevin McCarthy devotes himself to outing the pods, he finds himself part of an ever-shrinking minority. ("I'm not crazy. Make them listen before it's too late." Who hasn't been there, or thereabouts?) Imagine our planet completely populated by Uncle Basils. A chilling prospect. ("I'd hate to wake up some morning and find out you weren't you," our hero jokes, when it is still fairly early in the film and the prospect still unbelievable.) And so the question arises: in a false world, what does it mean to be genuine?

Film buffs will realize that I've conflated the 1956 version of *Invasion of the Body Snatchers* with the 1978 remake, the latter of which is generally agreed to be inferior, the Leonard Nimoy bit notwithstanding. Certainly it has proved far less memorable and less moving than the original. Remakes have ever been the opportunistic pods of the industry.

ॐ

Let us persevere with a moderate spirit: if we must not grovel, neither should we strut. Woe to the emperor who, having banished every tailor from the realm, has gone naked so long that he never feels a breeze.

And yet, his subjects still crane their necks to see him wave from the balcony. They would be disappointed if he did not make an appearance, and, possibly, a little afraid.

In mythology, Perseus survived by indirection, looking at neither the Medusa nor his own reflection dead on. Impostors all, we, too, must only obliquely approach what we hope to be, even as we avoid what we fear we might be after all.

Nearer

[T]he sense of actuality or reality . . . originates in
reversal.
    —Robert L. Caserio, *Plot, Story and the Novel*

Of all the inevitable failures to instill your children
with your own values, one of the subtlest and most devastating pertains to taste. Sophistication is just a style,
I suppose, but let's not underestimate the importance
of style.

Now this assessment will seem strange to anyone
who knows me very well. With the exception of my
tendency to scowl at the bestseller tables at Barnes and
Noble, I could never be accused of refinement. Good
wine is wasted on my palate; my powers of discrimination extend no further than differentiating red from
white. Pretty much any music will help the time glide
by as I drive—Motown moves me down the highway
as reliably, and as unconsciously, as Mozart does—and
the car radio pleases me no less than systems that offer
higher fidelity at higher prices might. Even when I
travel on the college's dime, I am content to spend the
night in modest accommodations, so long as there are
fresh towels and clean sheets, and I am happy to pass on
five-star restaurants and simply dine in unrated dark-

ness. Truth be told, my upbringing brings me closer to the bowling alley than to the Sorbonne, and despite my having spent my professional life working with intensely educated, densely credentialed people, I am in most things about as cultivated as a mall parking lot.

But I'm a stickler when it comes to movies. Not that I repudiate American movies for foreign cinema. (Make that cine*ma,* accented with knowing elevation on the final syllable by audiences who willingly watch tendentious art films for hours without benefit of a single Milk Dud.) But even among the car chases, shoot-'em-ups, and slapstick comedies, I am guided by definite biases. As we eat together at McDonald's before the show, I try to impress them upon my daughter. Even middle-brow art must surpass middling standards, I explain to her. Some Disney movies are consistently winning, like *Pinocchio,* and some, like *Atlantis,* are underdone. There are creative creature features, and then there are monstrous concoctions that should never have been allowed to leave the lab. Some movies are pitched as camp and intentionally clever, but in failed camp no intention digs in at all. Preferring half-baked, half-hearted movies to fully imagined entertainments, I tell her, is just as unacceptable as dipping your chicken nuggets in mustard.

The fact is, I may not betray that special squint that indicates a lifetime of unbending etiquette, but I am rather particular about what screenings are worth the bother. And whenever the opportunity arises (as part of an eccentric series sponsored by the college, say, or when I happen to tune in a movie channel secreted in the nether reaches of cable), I corral my daughter for one of those egregious sci-fi flicks of the 1950s I worshiped and still enjoy today. I may be permissive in almost every other cultural respect, submitting without a whimper of complaint to her choices in clothing, comic books, and boy bands; but my absolutism comes out when movies do. I want her to appreciate how some megabuck productions are meager at the core, whereas some B-movies make the grade. And when I chance upon a beloved one from the birth of the nuclear age, I treat it as a parental prerogative to make her learn to stop squirming and love the Bomb.

During the 1950s, it seemed as though Hollywood was enveloped in a radioactive fog, which spawned dozens of science-fiction movies featuring mutated creatures great and small. The twin threats of atomic testing (which compelled otherwise sane people to cower indoors) and television (which compelled otherwise sane people to cower indoors) caused moviemakers to turn to gimmickry to bring audiences out. Enlarging the screen itself was one such strategy—this was the burgeoning age of Panavision, VistaVision, and Cinemascope. Bombarding characters with gamma rays and sets with special effects was another. Consequently, some stars grew colossal, some invisible, some vulpine, some scaly, and some with raised veins like the piping on baseball jackets. As if respecting some evolutionary Boxing Day, humans and insects exchanged dimensions and destinies. Our underground testing disturbed the earth like indigestion, and out of its bowels rose every imaginable amalgamation of menacing tentacles and weird cilia, the fanged and festering effects of our technological presumption. For over a decade's worth of moviemaking, the wrathful planet positively seethed with unprecedented beasts, all angry magma and malevolent ooze. And the skies were visited by countless forms of exotic personnel, arriving in sleek vehicles sporting more lights than a Las Vegas hotel. The visitors themselves—low-budget, rubbery beings, roughly corrugated and pustular or, with apologies to Hopkins, shining like shook foil—may have defied penetration by any word or weaponry, but they were usually bipeds with more or less identifiable hands, mouths, and motives. In this way, the obviousness of the suppositious aliens encouraged two kinds of hospitality. Because they were, for all of that costuming, transparent, they were not scary, and were therefore viewed as wholesome fare for the kids. And because their humanity showed through the seams, they implicated us. "You! hypertrophic lizard!—*mon semblable—mon frere!*"

To my taste, the best of the atomic repercussion genre was the 1957 film *The Incredible Shrinking Man.* I say this despite my accidental refusal of the film's own shrill promotional terms. (By my mother's account, I mispronounced the title as *The Credible Shrinking Man,* which she presents as evidence of how endearingly daft I was at four. On the contrary, I maintain that I was a prodigy of nonchalance.) "A fascinating adventure into the unknown," read the original tagline. More accurately, it was a fascinating adventure into the known, in the sense that we were witnessing not unfamiliar environs, organisms, or machinery but familiar ones seen through new eyes.

In this movie, the hero, Scott Carey, succumbs to a mysterious dark cloud while sunning himself on his brother's yacht. (So much for trusting in recourses like backyard dugouts and duck-and-cover drills to shield us from fallout.) As a result, he begins a steady declension of the self, losing about an inch each day. It is funny and strange at once to see him fail to fill his clothes. It is funny and strange at once to watch him and his wife worry, argue, and commiserate over his fate, for as he shrinks, their interchanges alter in appearance, too, so that wife and husband start looking like mother and son, then human and house pet. It is as though they were on adjacent escalators, with her slowly gaining height as he, at the same insanely graduated rate, descends, putting one in mind of Maggie glowering over her guilty, diminutive Jiggs. In my case, I thought of the self-contained matryoshka dolls that decorated the mantle of a friend's house, which could be taken apart to reveal an ever-diminishing corps of inner dolls—a concentric, serial model of maternity. As he is subtracted cell by cell and scene by scene, Scott Carey demonstrates that same nested essence.

Meanwhile, thanks to optical illusions that by current cinematic standards seem rather quaint and charming, his home is turning into an endless Claus Oldenburg exhibit, with usually negligible household objects exploding out of their normal proportions. The increasingly prodigious silverware, for instance, sparkles with hazards: butter knives become propeller blades to duck from, forks flash like dinosaur claws, spoons loom. The more he dwindles, the more routines, pleasures, and habits he has to abdicate—even crossing the living room carpet, he risks being swallowed up like a golf ball in the gorse—until, for safety's sake, he takes up residence in his daughter's dollhouse.

As his constrictions multiply, Carey undergoes a psychological process similar to that described by Doctor Elizabeth Kubler-Ross in response to the diagnosis of death. The analogy grows more acute when he is terrorized in his toy lair by the family cat (the pet evidently too precious to put outside). Like the fairytale wolf pressing in on a barricaded little pig or an irascible landlord demanding his due, the cat forces Carey to flee for his life, and he ends up slipping down a crack too narrow for anyone else in the cast to pass through. For the rest of the movie he is marooned in the basement, which from his perspective is as unforgiving as any Martian terrain. A tiny minister of contrivance, a Crusoe of the Atomic Age, Carey must continually make do with whatever jetsam lies before him on the yawning expanse of basement floor. When he spares a few seconds' inventiveness for dreaming—leisure, too, has shrunk nearly to nothing—it is only to gaze helplessly at the Himalayan staircase he'll never scale. When he cries, the sound is too faint to reach the far horizon where a line of light glimmers beneath the basement door.

We iris further in. It is now, with our hero bereft of human company or consolation, that *The Incredible Shrinking Man* becomes relentlessly harrowing.

Survival is his sole concern, as even the least effort requires him to engage in elaborate military exercises. Rationing his pinched capacities as best he can under the circumstances (not to mention undersized, not to mention underfoot), Carey conducts a furtive reconnaissance around table legs and wicked drains, patrolling the baseboard perimeter. In what is perhaps the signature sequence of the movie, he is reduced to dueling a spider over a few stale corpuscles of cheese. Think of an infinitesimal Douglas Fairbanks or a whittled Errol Flynn—their dashing scaled down, to be sure, but deadly serious.

And yet, even so thoroughly reduced, some portion of Scott Carey proves irreducible. The core of Scott Carey persists in miniature, a tenured remnant of self able to stave off the severest contractions. As I see it, that is the saving message of *The Incredible Shrinking Man*: like a trademark stamped somewhere ineradicably deep in the cells, there is a soul. Every kernel of Scott Carey contains him.

I guess that this interpretation appealed to me because it anchored me as well. The lesson I took from *The Incredible Shrinking Man*, the lesson that the movie offered in the midst of travail, despite the defining dislocations of the age (and mine), was that there is a watermark of me that weathers any alteration and outlasts demise. Long before any whisper about DNA would reach me, I recognized this assurance of a world in a grain of sand and, furthermore, that each grain of sand guaranteed the beach. Something in every sliver of me remembers me. A meager meal, true enough—a morsel of cheese at most—but enough to get by with. As I watch the movie as an adult, the lesson still resonates. Unaccounted for, Scott Carey still counts. And as he continues to recede from view until the end of the movie, until he is nothing more than a voiceover, he manages to cling to this consolation. "Smaller than smallest, I meant something too," he declares. At this point, the very large and the very little converge, comprising the same wonders. In short, the atom makes or breaks the universe—the Bomb showed us so.

Identity endures even this. "To God there is no zero," Scott Carey realizes. "I still exist!" His exposure and exhilaration remind me of Emerson's confession in "Nature" on the verge of opening himself to the Ultimate: "I am glad to the brink of fear." And if it is fair to extrapolate from a thing so small, here is the promise I was looking for without knowing it: even on the verge of obliteration, we remain.

In keeping with Carey's predicament and the movie's conclusion, I also recall those pioneers of science who peered through the earliest microscopes to spy on sperm. In their enthusiasm, they claimed to observe that the sperm held the unborn child entire, whom they deluded themselves into detecting tucked into its gluey case like a baby in its crib. I remember the drawing from my high school biology textbook—one of only a few images from my shipwrecked memory of the course to stay afloat in my mind. The preformed creature was crouched hard up against the slick, translucent canopy, guided by an initial glimmer of instinct, ready to pilot the slithery teardrop toward improbable purchase. Imagine millions of mission-driven emissions, with all but one of those manned spermships doomed to kamikaze, all but one fated to come to nothing.

That theory's attraction as metaphor transcends its bankruptcy as science. This must be why a vision of an intrepid homunculus cockpitted in a droplet stays with me today. So does spontaneous generation, which was just as memorably depicted in the text and, in terms of its scientific validity, just as intrepidly wrong. Researchers of this persuasion were convinced that the proper mixture of soil, sun, water, and patience would result in vegetation (*had* done so, so they maintained). Similarly, maggots did not simply nest in rotten meat but were sired by it. Flies were the progeny of the shit we saw them in, thereby providing a scientific basis and vital repercussion for Yeats's contention that "Love has pitched his mansion in / The place of excrement."

My appreciation of those misguided scientists who embraced these beliefs undoubtedly had something to do with the satisfaction that I was not the only one having difficulty with the subject. (No matter how much I struggled in biology, at least I had the jump on *them*.) Today, however, I am still impressed by the assumption that civilization is implicit in every atom, that there is nothing that doesn't teem or engender. I carry their unfounded arguments with me for their shared refusal of the void. Indeed, when the surrendered Emerson proclaimed that he was "part or particle of God," he meant that he was no different than any other common, conspicuous, sacred thing in Creation.

What luscious effrontery! What heroic error!

Excuse an English teacher's dilation, especially what with Scott Carey—dimension's reject, stature's refugee—stranded on his cellar's darkling plain, glorious and forbidding as a literature syllabus on opening day. Frankly, apart from the videos I inflict on family, I have little opportunity to hold forth on film in any official way. (Let me note that the vicissitudes of student demand and the specialties of recent departmental hires, and not my idiosyncratic record of movie rentals, are the reasons for my having been restricted to print.) Nevertheless, because Emerson and so many poets on my course list anticipate Scott Carey in declaring war on the concept of ordinariness, this is no deprivation. Nothing is: slide any part or particle under a polished lens—"lift down the eye," as Hart Crane puts it in "The Broken Tower," so as to gather God back up—and like a visiting general inspect the ranks of knobby molecules. Bring focus to the usual soup, the routine confusion, and discover what Victor Shklovsky might have meant by defamiliarization had he the right equipment on hand. Remember the trick photographs in the *Weekly Reader* they gave out in grammar school? A bunch of pencils in close-up became a Platonic copse of yellow poplars. A magnified palm revealed countless crosshatched avenues of grain. There was the complicated raiment of fish scales. The bleached brain contained in a bit of cauliflower. The bristling infinity imbedded in a bit of fabric. The minutely incised coastline edging every potato chip. The galaxy trapped in a light bulb. (What rare, miniscule beings might inhabit *that?*) Those upgraded, high-definition visions were regular features to look forward to. Then somewhere along the way it was decided that they were no longer news.

Did it make the papers when an exhibit entitled Global Myopia arrived at the local museum? It belongs to an obscure Uruguayan artist, who uses toothpicks, X-Acto knives, and scalpels—employing the tools of presumably disparate trades—to score apples, etch aluminum foil, carve reams of white paper, turning prosaic materials into intimate, labor-intensive works. You almost have to put your nose against each object to see the complex, delicate engravings, which remind you of transistor circuits or hidden codes. They suggest a language, barely legible but extensive, and doubtless profound. The hieroglyphics of Lilliput, perhaps, or the semiotics of a city seen from space. They are at once maps to help explore the territory and the territories to be explored themselves—places of quietude and beauty that we encounter daily but have never really known. According to the artist, our task is to liberate our minds from and through information overload. "Our world is full of signs that we cannot understand: new circuits, old alphabets, atoms, dolmens, cells, biologic or urban fabrics, encrypted messages, mutant viruses," he explains. Reading them imitates the maker's labor, as well as his patience and love.

Only last year—less? is it possible?—Scott Carey was a man of vague plans and muddled hungers. He could get by despite having his thoughts, hours, and actions scattered like loose change—the inadvertent largesse afforded larger people with larger means—and still effectively manage his affairs. Now he's on a stricter allowance. The tolerances have tightened up. To survive, he must perceive and operate exactly. As the room expands on him day by day like a dying orbit, the room for error erodes to nothing.

Whether on a canvas or a contract, a page of poetry or an infested stretch of cellar, scrupulousness is the most dependable scruple. ("What is the purpose of poetry, friend?" asks Jorie Graham in "The Region of Unlikeness." "The floor which is cold touching your instep now, // is it more alive for those separate instances it crosses / up through your whole stalk into your mind?") In this, the writer differs not a jot from the scientist, all that clamor over the two irreconcilable cultures aside. "What falls away is always. And is near," Theodore Roethke confides in "The Waking," meaning that focus is an ethical priority, which is why, so as not to miss a bit of divinity, "I take my waking slow." For that same reason van Leeuwenhoek meticulously ground his lenses down to observe the vivid prosperity of previously indiscernible materials. (To him, writes Joanna Scott in "Concerning Mold Upon the Skin, Etc.," "there was hardly a difference between discovering life and creating it.") A. R. Ammons also cherishes the local because, as he explains in "The Dwelling," human destiny and the heart's cravings are perpetually "flaring bright into near / exemplifications"; his title alludes to the "plainest majesty" of this very, this veritable earth of ours. No wonder, with such wonders around, Robert Frost decides in "Birches" that "Earth's the right place for love."

In this sense, it is perhaps more accurate to say that these writers are not waging war against the ordinary so much as they are combating the tendency to treat anything *as* ordinary. Put another way, when Scott Carey tumbles into the basement, much like Alice taking her famous, lovely plummet down the rabbit hole, he is no more fatefully displaced than any willing reader enclosed in a poem. William Gass calls this condition a "kindly imprisonment," which, while it is admittedly temporary and usually less terrifying than what Scott Carey gets sentenced to, can be just as . . . well, for want of a better word, extraordinary.

My daughter latches on as best she can to my meanderings, much the way she clutches my hand when I mean to lead her through a crowd. At this age, she more or less puts up with me, she goes along. "He's not too little to find, Daddy." It is not just sentiment that confers on children the mantle of "natural poets," nor is it simply the fact that they make those sorts of endearing mistakes with language. (Every parent has his or her prized malapropisms to regale the party guests with, to the kid's chagrin, but unlike the prediction based on the boy's fondness for mixing soda pop with kitchen cleanser that Johnny will undoubtedly become a chemist, no career necessarily attaches to their diction errors. As if any parent would rush to commit the college fund to a literary apprenticeship anyway!) No, we extrapolate the poet from the child's steady, screwed down posture before an anthill, from that quality of apprehension, ever culminating, like the anthill itself. In your son's monkish deliberation over a favorite player's statistics, in your daughter's capacity to be fascinated for hours by the same motley dolls, lies the salvation of the race, for they guarantee any larger purpose you'd hope to preserve. So claims Nicholson Baker, who champions the essential activities of "busy, cheerful angels of detail" and salutes all the unsung curators, archivists, and microhistorians among us. He sends his blessings to "that excellent low-key sort of man who achieves little by external standards but who sustains civilization by knowing, in a perfectly balanced, accessible, and considered way, all that can be known about several brief periods of Dutch history, or about the flowering of some especially rich tradition of terra-cotta pipes." Dismissal of trivia—dismissal *as* trivia—is a failure of discrimination far worse than forgetting which is the right wine to choose. When we scant the atom, as all of those Bomb movies prove, we do so at our peril.

If you want to know treasure, go through your children's pockets at the end of any day. The way children cherish collections, sensations, and surfaces keeps that much more of the world from coming to grief. If an impromptu convocation of kids around a dog that's been run down in the road—talk about spontaneous generation!—or poring over collections of Pokemon cards will never inspire the eloquence of the Algonquin Round Table, they may nonetheless yield a high interest rate. Let Vladimir Nabokov speak on behalf of his penchants and his literary profession about the merit of attention yanked taut:

Bending from my warm seat, I liked to press the middle of my brow, its ophryon to be precise, against the smooth comfortable edge of the door and then roll my head a little, so that the door would move to and fro while its edge remained all the time in soothing contact with my forehead. A dreamy rhythm would permeate my being. The recent "Step, step, step," would be taken up by a dripping faucet. And, fruitfully combining rhythmic pattern with rhythmic sound, I would unravel the labyrinthian frets on the linoleum, and find faces where a crack or a shadow afforded a *point de repere* for the eye. I appeal to parents: never, never say, "Hurry up," to a child.

The precision of sensuality, the sensuality of precision. And yet, just try baiting typical college students with that chiasmus and see how few will bite. After all, they were weaned on speed. Faced with intricacy, often as not they punch the accelerator. They would vote to cut down the forest that inhibits their vision rather than take an extra second's account of a single tree. They would flatten phenomena the way bureaucrats vote to blast out the landscape to accommodate their cars. I've seen them slalom down the slope of the page, skimming frictionless as if the ironies were utterly iced over, as if not a figure interrupted the course, passing heedlessly over the ubiquitous Braille of the everyday. "I know you can finish this poem in thirty seconds," I tell my students. "Let's see you do it in thirty *minutes.* Instead of whisking through this Coleridge poem as if you're afraid the redoubtable Khan might catch you loitering in his court—wham-bam-thank-you-Sam— linger to learn what a pleasure dome a poem can be." As Shklovsky explains in "Art as Technique," reading is by design a measured, if menacing, progress: "[W]e can define poetry as *attenuated, torturous* speech. [. . .] The language of poetry is, thus, a rough, impeded language."

With so many snarls and marvels around, Scott Carey takes pains. He moves with care through the shadows and the sudden light. As Roethke advises, he takes his waking slow. "And, lovely, learn by going where to go."

That's the drill, anyway. Unfortunately, what for younger children seems a natural inclination to draw near, to wait for the miraculous to peek out of the mundane like a kitten hiding under the bed, is for adults by and large subordinated to adult matters, or just plain lost. As E. E. Cummings mourns, "Down they forgot as up they grew."

Childhood is just a romance, I suppose, but let's not underestimate the importance of romance.

"Listen, Daddy. Look. Closer." What will prevent my child from having her own passion for detail undone? Just last week she told me how much she liked the black patterns left by the previous night's rain on the neighbor's privacy fence. She delayed our driving off to lunch—the temptations of McDonald's, mind you—long enough to trace an especially grand corolla for me. She took my hand to show me, to help me see. (At this range, it may be hard to distinguish appreciation from pity. Down they forgave as up they grew.) Earlier this summer, while rollerblading around the deserted campus, she circled back to where I was sitting to share the sound the rubber wheels made against the pavement. To make sure I could appreciate it, she made several slow, close, stalking passes, demonstrating over and over their growly, guttural rub. Rich, unmistakable, reassuring, and crucial.

"So close, the infinitesimal and the infinite," muses Scott Carey. "But suddenly I knew they were really two ends of the same concept. The unbelievably small and the unbelievably vast eventually meet, like the closing of a gigantic circle. I looked up, as if somehow I could grasp the heavens, the universe, worlds beyond number."

At the same time, almost daily, they seem to grow more distant, don't they, our venturesome daughters, our doughty sons. Down they forsook as up they grew. Perhaps that's just a trick of perspective, an optical illusion of love, but let's not underestimate the importance of perspective, or of love.

You used to prop them up to see over the dinner table, where eventually they'll rise up to announce their determinations, their disavowals, and your reflex will be to want to unravel the labyrinthian frets for them, as Nabokov put it. Or given your post-atomic training, you may just want to duck and cover. What is each day's distance from your kids but another bomb detonating?

Nearer

That was *close,* you think. Too close.

Or it is as if you are on adjacent escalators, with their ascent a factor of your decline. There's a special effect for you. Incredible, if you've developed the taste for it. If you hope to see them at all, you have to draw nearer.

Chosen People

On the day that Ira's grandfather was found weeping in the bread aisle of the Jewel Food Store, Ira and I had been haggling over who would get to play quarterback. I was the better passer, but it was his ball. Playing football in the street already put a considerable strain upon our ethics. It was up to us to admit our own interference penalties, to time silently the delay before coming with the rush (a count of three "Mississippis," typically), call ourselves out of bounds, and admit to being down when a defender's desperate swipe caught even the least piece of shirt. If an oncoming car disrupted our concentration or forced one of us to break off his pass route, that judgment, too, belonged to the player disrupted or forced; and while the defender might have grumbled, he did not contest it.

Therefore, the additional burden of deciding how to distribute player assignments was very much in keeping with the general tenor of things. Basically, it came down to the question of what "fairness" meant in the context of a game of touch. From one perspective, it made sense that athletic prowess should be the sole determining factor, whereby the most proficient (meaning me, by my own and any objective reckoning) would quarterback the team; the swiftest, such as Arbus,

Weisburg, or Helberg, would consistently split out as ends; and the laggard and lame—the Adelmans and Groners among us, the irredeemably sluggish and lost, the inveterate right fielders and those born to the third string—would always stay in to block. From another perspective, "fairness" could be understood in terms of rotating the choicest positions. Following comparable Communist logic (so far as we understood Communism or logic in those days), Arbus, Weisburg, and Helberg could not all be picked for the same team, or else it would just be a slaughter, and no sane person would take any satisfaction in slaughter. So it was playing fair versus fair play—a real ethical stickler—and a debate could have hypothetically extended well into the afternoon were it not for one essential fact: if we wanted to play with Ira's ball, we had to let Ira call the shots.

Glen usually brought a football, too, but its tumors were worsening kick by kick, and its black bladder showed mortal bubbles through the seams. Mike had one, but its original grip had been restrung with a shoelace, and anyway, the ball had been left out in the rain so often that it defied all geometry. (Actually, Mike just left it out permanently next to the curb—who would bother to steal it?) But Ira had a "Duke"—"The Official Football of the National Football League," as it declared in proud black script—which his grandfather had given him for Chanukah and which was the only suitable conveyance for all the vicarious cargo we brought to touch football. So we always called Ira to join us when we got a game together, taking pains each time to remind him to bring his ball. And so we always made the effort to keep him happy in order to prevent his taking umbrage and his ball home. And so, again for the sake of fairness, we took turns enduring Ira's quarterbacking. We shared the problem of trying to master the wacky patterns he drew up and strained to haul in the pathetic, wounded ducks he delivered, all the while doing such rough justice to the Duke each time one of his impossible passes thumped a fender or scuffed against the street.

Ira's grandfather was a rarity. In the rest of our houses, old folks either went slack, puddling in chairs that would remember their stench forever, or they tapered toward a few awful certainties until there was no other news. No technology touched them, and their grandchildren never passed age ten in their minds. But Ira's grandfather was clued in to the specifics of our consumerist dreams. He had not pulled any wholesale exchange on his grandson, passing off an ersatz brand on the boy—just as big and just as brown, true, but an obvious bastard nonetheless. He had not forgotten the only name that mattered. So as we recoiled from the wobblers that fell dead, all of us kept wishing that our own grandfathers would consecrate a Chanukah the way this one had and, with that one splendid gesture, set us free.

When Ira's mother interrupted my best post move with her blue Impala and forced me to call "time," she stopped the car right in the middle of the street, blotting out the goal line. "It's Grandpa. He's at the Jewel. Get in!" She didn't even let him get his ball. ("We'll bring it back to your house, Ira!" we cried, delighted by the chance to use the Duke with impunity.)

Ira's mother had received a call from the grocery store that something was wrong with his grandfather, and she had taken off without waiting for an explanation. Apparently, the old man had been tottering about the verge of calamity for some time—hey, who knew? who bothered to know?—so it could have been anything that was wrong, but it was probably one thing more than any other. Once we got over the euphoria of having the ball to ourselves, unencumbered by Ira's insufferable strictures, we began to imagine aneurysms and heart attacks (so far as we could envision aneurysms and heart attacks in those days) and were, for the moment, subdued.

As it turned out, nothing especially dramatic happened to Ira's grandfather, not that day, anyway. (He would die eventually in the hospital a few years later—"after a brief illness," according to the obituary.) Ira told us later that when they arrived at the Jewel, the manager led them to the bread aisle, where Ira's grandfather was sitting on the floor, weeping. Ira had seen his grandfather rage, groan, mug, laugh a laugh rich with spittle, and mourn daily the daily news, but he had never seen the man cry before. Not like that. A terrible, persistent, committed crying that shook him and brought up terrible stuff from his chest. The manager hadn't been able to do anything with him, so he took the liberty of going through the old man's wallet and calling home.

It was the bread, the old man finally said. So much bread on so many shelves, which stretched the full length of the aisle and higher than he could reach. It reminded him of Poland at a time when there was no food to be had. It reminded him of when a morsel of bread was a miracle that was nowhere to be found. The brunt of abundance had brought him weeping to his knees. The bread on the shelves also reminded him of corpses stacked in the streets and cousins he would never hear from again. Ira's mother thanked the manager for looking after him and apologized for the disturbance her father had caused. The manager waved her worries away, saying that he understood completely—imagine that—that it had been no trouble at all, and that, rest assured, he looked forward to seeing her the next time she was out shopping.

We lived in a suburb of Holocaust survivors. Nearly half of the residents were either refugees themselves or first-generation Americans from Eastern Europe, so implication pressed heavily upon us almost every day. I had grown up seeing blue numbers peek out the sleeves of local jewelers as they reached across the velvet ramps beneath their glass displays or betray the barber's tribulations as he laid the razor down. Most of my friends and I—pretty much the entire roster of kids who played football in our streets, in fact—were second-generation Americans, which is to say that our guilt was twice removed. As diluted Jews, we knew what our parents and our parents' parents knew, but never the way they knew it. And so, ruled by their ghost physics, we had to survive their survival. While nothing ever reminded *us* of Poland, we were regularly reminded that they regularly were. We had all of us been held once or twice too tightly while our mothers laid out photographs of people we'd been named for but never met or when they smoothed out the letters of the long-dead. We had been cornered by their griefs, which returned like the asthma that kept Adelman on the sidelines. We had all eavesdropped on the same petitions about why He hadn't blocked the bullet or unburst the bomb that did everyone's relatives in. We had all been forced to listen to the same stories over and over, word for word, as if we were understudies for the roles they would some day leave to us but which we could never live up to.

Not that they wanted us to live up to their lessons, only to live with them. This was a condition distilled from what might have been called the Grandparent Theory of History, whose two paradoxical tenets were "You should not have to know from such pain" and "You should never forget how you got here and who you are." On the one hand, they wanted to spare us, to swathe us with loving bromides and birthday dollars. Anything to thin the blood that flowed down to us like toxins leaching through layers of rock beneath us, anything to launder the squalor for their loved ones' sakes. It was a sort of unspoken witness protection program for *der kinder.* On the other hand, suburbia never really contained them. Unaccountably and anywhere at all, they might have broken out in a fit of history. Of course, when the past manifested, it bled out in Rus-

sian or Yiddish—the code whose occasion we anticipated but whose phrases we could not translate. Not
even an occasional cognate to latch onto.

In place of explanations, they distracted us with the
flutter and clucking of tongues.

Among the resourceful, almost any event could be
mined for its Jewish content or adapted to deliver usable
Jewish principles. When Sandy Koufax refused to pitch
on Yom Kippur, it was as much a victory for the Jews
who produced him and whom he inevitably represented as setting down Yankees for nine innings would be
when he ultimately returned to the rotation. However
focused on pitching Koufax himself may have been, his
out-dueling Ford or putting a third strike past Mantle
defied, for one gifted instant, our diminishment for us.
At the same time, when one Jew transgressed, all of
us were made to feel like accomplices. "Let it not be a
Jew," our parents would mutter when Walter Cronkite
led off his report with a late-breaking crime. And when
it *was* a Jew, when it was David Berkowitz who was led
off in the wake of unforgettable ruin, well, it was as
if THEY had been given one more reason to hate us
and to keep us down. For if we smiled among ourselves
over their jealousy whenever our people copped another Nobel Prize, we cringed before any possible justifi-
cation for their suspicions and blame. After all, David
Berkowitz may have called himself "Son of Sam," but
he was also, and before that, a son of Abraham.

It is no accident that there is no singular for "face"
in Hebrew. There is only *punim,* a plurality of faces,
because each face betrays the face of Adam and, by ex-

tension, is a palimpsest for the visage of God Himself. (No pressure *there!*) Similarly, every Jew carries his culture for the rest. Inheritance tails him and spreads like infection through the Chosen People. Every Jew is a swarming ghetto. Each of us is us.

ז

And who hasn't heard the joke about the man who asks God if the Jews are indeed the Chosen People. God assures him that it is so. "Could you do us a favor?" the man asks. "Would you mind choosing someone *else* once in a while?"

Referring in an essay entitled "Remembering the Unknown" to the post-Holocaust generation in France, Nadine Fresco compares "these latter day Jews" to "people who have had a *hand amputated that they never had.*" You reach for a missing limb to rub away the pain.

"The second generation is the most meaningful aspect of our work," writes Elie Wiesel. "Their role in a way is even more difficult than ours. They are responsible for a world they didn't create. They who did not go through the experience must transmit it." But bearing the past was like playing a game of Telephone: the baffled message had long ago broken down, somewhere back along the line of descent. By the time it reached us, it was mostly whispers that persisted. You had to stay on the line and wait for the static to clear.

At temple we contended with the ranks of Hebrew letters, primitive and undifferentiated, like intricate stitching across the page, sewing it up tight. Or they made a pattern like the complicated sole of a fancy running shoe. A colony of bugs, precisely crushed. The Torah scroll itself was all the more recalcitrant because no vowels were attached to smooth the passages you had to squeeze through. Even those meager decorations—an occasional dash beneath a letter like a windowsill to lean on, a few dots about certain words like salt sprinkled to flavor the verse—were denied us. There was only the bare, uninterrupted terrain of arid consonants, stony and unyielding. Trying to read from the Torah was like dragging yourself across gravel.

Say what you will about living in Illinois, knock its flat land and flatter dialect, say there's nothing to stop a car that pushes off from the East coast before it rolls up against the Rockies, but the fact is that you can't beat the soil in Illinois. Even around Chicago, you could start a garden anywhere. Stick a trowel into any prospective spot, even behind a deserted factory or beside a back alley where the garbage trucks run, and it comes up black. We were spoiled where I grew up, thinking that fertility, like deserted factories and back alleys, was matter of fact.

Here in southwest Missouri, though, the earth is girded against us. The soil is too solid to sink even a tulip bulb in or to let you decently bury the family pet. It's just one more displacement to adjust to, the way the dirt—more clay and stone than dirt—like a trump in a card game turns your spade into a club. You till the back yard for nothing. When we tried, we brought up enough red rocks to border a *dozen* gardens, but we couldn't get enough to grow to justify *one*.

You figure they must have to import every flower in town. Kids have to go to school to learn that vegetables don't grow inside of trucks. God knows what the grave-diggers do around here.

Any upper Midwesterner ignorant enough to try to take on the task without a platoon of entrenching pro-fessionals will get the message the first time his shovel blunts only three inches down and stuns him through the shoulders. Believe me. When we first came to town, we tried to make the place feel a little more like home, but the plot we'd intended would have none of us.

I am sure that the problem of Joplin's obstinate grounds occurred to many members of the congrega-tion when the rabbi reported on the condition of the synagogue's foundation. For years the building had been shifting and resettling like someone who couldn't get comfortable in a strange bed. Cracks were creeping up the outer walls like varicose veins. Now the integ-rity of the whole structure was in jeopardy, and there would have to be another increase in the annual dues to handle the repairs.

Funding problems do not tailor themselves to the size of a given Jewish community, after all. Even with the recent influx in college faculty and the expansion of the local hospitals, Jews around Joplin are scarce. About forty families constitute the temple membership, and even that number may be optimistic. The building itself must seem as alien as a fallen meteor or an opera house to most of the residents, who on Sundays slip into one of numberless crannies in the Protestant hive. Hell, just *try* to find an "Ira" around here!

The first law of the local covenant, then, is accommodation. We schedule weekend services around Little League games. Working mothers pick up cold cuts and pre-baked cakes from the closest grocery store for the *oneg.* Anyone with a car and a word processing program can hold a temple office just by asking, and anyone with kids teaches Sunday School. As a matter of fact, the guy in charge of the eight-to-ten year-olds, who also teaches philosophy at the college, is an avowed atheist. But what can you do? If not us, who, right? So to keep the place stable, reupholster the rabbi's chair, or plug the ark, those of us on hand frequently have to up the ante. And now, here we were, sitting in a sanctuary that could collapse at any time, teetering like Noah's salvage on Ararat.

We asked questions whose answers we knew and knew we wouldn't like. Then we voted, because that was procedure, even though there was no doubt about the outcome. Speculating, postulating, tilling the difficult soil—these are some of our most endearing traditions, really, and you don't take them for granted when the population is small. And everyone kicked in. Now the temple is intact once again, ready to weather entropy a while longer. The joke we tell ourselves—who else would get it?—is that we have the finest temple in the entire four-state area.

ॐ

If the previous generation of Jews had to endure problems of survival, says Elie Wiesel, who is one of the most notoriously durable survivors we have, the next ones have "to face problems of the imagination."

Whenever I teach Wallace Stevens's poem "Sunday Morning," I like to challenge my students to try to invent heaven. Would they want the conventional compound of pristine clouds and perpetual Bach? When that scenario leaves them cold, I ask them what they *would* include if they were invited to be on the committee. Sex? Cable television? What would they bar besides cancer? What would there have to be for them to know heaven when they got there?

As they hash out the afterlife, I remember that there was never any mention of heaven in Hebrew school when I was growing up. No hell, either, come to think of it. There was no J. M. W. Turner versus Hieronymus Bosch opposition to struggle with on the way to sleep. There was no Disney vision or hint that heaven was some sort of a restricted golf course suddenly opened to the public; nor was there any sense of hell as His kindled wrath, where the heat increased each time we copied off a friend's paper or snagged forbidden candy before supper. If there were no golden avenues where seraphim played endless football with perfect Dukes, neither would we be consigned to some impenetrable pit to have to dig through hopelessly forever. There was just closeness to God or distance from God. It didn't get any more elaborate than that. Intimacy or abandonment. That's all there was. That's all there had to be.

"Therefore I have uttered what I did not understand, things too wonderful for me, which I did not know." That's a line from Job. Another old joke. Another rock to have to plant in. God keeps His project under wraps. The point is that you'd better not to turn your back.

Memory can be a rotten job. As the saying goes, those who do not know their history are condemned to repeat it. Just like those who do.

The Porlock Principle

What is iconic is abidingly true, whether we like it
or not.
—Owen Edwards, writing for *American Photo*

By 1973, Willie Mays was no longer Willie Mays. The
greatest of all Giants had by then diminished to a Met.
Having been the best, he should have known better.
"They throw the ball, I hit it. They hit the ball, I catch
it." That was the Say Hey Kid, circa 1954, gifted and
gloriously unconscious about it. They say that after
the game you could often find him, his brio spilling
over the brim of nine innings, on the streets of New
York playing stickball with the other kids. Mays the
Amazing, all natural mastery and effortless fun. And
in truth, as late as 1973 he could still draw on the collective memory of the fans; and in fact, every once in a
while he'd still unload on a hanging curve or a sinker
that stayed up. But mostly his swings were incontinent,
even desperate. Where once he had better "get" than
anyone else in the game, decelerated, he labored in the
field. Sometimes he actually seemed *tired*—imagine:
Willie Mays, tired from playing baseball!—and the
once-automatic chatter had to be rationed. He seemed
to have to lift his celebrated smile like a shade. Much of

the time, though, he just seemed confused by his loss of aptitude, looking like some befuddled husband loaded with groceries who can't locate his car in the lot.

I think of the fathers, for it's the fathers I sympathize with most. I think of the fathers trying to recall for their sons the Willie Mays whose uniform this phony had somehow gotten hold of. Fathers who had enough trouble trying to get across the concept of curfew or Korea to their kids now had to scrounge through the demise of Willie Mays in order to make sense of their own devotion. For the sake of helpless fathers and skeptical kids, Mays should have known better than to hang on.

Champions have to be furiously imagined, forcibly shaped to our craving. It's bad enough that an athlete perseveres beyond the body's endowments or keeps poking hopelessly at the embers of dead skills. What's worse is having to *witness* a Willie Mays tottering away from a third strike that unspooled him. Of course, reporters still focused on him after the game, seizing on his sporadic contact or flash of bygone deftness instead of bothering with other Mets, born unglamorous, who notwithstanding the occasional three-for-five would never ascend in their whole careers very much above bungling. "I'll play as long as I'm able. As long as I can pull this uniform on, I'll play," Mays would tell them. But—no one had the temerity or poor taste to say it to his face—but kids have uniforms of their own. Fathers can make it to "able" without you.

Rickety-but-unsinkable, Satchel Paige, permitted by the St. Louis Browns to throw well into his forties—Kansas City gave him an inning to work when he was fifty-eight!—used to say, "Work like you don't need the money. Love like you've never been hurt. Dance like nobody's watching." In other words, make a virtue out of ignorance. And so, as he pitched he pretended the stands were empty, while fans tried to deduce from the old man on the mound the one-time phenom they'd never seen. And so the biggest draw in the Negro Leagues, who when he'd hurled in the 1930s for the Pittsburgh Crawfords would occasionally have his outfielders sit on the infield while he struck out the side, drew out his career into the 1950s with a team whose previous publicity stunts had included a midget pinch-hitter and a one-armed outfielder. As the man says, you could look it up, if you can bear to.

Thank goodness they scrubbed that fight between a forty-nine-year-old Larry Holmes and a fifty-year-old George Foreman. Only poor pay-per-view sales saved us from the spectacle of over-the-hill heavyweights hugged by bulk, their trunks hiked well above their reluctant guts, delivering punches with more advance notice than Christmas sales. Who really needed to see Holmes and Foreman swimming in their skins like kids clowning about in their fathers' coats? Who could stand to watch them smudge one another's muzzles for the few rounds they could stand it? Not that the combatants weren't pumped for the event. "If they don't want to take it seriously that's up to them," Holmes said. "I'm taking it seriously. George is taking it seriously. George doesn't want to stop doing hamburger commercials." Well, a few would-be blows might have landed, I suppose, but they'd have come in jet-lagged from the difficult trip. Possibly, every other round or so, a counter punch, like an afterthought, offered up like regret.

For we had seen them discredit themselves for some time. Not only were these fighters sluggish and fat, they were sluggish and fat the way everyone else was sluggish and fat, the way guys at the racetrack were. Both men had succumbed to the same extra flesh that flesh is heir to. (One publicity photo, bearing the caption "Battle of the Bulge," featured Foreman attacking a double cheeseburger and Holmes downing a slab of cake.) You might as well have been at Wal-Mart instead of Caesar's Palace. We had seen Larry Holmes, whose jabs could once drive rivets, nudge his listless opponent like a worn-out wife urging her logy spouse out of bed on a Monday morning. We had seen George Foreman, whose hooks could once strip steaks out of steer, bump his gloves against a midsection ample as his own like mudfish against the hull. As for anything on the order of an uppercut, forget it. You'd think these guys were loading wads of wet laundry into the mouth of a dryer. "I could see the opening, but I couldn't get my fist to fire in time," laughed Foreman, panting in the wake of his last fight. One interviewer asked him if this was really it for him, if he might not reconsider if, say, he could get a shot at Tyson. Damn their stumbly surrenders and spent shells! Damn their blotchy hides!

Why doesn't someone stop it? every fan with a conscience should have cried. The thumps that did no damage, the dumb compulsion to bloodless cue, the weary jostling in the ring as though a couple of accountants were making their way through the door of the day's last train. Why can't they live fast, die young, and leave a beautiful videotape? Oh, the mere humanity!

Jim Brown had it right, quitting football while he was still inimitable, not simply still intact. He led the league in rushing the year he retired. Jim Brown dearly departed the scene, ascendant instead of ground down. Thanks to that, he retained the stature of myth. Swift-footed, dactyllic Achilles had made that same unselfish choice, sparing the gilded youth the sight of a slumped old soldier breathing too hard over his greaves. If you have to crap out, crap out at apogee—there's the moral. Jim Brown and Achilles: now there were a couple of trading cards you could return to without embarrassment.

But for every running back who ran off before running out, for every marmoreal Greek, for every Mozart gigged mid-symphony or Kennedy cut down, for every child prodigy who crossed against the light, millions fray their way forward, day by increasingly ordinary day. The long-time radio announcer whose attention drifts and consonants catch in his dentures, but who bogarts the microphone anyway. The arthritic rock star who, committed to an art where pertinence is as fragile as hearing, still won't quit the stage. The aging actor who, having specialized in action heroes, has to get by on special effects since even running for a bus is now too much for him. The ingrown politician who lodges like a mineral deposit in the public works. The decaying Casanova who can no longer maintain his carnal quota and who really should be home in his slippers penning his memoirs while he can still remember them. These and millions more dwindle and dissipate, along with the ultimately unblessed rest of us as we Doppler out and flake away, until you can barely track our dander back to our dim and distant primes.

In 1797, Samuel Taylor Coleridge awoke from a sublimely literate dream with the whole of "Kubla Khan" precisely revealed to him. By his account—and there is no other to contradict it—fifty lines into his recording session he suffered an infamous and fatal interruption by "the man from Porlock." Detaining Coleridge for an hour on some trifling business, the unnamed visitor managed to derail the poet's train of thought, leaving Coleridge coy and defensive about the abridged vision he'd had to settle for. As he put it in his 1816 preface to "Kubla Khan," "a marvellous origin and the man from Porlock could bear the blame and serve as a natural shield against criticism."

It may be mostly recalcitrant undergraduates who praise the man from Porlock's contribution to their lives as being equally marvelous as the remaining poem they have to prepare for the midterm exam. But the appeal of the editing principle exceeds this one event. How many authors, addicted to their own wordy churn, imply a plea by their umpteenth by-the-numbers publication: "Stop me before I write again"?

What we need is a society to assert the verb. What we need is to Porlock such people who persist beyond the desertion of their talents. To lock their pores, stop their unseemly leaks, shut their shoddy production lines down. For even on the anointed the oil will eventually congeal.

Imagine a board of review–an underground tribunal, if you will—dedicated to determining when a given player, poet, or other public grandstander is performing only a pantomime of prior striving. If only we could put out a call to stanch the flow of movie sequels that stream out like a sneezing jag or steal the formula that compels a detective series to continue for so many novels past novelty. I know that their royalty statements pauper mine, but is it jealousy alone that makes me think that someone might prescribe a mild sedative for Stephen King or gag Judith Krantz? When a clichéd conceit masquerades as stamina, when the tapestry of accomplishment begins to bare its threads, a Porlock squad would arrive on the protracted scene to remove the offender and thus restore his dignity, and ours. Or perhaps a battery of secret avengers—one delegate per each of the nine muses of mythology, for instance, dispatched as needed to protect their good names. Even a single scourge of old-timers' tournaments and seniors tours would be a boon.

I maintain that there is no profession that would not benefit from the clear-cutting of dead and dying wood. In my own discipline, such discipline is rare. I am not talking about the whole tenure controversy, with its images of superannuated professors still gamely clutching their health plans and crumbling editions of *Beowulf* that hold the notes they penned in seven presidents ago. They need not barricade themselves behind the doors of the bigger offices with the verdant views, with syllabi and service plaques girdled round—enviable digs for academics in these times of budget cutbacks, surely, but hardly pleasure domes stately enough to storm. Let them keep meekly to themselves, so modest are the marks they make on the majors, in the end, so quiet their tread on the stairs. No, what I mean are the insistent ones, the gaudy ones with the publishing runs, who tweak their themes just enough to earn another hardback rehearsal of an act they'd made their names and mortgages on decades earlier. I mean the ones who, having ridden their hobbyhorse to death, convince one university press to handle the beaten corpse, a second to print the autopsy. I mean the dissertation tonnage making the rounds of over-budgeted houses like that notorious barge of garbage out of New York no landfill would have.

Infiltrate the annual convention where the jobless stare darkly and the chummy and consummated drink and jaw, and ask yourself whether you should have packed a scythe or not.

How many trees must be downed to accommodate us, who compulsively pack our vitae with articles like insulation in the walls? What oven birds we are! How our busy little organs chirr! How about this? "Professor X is survived by his wife, five children, eleven grandchildren, some twenty remarkable sentences, and half a dozen solid reviews." All right? Now lie down while we get out the shovels.

And yet, when it comes to the matter of my own faltering, I falter. Naturally, tenure won't punch my ticket forever, either, much less keep the current running through this mortal coil. No special equity accumulates in my desk, nor will any exemption revive within me symphony and song. Mine is no miracle of rare device sustained by cadence like Coleridge's Khan. I may already have missed my stop, as Mays and other, better men have done before. Some day the knock will come, and it will not be a damsel with a dulcimer (To such a deep delight 'twould win me!) but Atropos, armed with her clippings of the unfavorable reviews that mark my falling off. And what then? Will I close my eyes with holy dread and strain to resume the dream? Or will I rise to my last occasion, in brief and decent valediction, and wordlessly (for once!) disappear into the dugout?

That's the plan, at any rate, when I join the majority. Exeunt, with forbearers.

Model Behavior

So it came time for me to cede myself.
   —A. R. Ammons, "Mansion"

Vladimir: Say, I am happy.
Estragon: I am happy.
Vladimir: So am I.
Estragon: So am I.
Vladimir: We are happy.
Estragon: We are happy. (Silence.) What do we
do, now that we are happy?
   —Samuel Beckett, *Waiting for Godot*

Jim and Paula are watching their daughter perform in the display window of the Fashion Conspiracy. An aspiring actress, she is one of four teenagers who have adopted voguish poses to show off the new summer line of beachwear. A small crowd has gathered here at the intersection of merchandise and tai chi to see how long these kids can hold it together. How strange to see teenagers, who are as a rule incurably available to diversion (a truth that mall merchants count on and high school teachers lament) looking so contained. Their frozen motives are meant to be obvious, iconic. One has a beach ball clamped at chest level and is presum-

70

ably about to launch it at her partner, who pretends to cringe in gleeful anticipation of its return; the other two, armed with fork and spatula, respectively, are beaming over invisible steaks on the prop grill.

The job pays just above minimum wage, Jim confides to me, but in the context of our town, it represents maximum exposure. (She also gets a twenty percent discount on anything in the store.) In that pastoral chamber—they stand on Astroturf, and a smiling cut-out sun dangles down, moving vaguely in the air conditioning—he can imagine her being permanently spared drudgery, complication, peer pressure, ovarian cancer, and despair. Everything safe is sacred.

Last week, his daughter performed with a different company in the same window. Jim referred to that tableau of syndicated identities as "Donna Reed's wet dream," a remark he warned me not to repeat in front of his wife. I saw that show, too: a still taken from a generic fifties sit-com about a purified family's Pompeii'd vacation. His Jennifer played the elder daughter in chic bikini ($24, S-M-L, in bone, sunflower, periwinkle, magenta, or jade), with the demure, anachronistic touch of an inflatable seahorse float encircling her waist. The rest of the cast included a mischievous little brother caught in the act of preparing to douse his sister with the hose; a congealed, abominable Mom, icily featured in unyielding disapproval; an enameled Dad, contentedly and forever collapsed in his lawn chair like his just reward; and a stuffed dog.

It is remarkable just how grueling a repose they strike. The players are allowed to thaw only at ten-minute intervals. They stretch and rub blood back into their hands, legs, and shoulders; then they refossilize into pretty much the same preternaturally normal scene. They are allowed little flexibility in their characters when they enter this sixty square feet of planned community. At least, I see nothing in the second performance that could be remotely regarded as extemporization on the part of anyone. Each mood and mannerism has been precisely snipped out of the same tin. I mumble something to Jim about *Seven Samurai,* but he waves off my comment, as if it would disturb the scene. My reference is to the Kurosawa film we saw together in college, particularly to the one warrior who was exclusively committed to a clean kata. Even in driving rain, even in the midst of battle, he maintained his sublime orientation. The unerring, textbook lunge. The perfect, pious parry. He kept cutting compulsory figures in the air, in a rapture of expertise, clear-cutting a path for tradition out of his vulgar surroundings as if downing obstructive jungle with his blade. The man was all matchless craft and exactitude—no other swordsman could stand against him. When the enemy finally attacked with guns, he drew his sword as always: the bullets dropped him while he was still in the grip of reflex.

But Jim, apparently unwilling to risk anything like last week's Donna Reed crack with his wife nearby, is seriously intent upon today's proceedings as they do not proceed. You might imagine (their latest fashions to the contrary) that the performers were standing for a daguerreotype, which had to gather a day's worth of nineteenth-century French light to guarantee an impression. Their perfect smiles—How marvelous the ceramic cuspids and bright incisors! Look! Those are pearls that were their eyes!—recall the martial smarminess of a children's beauty contest, except that this particular version of the American Dream requires no other talent than steadfastness. But I am not crass enough to mention it with so many parents around.

Everything sacred is safe.

Don't get me wrong. These are some of the good kids. In a society rife with the glibly cynical and overindulged, who reject school for scandal, they are hardworking and well adjusted. In a society frequently defined by tagged, tattooed, pierced, dyed, and riveted kids—kids stapled or banded like some delicate species released into the blighted wild—they are preserving the diminished frontier of wholesomeness. They belie the jaundiced kids in upscale jeans ads, with their signature slouches and precocious ennui, with their fixed expressions of disdain, knowingness, and loss. No, the teenagers mounted here are the types that help the elderly with the door. They go to the school assemblies that delinquents ridicule or skip. They can recite the symptoms of any STD, and, should the occasion arise, they know how to "Just Say No" in thunder. They never get into any newsworthy trouble. You know: good kids.

But it occurs to me that it's "good" as in "good baby," a distinction any infant earns simply by sleeping through the night. Put a full-blooded child behind glass and he'd mutiny in a minute. Oatmeal will stiffen in its bowl if you leave it out long enough, too, but where's the accomplishment in that? Sorry, but the prospect of that militant innocence and changeless state, where one's only task, like the pet cat's, is to soil the same moldy corner of the litter box and repeat to himself, "Posture, posture," as he squats . . . well, not for the kids *I* know. Never this cramped culture without verbs. Not for *my* kid, God willing.

When I try to picture my own daughter occupying the window with the rest of them, I can't manage it. Just turning ten, Elizabeth is the sort of girl who evaluates dresses according to how well they twirl. The best dresses easily take the shape of her spins, and I sometimes have the impression that she is spinning all the time. I enjoy thinking of her as being caught in a continuous squall of delight. She has her dark, centripetal times, to be sure, but most often she is lifting in my mind. The best dresses—the ones that she can hardly bear to hang back in the closet—pick up on her buoyancy. Then there is Jeremy, Joy's son, who in his six years of existence has literally never sat down to a meal. Seconds into the first course he's coiled in his chair. It could be anything that will trip his hair trigger for distraction and fire him from the table. All bundled torque, that boy. How either child could aspire to the oblivious rigor of these model teenagers is beyond me.

Although half a dozen parents would shush me if I so much as whispered one word about it, the clichéd repertory being staged at the Fashion Conspiracy manifests a quintessentially American brand of harmony—the sort of whacked-out sclerosis you find in mail-order catalogs. The closest counterpart I can come up with from my own experience is the playground game of Statues, in which all of us had suddenly to "freeze" on command in the midst of some centrifugal scatter. Already veterans of duck-and-cover drills, the best of us could last the entire recess out in suspended animation, until the second bell sent us back to homeroom and Mrs. Seifert. Above her desk were two brilliant yellow placards: ALTHOUGH PERFECTION IS IMPOSSIBLE, MAKE IT YOUR GOAL and SILENCE IS GOLDEN—FILL THE ROOM WITH GOLD. Hey, no problem there for the pre-hormonal, weaned on freezing and eager to please. As to whether those bright signs guided our play, or whether the strict etiquette of Statues followed us back to class, it is hard to say. Whichever the case, we were leading undeniably charmed lives, both inside and out. Even that young, we all knew how to assume the position.

In a sense, all of us got used to cozying up to simulations long before Baudrillard invaded graduate school and armed us with the terminology to scold ourselves for it. I like to teach Don DeLillo's *White Noise*, which positively swims with manufactured images. There the bath of television static, the drone of the broken smoke detector, the growl of the garbage disposal, and the leaky surround of a thousand anonymous devices strand consumers just beyond the reach of comprehension. What is the difference between secret code and blather, between dense texture and creeping death, between the *om* that urges revelation and the constant hum of household compressors? When the complicated world is too much with us, DeLillo's characters hunker down in front of the television like primitives before a fire; they pull up the ladder and batten down hatches. Or they try to shop their way toward nirvana, seeking the coordinated embrace of the local supermarket's Oversoul or the dazzling All of the mall. (Everyone is in on the Fashion Conspiracy, you might say.) "Here we don't die, we shop," Murray Jay Siskind, Professor of Elvis Studies, explains. "But the difference is less marked than you think."

My students—good students, mostly majors in this class—have their heads down. They take notes.

Nine-year-old Steffie Gladney has developed virtual capitulation into an art form. She participates in simulation exercises as a volunteer victim, training for demise should the next incident of fallout prove fatal. Her father comes upon her splayed in the middle of the street and "devout in her victimhood," with "one arm flung out, her head tilted the other way. I could hardly bear to look. Is this how she thinks of herself at age nine—already a victim, trying to polish her skills? How natural she looked, how deeply imbued with the idea of a sweeping disaster. Is this the future she envisions?" DeLillo's Director of Advanced Disaster Management concludes his pep talk by telling the auditioning casualties that they "are not here to scream or thrash about. We like a low-profile victim." Let's see. At age nine, Steffie could be my daughter's classmate. Or she would have been just about ready for Mrs. Seifert's idyllic island. That would have been an effective addition to her resume.

"Victims, go limp," advises the director. What *doesn't* melt us into the yield signs he's after? What *doesn't* tell us to lie down? In "Skin," the poet Lucia Perillo confesses that for years she believed in "laws of adulthood: no yelling out of cars in traffic tunnels, / no walking without shoes,/ no singing any foolish songs in public places." Remember McMurphy's amazement in *One Flew Over the Cuckoo's Nest* when he realized that everyone else in the asylum was there voluntarily? Maybe undiluted McMurphy would be too much, but we could all benefit from a regular dose of Murray Burns, that lovable contrarian from *A Thousand Clowns,* who knew you had to ambush ordinary life every so often, preferably just when it sits down to tea.

More than a few of my students could do with a quick goose in the elevator.

To be honest, I must admit that their settled kettles look all the darker from the cozy perspective of my own black pot. I teach from a discipline in which some of the most esteemed representatives, Murray Jay Siskind confides, "read nothing but cereal boxes," and in a town where you can attend church services on every other block but cannot buy decent corned beef or the Sunday *New York Times,* so I get cranky. My department is lodged in a climate-controlled building whose windows do not open and whose thermostats—one in every office and classroom—are not connected to any system at all. It's like working in a sealed museum case for the spirit to slumber in, which, given the general status of the humanities these days, is a metaphor chillingly close to the mark. As the students grow drowsier, passing back and forth the same confined air day after day, teaching sometimes seems like irradiating meat. And so school subdues the would-be gooser and the prospective goosed together.

And so who am I to declare "not *my* kid" when she's seated with the rest, up close to the culture? "I had not thought death had undone so many. / Sighs, short and infrequent, were exhaled, / And each man fixed his eyes before his feet." In the event of catastrophe, walk quietly in a straight line, and keep your hands to yourself.

Oh, sure, plenty of my college freshmen are raucous enough before the bell. A kind of contemptuous grunge dominates more than just their clothing. They can dismiss the curriculum quicker and with bolder vocabulary than their parents could. But it takes so little to out them, really. Just a bit of pecking from one of us tweedy birds will do it. Ask them to articulate a position, and they'd sooner deny having one than have to stand for it. Challenge them to challenge one another, and out comes the numbing diplomacy of "I'm Okay, You're Okay," or the preferred, fundamental relent, "Whatever." Afflict them with insistence, and for the reaction you get you might as well have urged them to risk a piss beneath a church pew.

This is the way William Henry Devereaux, Jr., puts the predicament in Richard Russo's *Straight Man:* "If I could teach Blair how to become invisible, she'd be interested, but she doesn't want to argue with anybody, and who can blame her?" Blair is his best student, by the way, which is to say that she is most accomplished in barricading the perimeter of her attentions.

It is so tempting to be ungenerous. Faculty will move more readily than most into a sunny, dinless subdivision of ironic distance. "They are barely able to betray a pulse, much less a conviction," goes the usual war story. "They are so used to driving up to the window and showing their money. In return, they want their order, nothing more and nothing else."

Actually, fashionable conspiracies catch them long before they appear in my classes, all trusting and trussed. Stunned and wonderless between hard rock and Ritalin, what chance do they have? Furthermore, it is not their fault that the principal lesson of their formal education has been obedience. Starting in elementary school, where how to compose themselves is as central a lesson as phonics, the good students—yes, that double agent of a term again—become little ministers of deportment. While long division proves impenetrable to many children, none would flunk a test in school procedures. Kids notorious for not being able to find South America on the globe know just where they are supposed to march to during the fire drill. It may be cheap socialism to say so, but in school you learn what sells so you can go out and buy, and buy into, better. *That* drill is common knowledge, too: school inspires nothing so much as systematic surrender. First-graders say the Pledge of Allegiance every morning without having any conception of what "pledge" or "allegiance" means—an ignorance that ensures their allegiance anyway. It's all wide-eyed compliance and systematic

surrender, until the kids become so addicted to supervision that they can't pick a crayon or plunge a thumb
into a lump of clay before an instructor okays it. Once
they become literate—that is, once they are able to follow orders and fill out forms reliably—they will be released to enter the legions of the inconspicuous. What
giddy kindergartner *doesn't* come home with a hand-
print set in plaster? Who realizes at the time that this
is emblematic of the fate education has always had in
store for him?

So the students themselves are not entirely to blame
when their ideas are bleached beyond the pale of pale.
We complain that our schools don't work, while in fact
they probably work exactly as they were designed to.
As Lewis Lapham, the editor of *Harper's,* reminds us,
"The schools as presently constituted serve the interests
of a society content to define education as a means of
indoctrination and a way of teaching people to know
their place." Most often, that place is snug in one's desk
or, perhaps, encased in a mall window like a commodi-
fied Sleeping Beauty in her upright glass coffin.

People who live in glass houses go stony.

As an artist of the dutiful, Jim and Paula's daughter must spend hours in front of the mirror dequirking
herself, subtracting her idiosyncrasies flex by inflection, flinch by flinch, patiently solidifying the way a
dry-stone wall tightens under its own dedicated weight.
("The thought of *my* attempting such a stay!") Such
grave rehearsal! She has to apply herself carefully. Tor-
por must be engineered, and Jennifer abides by a specific chiropractic code. She practices a meticulous em-

bodiment, a step-by-step aesthetic of dispossession. She must imagine her every intentionless atom quieted and queued, as if consenting to a single dimension. And yet, this description doesn't really do justice to Jennifer. Given time, any child can learn to yield to a store window or a Disney cartoon. But this girl has a special flair. "She doesn't merely try out her role, she abandons herself to it," Jim says. "And that's not just a father's pride talking."

Remember when there was a fire on the set of *Leave It to Beaver?* No one was hurt, but they had to take the show off the air temporarily in order to restore the Cleaver house. Come to think of it, it may have been *Family Ties* and the Keaton house, or *Happy Days* and the Cunningham house; regardless, the point is that they recreated whichever set it was precisely to conform to the original, and Spring, Oak, Timber, Lake, or Pleasant Dale, Ridge, Vista, Terrace, or Glen healed from its burns within a week or two. In fact, the writers decided to incorporate the event into the show itself, devoting an episode to a fire that destroys the Brady house—I'm thinking now that it was *The Brady Bunch,* but no matter. Whichever family it was escapes intact, and the children, smudged and clutching a few toys emblematic of their respective characters on the show, are consoled by the lesson that things don't matter, only family does. Anyway, an appointed parent promises that their house will be rebuilt "good as new," which is to say, indistinguishable from the way it looked before the accident. Sure enough, when the show airs again, the family is back in their familiar digs, and, in keeping with the modular nature of situation comedies, whose segments may be shuffled for convenient syndication and consumption, no mention is ever made of the fire again. Like the commercials that taught us how to defeat "occasional irregularity," the shows themselves absorb and erase contingency, which is one of the reasons we watch. To come back to the same old place in the same old way, returning to that tidy and delicious trance, good as new.

Jeremy, mere months shy of first grade now, zips past his mother on his way to their car, winning a race she isn't even aware is being run.

Better than new, actually, because status quo is now more deliberate than ever. People are still watching the display models, captivated by how captivated they are. They seem to hover there—you forget there's a platform and a promotion. Like decoys on a pond, they provide just a touch of the ideal, just enough to seduce the other ducks. Well, I'm here, too. Even my own daughter, for all I know, is out trolling.

Like everyone else, I guess I'll stop to listen to the junior high choir perform in front of Sears or let their classmates wash my car in the parking lot to earn money for a trip to our nation's capital. I agree with Jim and Paula that there isn't enough coverage of kids like this.

At lunch in the Food Court, they tell me about Jennifer's plan to go to Laguna Beach, California, next summer to try out for the Pageant of the Masters, in which artists draw in customers by dressing as life-sized works of art. They may impersonate Picasso's undulant ring of bathers, assuming whatever censors there may still be so close to Hollywood allow, or put on *Guernica,* if sufficient funding comes through to accommodate the cast a work of that scope would require. She may inhabit Grant Wood's *American Gothic,* standing with an equally rigid husband for the unbending sobriety of standardized Iowa; or she may get to nurse a cognac for a breezy evening in Toulouse-Lautrec's *At the Moulin Rouge.* Perhaps she'll reconfigure inside of Seurat's pointillist Sunday along the Seine or join the set of a lush Gaugin, a couple of plum opportunities, presuming the weather holds. Perhaps she'll be part of the slight, indefinite clientele of Hopper's *Night Hawks,* sunk in contemplation and blear. With her mall background, she'd be a prime candidate to ravage Degas's *Millinery Shop,* musing among plushy hats. Doing a Renoir would surely enhance her vita, and what career would not prosper after a solid run of Mary Cassatt? "We're keeping our fingers crossed," Paula says.

I don't expect Jennifer to stick around here for college—her prospects are too exotic for Joplin to contain her. I am not planning an intervention on principle—I wouldn't even think to smudge the glass. But if she did somehow stumble into one of my sessions on *White Noise,* I'd be curious to see her deal with a favorite exercise of mine. Jack Gladney, the novel's protagonist, discovers that he has been infected with Nyodene D, a mysterious toxin about which little is understood except that it is lethal. This is upscale, prestigious dying, dying at unprecedented levels of technological advancement, dying by one's own condemnatory data, but dying nonetheless. There is no way to tell how long it will take for it to kill him—there is a good chance that he will die long before the contaminant does him in—and tenure was not about to prevent his death otherwise. But the crisis is that now Jack Gladney is aware of his mortality. Everything sacred is no longer safe.

I tell my students that I awoke this morning from a prescient dream, in which came to me the irrefutable dates of their respective deaths. I pass out a sealed envelope to each student with his or her name upon it. Here are your death certificates, I tell them. Open them or not. But before you decide, ask yourself if you really want this information. Admittedly, it would enable you to plot wiser investment strategies, but you'd begin to see the future, however much future you have bequeathed to you, not as a far horizon but as an oncoming train. And if you know that your death is coming, how do you change your lives? *Do* you change your lives? And if you do, how? And if you do, why bother with the envelope, as if what it contained were the sole disqualification of what you are without it?

Heads up! I cry. The ball has landed smack in the middle of your yard. How about a little help here? I have to tell my students when I'm not being rhetorical, when their response is not an interruption but a collaboration. Grab a bucket and bail, somebody! We're going down!

You may think this is stupid stuff, I continue, but the fact is that I have had this dream before, and I have never missed the mark by more than forty or fifty years. Given the incalculable expanse of time, that's pretty good shooting. Today is the first day of what's left of your life. Do you want to open your envelope or drop it in the trash can? And what do you want to do *then*, Jennifer?

No one looks forward to being graded on the novel. The trouble is that it will not stand still, like a sun moving ambiguously in the air conditioning. Everything is sacred. Nothing is safe. Nothing is sacred. Everything is safe.

The Cast of Characters

Now begin to combine a few or many letters, to permute and combine them until thy heart be warm.

> —Rabbi Abraham Abulafia

"We are here to carry out the pattern. A small patient task. You have the word in English. Abecedarian. That is what we are."
"I don't know the word."
"Learners of the alphabet. Beginners."

> —Don DeLillo, *The Names*

CAST
(in order of appearance)

A is sturdy and redoubtable, the formulaic first son, with his feet set wide astride a hypothetical chasm. Go ahead and lash your horse to that stable center rail—it will hold. Drive your pick into either sheer face with assurance and keep climbing. Suppose a couple of toughs are chasing after the class's hapless toady. They corner the climactic alley . . . and a brace of A's is there to save him. For A is the emblem of moral gravity, guardian and herald of all the alphabet. With an A at her side, even Hester Prynne was able to brazen out a novel's worth of derogation. Yet for all his resolve, A remains unglamorous, like an inverted Atlas, with everything dependent. No companions ever beat congratulations against his back as if putting out a fire. For while prodigals get the glory for recoveries we never entirely trust, the steadfast simply stand their hammered ground, anonymous and unthanked.

B strains to bursting in her corset. So buxom and full of cushiony promise, she offers herself unabashed. A pair of lips, swelling breasts, ripe belly, embodying in a single form the carnal properties Solomon found dispersed and had to wed hundreds to secure. Inevitably gentle, she bumps out the mouth and up against a proximate ear, hardly acknowledging, coy as her sly presence in "subtlety." Her voice is like brushing—so delicately!—against a beauty in a subway, just enough to be able to trace the belated shudder back through the door she departs from.

C gapes on invisibilities. A clamp in search of purchase, C is the way that all craving starts. Tongueless, toothless jaw, he opens everlastingly on absence, serving some vague, yet still insistent, appetite. What prospects left so indelible an impression? What pressure does that scything curve recall? A thumbnail's dent in the bread dough, a hoof in the dust, the jut of a corpse's chin. In any event, C suggests a rigid, vanishing insistence.

D hides like a side pocket, which itself hides . . . what? Some homely property, no doubt, hardly worth discretion, much less secrecy. Frisk her for richer symbolism, and all you come up with is a few coins, a bramble of keys, a grocery list impaled on a ballpoint pen. Of course, no matter the size of the secret, secrecy breeds intrigue on its own, and this understated tuck could be cultivated to serve that purpose. (It is whispered that D is far along in her pregnancy. Whom among her consorts do you suspect?) Alternatively, you could conceivably seize her by the vertical and slice with that whetted arc. Figured this way, worn close, D would threaten the bearer whenever he budged, so that the secret could cut whoever carried it.

E pretends to be dedicated to a policy of full disclosure. Certainly, no one is cast more often than E, who tends to disappear into his role like salt in solution. Take a paragraph at random: watch the E's convene like crows come to edit a carcass. Yes, it is a forbidding simile for so common a character. Why do those three inky fingers disturb you so? The withered hand of the last of Dickens's Christmas ghosts emerged from a black sleeve like that, too. A specter silent and final as E can be.

F is either flying a banner or flagging down help. If you accept the argument that bravado really conceals insecurity, possibly it's both. F may be beckoning or waving goodbye. Her arms may be raised to await an embrace or to stave off assault. Motives are a complex business. As in any relationship, knowing whether to commiserate or to steer clear is key. Haven't you been bristled at for failing to understand and for trying to? What does F expect from you, anyway? Nothing much. And a lot more.

G is bent on inwardness. You have apparently caught her at the instant of recoil. Either shyness or an attack of conscience has begun to ball her up. It may be a sign of autism—you expect G to begin to rock back and forth, keeping you at bay with an unintelligible volley of gutturals. For want of asylum or shell, G lies doggo and denies you, a knot you might bother or budge but never undo. In just another second that last access will suck flush, so that nothing—not counsel, not compassion—can enter. For G has already issued its preemptive strike and assumed the worst of herself, and of you.

H recalls the goalposts that the winning kick cleared, but celebrations take place in the shadow of the gallows. That is the double lesson H affords: all success must be reconciled with demise and must take its measure from it. That is why a Jewish groom grinds a goblet beneath his heel when he marries, thereby remembering the destruction of the temple even as he and his bride begin to build. Their ceremony takes shape beneath a *chupa,* another H. The lesson of H, you might say, is that there is no such thing as an unadulterated good time, which, admittedly, is an arch way of putting it.

I announces the first person. To begin at the Beginning, the first first person was Adam—the first in the Bible to poke his I out—after whose fall a series of rapid-fire begettings spread selfhood like sin. Prior to Creation, the Lord likely had to manifest without an entourage. All I's were on Him. Afterwards, He continued to emphasize that He is beyond accounting, His circumference too swollen for any first-person singular to surround. Only fitfully does the God of the Old Testament fit His Pluribus into a Unum. Thus while every frenetic Hebrew plots his or her individual departure in Exodus, He goes We, We, We all the way home.

"I heard you in the garden, and I was afraid because I was naked, so I hid," Adam stammers, trying to hide behind those I's like a stand of leafless trees. Whereas God's word fleshes instantly, making every utterance an assembly, man's can't even cover him.

When one Book later our fate is lateraled from Adam to Moses, the pronoun is still whittled thin. "Who am I, that I should go to Pharaoh and bring the Israelites out of Egypt?" His I strikes even Moses as an inadequate staff. It is all well and good that God announces that "I am that I am" is self-sufficient, but for Moses, that poor iamb "I am" scarcely flutters a pulse, much less fazes Pharaoh, until heavenly reinforcements arrive.

Interestingly, while not even God's prophets robe themselves in plurals, the Pope enjoys the prerogative, as do kings, who use the royal "we" to indicate the whole kingdom. (Thus when France enters in *King Lear,* the entire country has symbolically come to call, and offstage the cook frets about stretching the soup.) Editorialists also employ this rhetorical trick, which presumes solidarity and the group hug of consensus, although it sometimes smacks of a bully relying on brawny buddies to back him.

Surely the most wide-I'd example you will find comes from Walt Whitman, the Grand Panjandrum of selfhood, whose I means a multitude and parades en masse throughout the canon. While for the typically retracted rest of us the I is a solitary stitch in time, his is the most potent vocable in American poetry, the cynosure of existence and universal homing device, as this Whitman sampler will serve to demonstrate:

I know I am deathless,

I know this orbit of mine cannot be swept by a carpenter's compass,

I know I shall not pass like a child's carlacue cut with a burnt stick at night.

I know I am august,

I do not trouble my spirit to vindicate itself or be understood,

I see that the elementary laws never apologize . . .

What ostentation and clamor! What an unprecedented barging in! This I is a battering ram. So much for the glazed urbanity of a T. S. Eliot, whose persona picks so carefully through the waste, with pinkies out. Not for Whitman the maimed orthographies of E. E. Cummings, with his tiny i's rubbed raw (not to mention his meager, stripped t's). Even a period would offend so sweeping and perpetual an entrance: "I exist as I am, that is enough." Not since the commodious

Old Testament Lord has so sovereign an I surveyed the scene. If you are looking for the stuff that main characters are made of, the I's have it.

J is a hook dangling in unimaginably placid waters. Cast that capital; feed out however much line behind it professional technique requires. Wait. Not a shiver. Never at all. Anticipation cannot last against peace so absolute as this. The whole scene feels posed. Poised. Incised. Pay out more line if you wish, but for what? What do you mean to catch? What do you hope will find you?

K has all the tenderness of a clock gear and sounds as if some widget went down the wrong pipe. K sticks in the throat. K seems about to deliver the kick that K initializes, but the kick never comes. K stays the execution. And so, K connotes the precipice, the second guess, the misgiving, the purse snapped shut in spite of the urge to spend.

L defends a lonely outpost with centurion detachment. Chiseled and fixed in his convictions, L brooks no debate. What steadies his eternal rectitude? What private imperative feeds steel into that spine? Or is he just stuck in a lull? L persists like a flagpole planted in a vacant lot.

M is rigid as a pillory and as stern. You might remember Shelley's Ozymandias, or his imperious remains: "Two vast and trunkless legs of stone" empedestaled in the desert. That is the way M rules the environment, an altar unto himself, while "boundless and bare / The lone and level sands stretch far away." Accordingly, M maintains that isolation is the true test of majesty.

N is so intractably, predictably cynical that irritation is the only reaction you can manage. The sensation of that consonant is like a needle in the teeth, until the unbending "no" or "not" or "negative" begins, and you know what's coming before N's full dissent gets said. "Oh, what can you do with a man like that? What can you do?" asked the exasperated narrator of a John Cheever story. "How can you dissuade his eye in a crowd from seeking out the cheek with acne, the infirm hand; how can you teach him to respond to the inestimable greatness of the race, the harsh surface beauty of life; how can you put his finger for him on the obdurate truths before which fear and horror are powerless?" He had contended so long with an inveterate N of a brother that he actually ended up, like Cain, clubbing him. Yes, the verdict in the Bible came down quickly and clearly. But be honest: who, met with an N of his own, forced to endure for the hundredth time the usual smug dismissal and sneer, hasn't thought about picking up something blunt?

O is the letter you can look through, a womb with a view. A decorous little void, not only the navel gazed into but the gazing eye invited in as well. Not to mention a blind orbit, or a ball, to boot. Or try the site of some compact implosion, possibly, or a cold, uninhabitable planet. An inestimable depth. A black hole. Any analogy you might contrive intimidates you. For the story of O is insularity. Hers is an entrenched, recessive character, withdrawing evenly at every border until she is perfectly immured. Sounds of mourning, disappointment, regret echo unremittingly within that empty chamber. An incessant, lowing O, utterly self-absorbed. The scrupulous zero O might be mistaken for offers nothing either. O is the drain you circle. Do not draw too close to the rim.

P turns heads. "Ample, but not fleshy," as Edward Albee described Martha in *Who's Afraid of Virginia Woolf?*, P seems always about to topple (like Albee's Martha, too). It must be difficult to uphold that perfectly rounded pout, strict inhale and permanent flex. You may salivate or scorn as you pass that Amazon by, but walk a little softly: P is a prisoner of her own silhouette.

Q has the nuance of a mollusk, whose indeterminate appendage suggests a tongue, tail, antenna, leg, or genital, according to your predilections. It is that little kickstand, that slight hint of reluctance, more akin to a lick than to any substantial anchor, that dominates your attention. Provocative and—it must be acknowledged—vaguely lewd. But its vagueness warns you against indignation, for it might be a cripple's infirmity dragging after, after all. You yourself undoubtedly trail some imprudence or other, and thus dare not judge. (If you find a single, wiry, gray hair poling out of your groin, are you able to reconcile the finding with what you believe yourself to be, or ever will?) Alternatively, consider the ladder lowered from the landing module, which, given the least sign of duress, might be retracted. So Q begs tentativeness and, whatever the case, counsels caution.

R depicts the perils of inbreeding. There is something jerry-built about R, as if each member of the consortium behind its creation had been asked to compromise in one particular or another. (More than any other character, R cries out for career counseling.) Clearly, no one designer got everything he wanted. Nor would it be surprising to learn that the project director was in fact the president's son. One thinks of the platypus, that disastrous rough draft of an animal. One thinks of the chimera of Greek mythology, at once plagued and punishing, as ungainly as anything ever agreed upon by a committee hungry for lunch. One of the balkier members of the alphabet, R occasionally plays the growly uncle who raps his cane like a petty tyrant and makes Thanksgiving a chore. You want to sympathize with him—some trauma, surely, has him so bent out of shape—but his personality makes it difficult to do so. More than once you've pictured R in that very posture on the ground—the corpse the cops have chalked around.

S slithers sensuously, sibilantly, seductively, and so on, inviting one obvious crime of consonance after another. The serpent in Genesis sloughed his name along with his legs as he wound down the ages, but the snake he became through current consensus never shed its essence or its character. S has also served with honor, adorning the caduceus, as well as a few emblems of nations situated near the equator. And yet, having earned higher station, S has still never won much trust. Emily Dickinson's feeling of "tighter breathing / And Zero at the Bone" continues to hold sway. (Dickinson also confessed, "Sometimes I write [a word], and look at his outline till he glows as no sapphire." The poet was ever prey to humble seductions.) Frankly, it is hard to come up with any form of civil service that S might perform that will convince anyone otherwise.

T puts his foot adamantly down. Standing for the Cross—envision T strewn with raiment, a risen clothesline—he can be priggish. T names the principal spirit of etiquette and restraint. Pronounce the consonant, and you sound like a matron chiding a servant at a formal dinner party for failing to set out the proper condiments. So for all his stalwartness and intimations of transcendental stature, T is always too concerned with what others might think. (What character is more fanatical about posture than T?) Broad-shouldered, he is nevertheless, at base, something of a stick in the mud.

U has that allusive droop to him, intimating demise. From pouches under the eyes, to the slump of despondency, to the shovel that instigates the grave, this character carries a narrative so inevitable, so inevitably miserable, that the middle collapses. The weight of foreknowledge stops his progress, breaks his back. Feel U rumble deep in your throat like something ungulpable. No enchantment can lend a vector to him. No predicate can compel a progress out of that sad sack. Worse still, this is the character that names you, and although you tell yourself that no superstition clings to you, you can't help but worry just a little, just enough to take the trouble to look for evidence of this irrevocable U in the mirror.

V is that limber, leggy lover you fantasize about, whose availability would be Victory, indeed. To be so deftly scissored at the hips by her—the prospect thrills you, but not enough for you to rouse your embedded partner, who lies pooled in indiscriminate sleep beside you. How can you settle into your familiar sleep again when dreams of angles assault you each night? What consolation can smooth desire so acute?

W carries the proof of rough forces. Your first impulse is to prescribe potassium for so bad a case of cramps as that, but indigestion alone cannot account for such an extreme a condition. Plate tectonics, perhaps, or some other indifferent pressures caused it. W is durable, yes, but he wears durability's price permanently. The honed declivities. The escarpments that fill with darkness as W bites sedulously down, digs in.

X arks the spot that the map values most, true enough. Convention directs your attention to the center, where the intersecting forces are cinched. This is the forgotten prisoner, gutshot while he hung manacled to the wall. This is the site of the inoculation, where the treasure's been injected. You score what you mean to return to, hence the forbidding quality of this character. (Beware of the poison that lies behind that aspect.) No wonder Wallace Stevens was stopped cold in his tropes by "the vital, arrogant, fatal, dominant X." Yet you could just as well focus on the vectored stretches as target the core, as if the notorious spot were the epicenter of some Euclidean burst. Consider, in other words, those implied forces as centrifugal, not converging like sparrows on one fluff of bread but obeying a contract of departure. Thus those X's on your calendar that began the month as meetings ended it as adjournments. What if X's appendages were lashed to four simultaneously incited horses? A gruesome future for one so dutiful, whose allegiance has never been questioned: the character keeps your metaphorical foot in the metaphorical door while you venture elsewhere. And to further enchant the figural-minded, X is an ideal example of chiasmus, a most committed mark marking most commitments.

Y is so plaintive, naming its wish and wonderment at once, reaching her arms to plead or receive. But does anything fall upon the supplicant—bare, forked tree—from that extrapolated sky? Not even a drop to wet this good wineglass, which has been set out in the hope that company might come? Philosopher or poet, eventually you have to acknowledge the truth: the white surround is final, a dividing and indifferent hue. Despite her heartfelt cry, Y's page always goes unanswered.

Z cringes before intimidations you can only guess at or suffers some ambiguous crush. He endures like Atlas the weight of the world. Indeed, the entire alphabet presses consequence upon Z. Your automatic reaction would be to offer condolence, if only a brief embrace to soften such obvious grief—you are not stone!—but Z responds sharply, offering no contour to caress and nothing to love. Ironically, the truculence that sustains his solitude keeps Z unrelieved. He will not be coaxed out of that crouch. Indeed, were Z to relinquish his condition and straighten up to accept you, you would not recognize him. No, Z's resignation is his resolve, and the voice of Z is a snarl. In the end, you back off.

Some One-on-One

It begins as a dance, as edgy and unpredictable as dating, and like dating, it includes prospects for both conquest and humiliation. A couple of solitary players are shooting at adjacent baskets. Say that one had been watching a game on television and caught the fever; say that the other has come to work out his aggressions by working up a sweat that, for the first time in a week, does not originate in anxiety. Whatever their respective motivations, chance has brought them together, or nearly together. Now, in strategic proximity, the enticement—the game before the game—begins.

From time to time, they catch sight of one another as various caroms off backboard or rim dictate. Neither one wants to reveal his needs, so each pretends to be engrossed in his practice. Each player labors to suggest that his solitude is not loneliness but self-sufficiency. Each implies in his feigned preoccupation that taking unconflicted jumpers and corraling his own misses is enough for him; within his charmed radius (from the three-point line in) he is content to abstain from company. But they sneak peeks, size one another up, and, detecting an impending dare, do not show everything in their arsenals. Five minutes of sometimes syncopated dribbling pass. Ten.

Finally, one breaks the ice. "One on one?" According to protocol, the petitioner makes his offer casually, so as not to betray interest or dependency. Play or not, it makes no difference to me. We're both here, so why not? But make no mistake—I'm entirely willing to keep on as I am. Protocol dictates that the second player delay and consider his answer, so as not to betray interest or dependency. I just want to make sure that you are the last resort, so I just want to survey the gym one last time to make sure that nothing better (which includes my continuing to shoot around on *my* own) presents itself. Thus the competition is keen even before the score is kept, with the wooer unmoved and the wooed unwowed.

Whether the one who approaches or the one who's approached suffers the greater exposure has eluded sociologists so far. It suffices to say that the semiotics of Friday night at the local bar are no more fraught with tension or decorum than this interchange.

Probably because my game is so unencouraging, I usually end up taking the initiative. Or perhaps it's because my gear is so unprepossessing—my gym shirts boast logos of companies that long ago went under, celebrate the exploits of disbanded teams, or advertise slogans so obsolete that my opponents do not recognize them—that I spark no serious notice. You may talk to me all you want about putting away childish things, console me with evidence of my professional standing, whisper lines from my vita like a lover's assurances, but the fact remains, if given cosmic carte blanche, I'd choose to command the lane rather than reign over any committee.

Oh, sure, I take pride in what I've published, but I'm still nagged by the belief that publishing is the prowess of the last kid picked for the team. Seriously, now, who in academe, that elaborate bastion of compensation for constrained physical gifts, wouldn't surrender tenure for a lethal curveball or a four-three forty-yard dash? A typical weekday finds me wading through freshman essays, trying to keep my aesthetics aloft while passing through gauntlets of grievous grammar. Don't imagine that I'd put the head coach on hold to pencil in another set of corrections. And you needn't recite the symptoms of burnout to me. Job counseling won't cut it, either. What difference would it make if I were to push other paper in other directions? Ascending the corporate ladder cannot compare to rising above the rim for a ringing slam. Face it—Faust squandered his chance. He might have dared to aspire even higher and bargained with the Devil to let him dunk over Michael Jordan. He might have manifested his vision of influence and renown not in some musty library or remote German village but in Springfield, Massachusetts, consecrated site of the Basketball Hall of Fame.

A few years ago, my mother called me because a conversation with my younger brother had distressed her. He is an attorney, with a wife and three healthy, talented children and an impressive home on a pastoral-sounding street in a pastoral-sounding suburb of Chicago. The guy's flush, in other words, and to be honest, in view of the somewhat erratic kid he was, a pleasant surprise all the way around. I guess that they had been reflecting on how far he'd come, and my mother, sitting in his richly appointed living room—it has blond paneling and tasteful French doors that open out to the patio, with its built-in gas grill—asked him, innocently enough, whether his legal career still made him happy. He said, "Well, I guess if I can't play centerfield for the White Sox, it's fine." So my mother called me. "He still wishes he could play baseball," she mourned. I explained to her that this was not news, that *all* of us have similar dreams that similarly endure. (Basketball is my game, or rather the game I pretend, in faithful Walter Mitty fashion, to suit up for, but I can still commiserate with my brother about his true ambition.) No one grows up hoping to work in Accounts Receivable, I explain, or waxes poetic over the prospect of becoming an actuary some day. These are honorable professions, no doubt, useful to society and dependable means of feeding a family, but these are points one makes when he's ceased to score any other way. Is the identity a person has established in sales so precious that he wouldn't wager it against the chance to go to work in a jersey? Who wouldn't back-burner everything else for a try-out with the pros?

Jeff continues to play ball—softball on Saturday afternoons when the kids don't need to be shirpa'd somewhere or other, and hoops at the high school on those Tuesday nights when work hasn't followed him home or when too many errands are not lying in wait for him when he gets there. My mother and my sister-in-law, both sensible adults, call it silly and sad that he keeps at it, an estimation that is silly and sad, or so I'd say to both of them if it weren't cruel to do so. "Don't take it seriously," I say instead. But I remember the captivating squeaks of gym shoes sounding like a great caucus of rodents, the rabid crash and gallop of committed bodies forcing a fast break, and the *hoosh* of the good shot as the nylon gives way—yes, the image is sexy in *any* context. I beg off the phone because unless I do laundry, I won't have shorts for tomorrow.

And so I persevere. My jumper is still legitimate, if not inspirational, although "jumper" does it more credit than it deserves, for what little "ups" I may have had in the past have now deserted me completely, leaving me no elevation to speak of at all. (Goaltending, which had always been a vain desire of mine anyway, is something I no longer even fantasize about. Even in my dreams I am rooted to the floor.) Call my play capable or earnest—think of the guarded adjectives reluctant letters of recommendation rely upon. I have all the lateral alacrity of a giraffe in splints, and I go to my left about as often or effectively as any member of the Reagan cabinet ever could. Meanwhile, an over-developed sense of self-protection and wariness over my medical deductible have combined to make my rebounding random at best and too rare to rely on. But because I am in the end better than nothing, I usually prevail, and the game is on.

At this point, my opponent recognizes his predicament. I am old for the game, still pushing against my more-and-more constricted perimeter as I push fifty. When a player young enough to be my son takes me on, he cannot reasonably expect anything much from me, leaving me essentially immune to disgrace. Indeed, because I was never swift, the attrition of my speed—no, there is no way for me to allude to "my speed" with a straight face—has been for all intents and purposes indiscernible. Having had so little to lose, I handle the fact that my meager speed continues to leak away as the seasons pass with aplomb, to be supplanted by "savvy," that transparent euphemism for "slow." For the older I get, the more respectable my talents become. Whatever I ever possessed remains intact: I've lost nothing on my shot, and my passes remain true, even on occasion impressive. (This second characteristic is irrelevant to one-on-one, of course, but my gift list stops at two, so indulge me.) In this way, while I was a mediocre basketball player as a teenager and through my twenties, I was deemed fairly decent in my thirties and have gotten even better reviews in my forties. If I can sustain play into my fifties, I look forward to surprising denigrators with my modest but essentially unblemished skills, until one day I'm known as being "not bad, for an old guy" and can even lie convincingly about having once played college ball. And with each game he agrees to, like the eager thoroughbred that explodes from the gate only to come inexorably back to the pack, my tiring opponent finds his dominance diminishing over time, whereas my own level of play, which basically began in the basement anyway, has not sunk any further.

That's the plan, anyway. When a superior player breaks me down like balsa with his dribble, I bear no blame—I'm old, remember, and it's miraculous enough that I got back on defense at all. If I score on *him*, however, that lands a blow to the heart and may subject him to the jeers of anyone who catches sight of it. Thus, notwithstanding my stumbles, I am ideally positioned, in that any solid play I make on the court is a bonus no one counted on, and any lapse is forgiven since no one really imagined I had all that much ability left to lapse in the first place. In short, beat me and you've defeated a father, which is a questionable victory anyway; lose, and you've lost your dignity along with the game. You cannot win for trying. Live with that, boy.

I usually do take the advice I gave my mother and don't take it seriously either, my eternally ragged play. I have perspective on all this scuttling across the floors of local Y's. Yet there have been times, even recently, when my vestigial ego has been rooted out for bruising.

For instance, there was the day I came upon a demigod holding court. He was probably in his late twenties, about six-foot-six, and knife-lean. To my surprise, he deigned to play me. Perform for me, rather, since I could not really give him a game. His jump shot had the balanced action and sweet release aficionados ascribe to the finest hunting rifles, and his aim was just as lethal. When I tried to play him close, he shed me as easily as Bogart in so many movies shook the novice cop's tail, and it was death by a thousand merciless cuts to the hoop. His calibrated crossover dribbles and drives had me backpedaling more awkwardly than a city councilman at a news conference. When I played off him, or rather, when he grew weary of uncontested jams, he simply drifted back beyond the arc and rained ideal threes that seemed to drop from Platonic heaven. His own defense was adhesive, and when I did free up for a shot, that meager success was tempered by my suspicion that he had merely relented, much the way its handler lets his dog run after he has maneuvered the unwitting creature into a fenced-in yard. For the record, I lost the first four games 15–6, 15–5, 15–6, 15–2, thereby denying me even the faith that the passage of time would even us up somewhat. Nevertheless, between gasping and gulping water, I begged a fifth game.

Hubris is the last sin the aging player is likely to relinquish. Clearly, I wasn't going for his nose, but I may rightly be blamed for overreaching. An errant elbow of mine caught him flush on the bridge, and the blood spouted freely, rendering him for the first time in our acquaintance awkward in some way. He waved off my help and apology, but collected himself as best he could under the circumstances and headed to the front desk for repairs, his nose poking skyward all the while like a periscope. Ten minutes later, the guy who came to wipe away the Jackson Pollock our unintentional collaboration had left on the floor told me that another employee had escorted him to the hospital. "Do you need a hand with that?" I asked, hoping to make myself useful. "I got it, I got it," he replied, having pegged me, I suppose, as clumsy in every regard. There was nothing for me to do but shower off and duck out of there.

Three weeks later, while getting a locker key at the front desk, I again spied this Achilles in the gym. He was shooting on his own as before, and neither his face

nor his expertise appeared any the worse for our colli-
sion. He was in his element once more and zoned in,
utterly absorbed by perfection. Not only did I not interrupt his practice this time, I hurried past the gym
to the locker room, deciding to settle that day for the
anonymity of the weight room.

In the enlightenment that has succeeded Title IX,
the prospects for the demise of one's self-esteem have
increased and become more varied. That is to say,
one never knows when the next player to show him
up will turn out to be a girl. Once upon a time, there
were no sports for girls to attempt, much less to hope
to play professionally. Girls were segregated from the
gym altogether, or so it seemed, and during recess not a
hint of estrogen shadowed the blacktop or scented the
softball field, creating, as it were, an apartheid of the
playground. In gym class they primped and stretched
in preparation for vague rituals like "rhythmic movement," a pseudo-exertion that required no competitive-
ness and left no sweat. Left to their delicate conditions,
girls never imposed, and whatever challenges to boys
they represented were never athletic but sexual and distant. I tell this story to my skeptical daughter when I
run out of fables about witches and dragons. She finds
that bygone world of female apathy and incompetence
as fantastic as any Camelot. Since she is exhausted from
soccer practice anyway, she sleeps easily.

So nowadays I occasionally find myself up against a
girl whose basketball skills, freed to flower by contemporary feminism, threaten to prove too much for me.
Nevertheless, I can't help holding back when defend-

ing a girl, reluctant to "play up in her shirt" as coaches always urged us to do for all I might accidentally find there. Reaching for the ball, I might cop an inadvertent feel, catch an unsettling, unmistakable softness, and go suddenly buttery in the legs. I recently took on a girl who was sheathed in black, her legs tightly holstered and gleaming, her torso only half-concealed by a kind of halter-top. Defending against her midriff—the conventional wisdom is that the body always follows the belly, so do not be misled by jab steps, feints, and ball fakes—I could not help but wonder at the humming-bird tattoo displayed there, with its beak discreetly dipping into her navel, as if it were about to drink from the silver piercing there. As it happened, she was no match for me. I was too strong, or at least too heavy, for her to dislodge from the paint; furthermore, I was a good six or seven inches taller than she was, so that even when my transfixion allowed her to slip past me, I could still swat down the shots she hoisted (emitting each time a barely perceptible note somewhere in the vicinity of F sharp) like late-summer bluebottles.

I succeeded in winning every game—don't talk to me about chivalry when it's 13–12—and to her considerable credit, she handled it with a grace that more than lived up to the avian image she bore. (If it isn't too sexist to say so, sportsmanship comes more naturally to women, who may be by socialization and by nature alike quicker to mature, wiser about priorities, and better disposed toward cooperation than men, who certainly receive precious little instruction in that discipline from the sports they see on television.) Amiably, she accepted my chaste tap of congratulations for a game well played, and she disappeared into the women's locker room and, I presume, into one of any number of promising futures available to young women in today's America.

It is with this awareness that I once in a while coax my fifth-grade girl out onto the court with me. I'd just as soon just shoot around with her, honing her fledgling skills and our relationship, but she wants a game. It is a difficult balance to maintain between taking it easy on her (I would never risk fouling my own nestling) and insulting her by too obviously not trying. But on offense, it is all she can do to maintain a dribble, much less worry about getting by me or launching a viable shot; she slaps at the ball assiduously but tentatively, as if she were chastising her puppy for chewing up one of her *Archie* comic books. On defense, she's as persistent as her physical limitations let her be, and for a while, anyway, she clings to me like a pilot fish to a shark, knowing that any advantage I might take of her would never menace her in any significant way.

Puberty is not all that's burgeoning in that little body, I think. She'll need that tenacity elsewhere as well, when she's up against something less forgiving than her dad. I know more acutely than she does that lurking just past junior high lie seductions more dire than the deadliest jumper ever could be.

Let her delude herself otherwise in fun, I figure. We both realize that no matter the nature of the game, I am always on her side.

When she is in her defensive crouch, my dribble rises to eye-level. I easily evade her telegraphed lunges, dribble around and through her legs, even give the ball an exaggerated bounce over her head and go in for the lay-up before she's recovered. Instead of get frustrated, though, my ungainly girl gets giggly. Eventually she is grabbing at me instead of at the ball. She assaults me crudely, over and over—"Play clean!" I cry, in mock consternation—until I finally let the ball go and hug her close. When I release her, she shrieks, rushes over to the abandoned ball, and heaves it off the backboard and in.

"All right, all right," I say. Temporarily, and not for very much longer, her winning is up to me. I let her win, in other words, because for the time being, I can. "Good game," I tell her, and that is mostly what I want her to get out of this afternoon, and for as long as I can keep it up. This lesson, expectation, and just desert. "Good game."

Memorial Haul

The crudest scroll-work says "commemorate." . . .
—Elizabeth Bishop, "The Monument"

And least will guess that with our bones
We left much more, left what still is
The look of things, left what we felt
At what we saw.
              —Wallace Stevens, "A Postcard
                      from the Volcano"

"Never let it be said that I didn't do the least I could
do." This is a favorite expression of mine, my disclaimer's mantra. As I have found myself confronted more
and more frequently with situations that require my
peculiar brand of insufficiency, it has proved increasingly useful. For instance, it was how I concluded a
prolonged telephone conversation with the president of
our local historical society. Having somehow learned
that it was "common knowledge" that I was an accomplished speaker (read: willing to work cheap), she had
decided that I was the ideal candidate to give the featured address at the centennial celebration of our county courthouse.

The event had been swelling for months. A squad of boy scouts, a selection of prosperous city fathers, and all manner of middle-grade governmental eminence had already been scheduled to populate the dais. Everyone who was prominently anyone in our community was in one way or another pitching in, variously lending his or her efforts to recruiting, organizing, fundraising, printing, transporting, and baking. The high school band would be playing an extensive program of patriotic music. Magicians would be working the crowd, along with clowns and ice cream vendors, to keep the younger kids intact. Scores of volunteers of every relevant talent and trade had been commandeered to ensure that whatever needed to be hammered together, festooned, or wired for sound would be seen to. That left only the featured speech—the centerpiece and *sine qua non* of any grand occasion—and, as I was informed, my reputation preceded me.

"Like an odor?" offered the fish with the hook fast in its mouth.

"You see? That's just the sort of humor we are looking for. So we can count on you? Please, Art. What with everyone working so hard to make this a success, it's the least you can do."

I did not miss my cue. "Never let it be said," I said.

With predictable efficiency, she dropped off an impressive folder of smeared Xeroxes inside my screen door the very next afternoon. I read about the tempestuous rivalry among Joplin, Carthage, and Webb City—hey, it was in all the papers—about where the county courthouse should be built. I read about the in-

famous 1894 council meeting that led to physical vio-
lence before compromises over the chosen site and tax
deferrals were reached. I'm a slow twitch sometimes: it
was almost an hour into the documents before I realized that the building I had been commissioned (com-
mission-free, mind you) to commemorate had been de-
stroyed by fire in 1911, due to the explosion of a can of
disinfectant in the basement. (Quick-thinking officials
had flung threatened records into a vault before leaping
from a second-story window.) In other words, I'd be
honoring an emptiness already eighty-three years old.

All that had been preserved from the courthouse itself was the cornerstone, which would anchor the monument. Like the Peary expedition presuming the Pole,
researchers determined that its original location was
currently and unconsciously occupied by Ray's Clutch
and Transmission, which, even for the sake of nostalgia, could neither be bought out nor budged. Happily, a century after the original dedication, the spirit
of compromise remained unbroken: those businesses
sharing the closest available parking lot—a branch
bank, a dictation systems office building, and a paint
supply store—agreed to suspend arguments over the
parking trespasses of one another's patrons and ceded
five square feet to the monument.

And so about two hundred citizens mustered around
an invisibly displaced building to pay tribute to nothing that was not there, and the nothing that was. The
police had used yellow tape to cordon off the void,
much as they might have roped off an open manhole.
For my part, I tried my best to live up to ambiguous

expectations. I played host to the vanished edifice and the mythical assembly one hundred years gone. I noted that if the courthouse had been any larger, we'd have needed a bigger vacant lot not to put it in. My delivery was cheeky but clean, and video-clippable for the evening news.

What I did not mention was the fact that every memorial, from the most elaborate headstone to the dime left on the putting green, marks an absence. I said nothing about futility or belatedness or the unhousing of justice or time's sleight of hand or trials by fire. I did not reference Mark Strand's lines "Wherever I am / I am what is missing," as well might be said of any of us, although I said nothing of the sort. I opted not to philosophize at all. I simply did my requisite fifteen minutes, then stepped aside to let the mayor, the president of the chamber of commerce, and our state senator weigh in. One harmless, rickety hour later, we dispersed. Because the monument had had to be cemented into place a couple of weeks prior to the ceremony, there was not even an unveiling per se. You can find it on Virginia about half a block south of Seventh, if you care to, although, so far as I know, no one does. Not even graffiti artists have troubled to deface it: a squat brick and stone affair about five feet high, small enough to miss but substantial enough to threaten the employees of any of the sponsoring establishments who back out too fast at five o'clock.

I suppose I owe a debt of thanks to the grad student who commanded the desk that fell to me when he left the university for a more stable fate. Wrestling out the stubborn center drawer, I found a bundle of used pipe cleaners, a few wads of Kleenex too repellant to inspect for content, and a tin of breath mints, which did not contain breath mints but a collection of his fingernails and—what else could they be?—his toenails. I realized that were this box a saint's salvage or a reliquary for Elvis (whose own sweat-soured towels, smuggled from various concert appearances, brought in four-figure bids at auction), I'd have been flattered. But if my implied task were to finger through the entrails for insights like a haruspex, revulsion overcame any curiosity, and I just bagged and junked the remains.

Undergraduates at the college I teach at today are less oblique about their leavings than any prospective English professor would be: they score the bathroom stall doors with curses and caricatures; they knife their sentiments into their desks. Thus did Hansel and Gretel deliberately mark their departure with crumbs, their ellipsis trailing off into the indeterminate, by which they thought they might always find their way back. Even criminals leave their inadvertent prints, threads, hairs, dots of blood, or smidgens of DNA to retrieve them by. I was unable to conclude whether my predecessor (like many grad students, he was partly a fabulous child with foiled intentions, partly on the lam) had meant by his unique deposits to remember Illinois or to be remembered by it. But why wonder now? As I said, I threw it all away, anyway.

ᚶ

My Aunt Dorothy, part of the California contingent of
our extended family, was renowned for her malapropisms. They were a source of reliable, recurrent fun for
all of us, Aunt Dorothy included. At least, whenever
someone reacted to her tearful account of a particularly "heart-rendering" movie or remembered at a holiday
gathering her disdain for "pestimistic" people, she was
a good enough sport to join in on the laughter. When it
comes to family—when it comes to most interactions,
actually—that's pretty much what you rely on to get
by: good sportsmanship.

A particularly splendid blunder of hers had to do
with her belief that she was gifted with special intu-
ition. My mother might call her up from Chicago, and
she'd say she knew it was my mother before picking up.
Or an inkling of impending trouble would trickle down
the back of her neck from the atmosphere, and she'd
phone in her latest presentiment: Be sure to shut off
the iron before you leave for San Diego. Don't take the
Volvo tomorrow. Don't buy the smoked fish at Kroger's.
And once, when we were visiting one summer, she was
ready with a bag of my favorite candy (hard raspberries
with sweet, rubbery cores) before I'd asked, hungered,
or described it. Seeing my surprise and delight—unanticipated gifts always impress us most—she moved in,
conspiratorially, and confided, "I have RSVP."

As I write, Aunt Dorothy has for many years been
suffering from one of several dozen undefined kinds
of dementia. The doctors maintain that it is not Al-
zheimer's, not in order to offer anyone hope so much

as for the sake of accuracy. Some hoses are kinked in
her head, or something. According to Uncle Herman,
she has her better days and her worse. She flickers like
a bad channel. Some days she is alert and available and
aware of who else is in the room and why. Other days
are . . . otherwise. The doctors can only guess what it
must be like for her. Maybe like being at the bottom of
a high, lightless tower, with sheer, slippery walls. Poetry is the least they can do, but, medically speaking, it's
not all that sound. In any event, she isn't saying. She's
in, she's out, that's all.

Under the circumstances, whoever happens to have
Aunt Dorothy in his charge becomes the de facto family diplomat. When she is up and about, she must be
reassured by whoever happens to be bolstering her that
the invisible blizzard she cowers from is indeed as obvious and irritating as she imagines. When she numbly
plucks at nothing, tries to turn an absent page or to
retrieve some unidentified, fleeting thing—given the
delicacy with which she extends her hand, a proffered
drink, perhaps, or a silk scarf—your task is to rescue it
from the cataract for her. Then, as you gently present
it, you must remind her just as gently who you are, so
that she will continue to trust you and keep hold of
your hand. (SURRENDER, DOROTHY, wrote the
wicked witch.) My aunt's jabs are paltry but unnerving
nonetheless. She would stay the impertinent birds that
seem to be bearing off the names of things on their
backs, which are somehow dragging umbra after them
like a gigantic tarpaulin over an infield. Her intentions
unmuscle in the air. Everywhere there are thresholds to

be negotiated, and you have to help her over. She would thank you if she weren't suddenly so suspicious about where you mean to take her (although the afternoon's itinerary is typically no more extensive than going from the living room chair to her own bed) or who you are.

Once Uncle Herman found her repeating the word "floor." She was down on the floor, a soft shamble, saying "floor." Somehow she had said it so many times in the course of her life that she'd managed to wring the allusion out of it, until there was no longer any sense to it and not a thing beneath her feet. Only a sound in her mouth, an unidentifiable, stale taste on her tongue. Floor. It was as if she had suddenly come upon a stranger sitting at her table. Her husband hesitated to come between them, he said, as if he were the intruder. She was given to these bouts of muttering, he said. Some small havoc going on just under her breath. Floor. She was on the floor, looking down and saying "floor," seeing if the word would reach it, inspecting the floor the way a dazzled housewife in a commercial might.

With each passing month, there are fewer and fewer circumstances that do not abuse her. One doctor suggested getting one of those adhesive guns to make name tags for absconding nouns. So she might feel a little more at home in her home, where Dorothy might be comforted to be reminded that her countertop is a "countertop," her shoes "shoes." She would then recognize the word for "refrigerator" before it creeps like a roach behind its reference, out of reach. A modest, legible bunker. And yet, even with the language right in front of her, she sometimes gazes at words the way that

119

an assault victim—nervous, unsure—stares at suspects in a police line-up.

On those increasingly infrequent occasions when Aunt Dorothy remembers me at all, it is not as the English professor I've become but as a child pining for treats. So she does not know, if she ever did, that the words that pester and dodge her like those devilish kids who blitz the neighborhood unsupervised and rip chunks of lawn with their bikes are what my bread is buttered by. If words are skittish in her kitchen, they are the smooth-handled tools of my trade. Irony can be a real bitch sometimes. With apologies to Ezra Pound, even in literature, it isn't news.

We still remind one another of Aunt Dorothy's accidental witticisms from time to time, but now that getting things wrong is no longer a joke she can join in on but a persistent symptom of something that cannot be defined or cured, our tone has grown kinder, elegiac. Since she has paid so much of herself out, we don't want anything more to come at her expense, I suppose. Propriety requires that we restrict ourselves to smiling and shaking our heads when we remember her especially ingenious mistakes. Nevertheless, despite the seriousness of Aunt Dorothy's current condition, the satisfaction I get out of the ESP / RSVP mix-up has not abated in the slightest. The notion of a psychic endowment that is at once reliable and polite, a capacity that has the decency when invited to remember to get back in touch, has not lost its capacity to gratify. And as you can see whenever light does find a seam in Dorothy's so-often-daunted expression, during that merciful hour or thirty seconds when she gets a clear glimpse of what's directly in front of her, memory is another one of those unanticipated gifts.

ᘐ

The east gate represents 9:01; the west gate, 9:03. In this way, the moment of the destruction of the Oklahoma City Federal Building is bracketed but not protected, which may not have been the intention but seems appropriate. You may approach the memorial compound from either end. Symbolically, then, as your mood dictates, you may either enter this snipped instant from an innocent distance prior to the blast or return to it from the direction of aftermath.

After the demolition, people kept piling flowers and messages and ribbons and photographs against the fence, or sticking them on top like piked heads of state after a coup had cut them down. Once the notorious Oklahoma winds kicked up, it was chaos, so the state had to step in quickly and build something official. A balm shelter, as it were.

There is a field of 168 empty chairs, which have been placed in nine rows to represent the nine floors of the building and arranged according to whatever floor a given victim happened to be visiting or working on. It would seem as though the building had been simply lifted from the site and its employees abducted from an otherwise ordinary day, were it not for the abstraction occupying the chairs that have been left behind. They are made of bronze and stone. Each rests upon glass. "By day, the chairs seem to float above their translucent bases. By night the glass bases illuminate as beacons of hope," we are told. (The designers wanted to avoid the effect of plutonic gloom, which soothes no pain and is, in the end, unproductive.) And yet, blazing row upon row, the chairs might look to some like tidy pyres. Another potential result of the field is the apotheosis of the workplace, as one envisions the 168 plots as magnified cubicles. This is office furniture for angels, with ergonomics descended from God.

Although it need hardly be said that this is no reflection on the relative stature of their absence, the brochure confirms that the smaller chairs stand for children. And somehow the thought of how commonplace the abandonment of children can be takes the eminence out of it. The kids have gone to recess.

The Survivor Tree is an American elm, representing resilience. (Deferring to sorrow, the designers were nonetheless determined to remove any sense of surrender.) The surrounding promontory provides the best prospect for viewing the whole memorial. The Rescuer's Orchard, an "army" of fruit and flower-bearing trees, rings the Survivor Tree like a retaining wall. Or a tribunal. Or a prayer circle. A necklace adorning the dead. The brochure saves us from darker figurations, declaring that, taken together, the Survivor Tree and the Rescuer's Orchard constitute a tableau vivant illustrating the organic relationship between natural and human devotions.

The Reflecting Pool, which replaces what used to be N.W. 5th Street, invites us to see the change in our own faces. The brochure presses serenity upon us: the "shallow depth of gently flowing water is intended to help soothe wounds, with calming sounds providing a peaceful setting for quiet thoughts." Redundancy is a comfort. The pool's surface is almost preternaturally still, ripe for mirage, and so smooth that even grief doesn't ruffle it. Like a drain, it draws us into it, and down.

In the wake of the bombing, so many expressions of encouragement came from children that a special Children's Area was also added to further guarantee the healing process. In addition to a permanent wall of hand-painted tiles, there is a series of chalkboards upon which children can continue to offer their sentiments. The idea here is to convey how memory is at once a fixture and a construction site, or so we presume, for in this instance the brochure offers no explicit counsel about how to react. But we might apply an insight from Don DeLillo's *White Noise,* when in the wake of another disaster—an "airborne toxic event"—the recuperating community takes in the splendor and ambiguity of the transfigured sky: "Certainly there is awe, it is all awe, it transcends previous categories of awe, but we don't know whether we are watching in wonder or dread, we don't know what we are watching or what it means, we don't know whether it is permanent, a level of experience to which we will gradually adjust, into which our uncertainty will eventually be absorbed, or just some atmospheric weirdness, soon to pass."

"The sunsets linger and so do we." We shift and look about, wondering how long it has been, and we wait for some sort of consensus to guide us out. A kind of anticipation charges the scene, but really, we expect nothing to happen. It is 9:02. It is always, interminably, 9:02.

☞

Total Baseball is the self-proclaimed bible of the sport, but unlike the better-promoted Bible, it forgets nothing. In *The Book of J*, Harold Bloom infers the evolution of the Judeo-Christian Bible, with its mysterious yet undeniable embroideries by J, E, P, D—those hoary, discerning initials standing for anonymous scholars through whose hands our heritage evidently passed— and the Redactor, Bloom's consummate editor, whose designation makes him sound like a villain out of Marvel Comics. But *Total Baseball* obeys no principle of omission whatsoever. From year to year, it is utterly additive in design, its steadily growing equity guaranteed by an editorial board that never edits out.

They well those passions read which yet survive. Every player who has ever played is inscribed for all eternity in the book of baseball's life. So while most are apt to consult *Total Baseball* to settle bets about the renowned, what is most satisfying is not that Gehrig or DiMaggio is firmly ensconced there but that they enjoy no priority that might upset the encyclopedic, alphabetical rigor—Hank Aaron to Dutch Zwilling—of the book. Just as the universe is unlikely to differentiate between my atoms and any magnate's or movie star's once we've all dissolved into our respective elements, so, too, is baseball's bible benignly indifferent to the relative status or lack of same among its entrants, all of them equally and forever assured.

So I urge you to postpone for a moment or two your eagerness to see the statistical tomb of your childhood favorites—refrain from tramping over the plots of the other dead to get a load of the more celebrated lost— and pause at the site of Frank Norton, who played for the Olympics of Washington, D. C., during the first year of the National Association of Professional Base Ball Players. May 5, 1871, was at once Frank Norton's debut and swan song: he struck out in his only at-bat. By anyone who bothers to know him, that is what he is known for. Live with that. Die with that.

Or regard the legacy of John Wood, a pitcher for St. Louis. In 1896, he made his first and only appearance, giving up one hit and walking two batters before being taken out, as it turned out, permanently. Hence his earned run average: a peerless and unassailable infinity. Look on these Works, ye Mighty, and despair!

☙

Mine is one of several states with pending legislation about removing those impromptu shrines that you find along the highways to mark where fatal accidents oc- curred. The interstate I travel most often, for example, is studded with an impressive variety of remembranc- es. Wreaths supported by wire frames, crosses made of kindling, painted cairns, placards urging drivers to be cautious or God to be kind—all of them offering ram- shackle love. They are as abundant as road kill and, given the generous speed limit, impossible to decipher entirely.

As the state's main arteries, highways must be kept as free of blockage as possible. But just what threat to economic health these shrines pose has never been clearly articulated. Actually, the arguments to clear them away have tended to center upon two points. First, they are eyesores. Not to disparage the motives of those who would sanctify the place where their dears departed, but heartfelt litter is litter nonetheless. Second, they are traffic hazards. Like cell phones and whining children in the back seat, these intermittent weigh stations for mortality distract us from the serious business of driving. Paradoxically, any effort to defend the shrines has maintained either that they are no more irritating or dangerous than billboards (hardly an affiliation that exalts the dead or their attendants) or that there is no indication that they have caused even one driver to swerve. Either contention seems to confess a defeated purpose.

What has stymied every bill on the subject so far is the realization that as soon as a shrine is removed, it will be replaced. Because the government has enough trouble trying to enforce the laws it already has on the books, no solution has aroused any sustained support. Add to this the fact that an under-funded police force is already spread too thin, and you can safely predict that, like kids who spray their names on overpasses or people who, rather than wait for the next Shell station, pull over to relieve themselves behind a convenient hillock, stanchion, or sycamore, those who stake claims to sacred ground will continue to evade the authorities.

క

If you are looking for an under-appreciated index to a lasting relationship, consider the strategic pairing of someone who holds onto things and someone who casts them off. Duplication of tendencies may be fatal. Two people who feel compelled to keep everything may suffocate together; conversely, two disposed to disposal may bleed out entirely over time. A healthy system circulates, with about as much salvage as secretion going on.

From the day my little brother left the crib to assert title to half the bedroom, I have lived exclusively with keepers. Jeff collected collections, which abided by no obvious principle other than the space they ate, and which, once they were stowed, were, like deferred annuities surreptitiously tapped from each month's salary, never again consulted. Ever since this single sibling, who crammed his portion of closet with ample crap to sustain twins, I have never enjoyed any but exponential company. I shared a tent with a boy who brought with him an attic's worth of toys (not to mention a second knapsack just for desserts, perhaps to bribe the guards) to make his stay palatable, as if he had been shipped off to some permanent ghetto instead of overnight camp. My roommate in the freshman dorm was nicknamed "Rat" for the packing he came to campus with and never found adequate space to accommodate. In graduate school I managed to buddy up with a guy whose daily peregrinations could readily be recapitulated by the debris he left in his wake. Nor have I ever loved and lived with a woman who was willing or able to relinquish the least particle of past.

Psychiatrists might track my unconscious attraction back to my mother, whose drawers are still stricken with chronic indigestion, thanks to all the indiscriminate bits she has forced them to swallow. Her purse, pendulous, still strains at her side like a full bladder or second belly. Nothing ever leaves her retinue. Witness her bathroom cabinets, chockablock with hairpins, Q-Tips, and enough cosmetics to maintain appearances well into the next decade. Pry into her nightstand, thick with pictures and clippings of incidents that, as far as I can see, were never news. Consider the boxed flotsam and jetsam kept from vacations whose only other trace is what they have added to the Visa balance. For my mother is and always has been someone who deems every inch of string a souvenir as crucial as the thread Theseus clung to in the labyrinth, and who for some reason sees in every random stack of magazines a potential Nevelson, not to be moved.

Therefore, I survive on a regular diet of purgatives. The next time you leave, I have said to everyone I've ever shared the premises with, I am taking an armload out of here. All you have to do is identify what's gone, and I'll return it. However, if you cannot tell me within two weeks what's been banished from your stash, it's gone for good. And I believe in the existential foundation of that goodness when I say so: the rare, oxygenated accomplishment of a clean, well-lighted place.

Yet when it comes to getting rid of things, I'm a piker compared to that paragon of dispossession whose story recently made *USA Today*. Here was a young man from Iowa who decided to liquidate himself absolutely, to melt down everything that could conceivably be seen as an asset, and started pumping. He inventoried every possession, all the way down to the worn dishrags, and put it all on e-Bay for sale. Obeying some obscure dispossessive mood—more thorough than even Thoreau would warrant, more unsparing than any Spartan could sustain—he took himself out in dollars as though all that was the matter with him were so much trash to be trundled to the curb. T-shirts, pens, paperweights, books, photographs, calendars—all the memorabilia to which no memory clung but his, to which no one else's stink would stick. The wretched refuse of a life refused, all of it, dumped onto an on-line auction site to see what would happen. Even obvious, ubiquitous items, each a subpoena to no conceivable consumer, answering no viable desire: a dented teapot, a well-worn Hawkeye jersey, ice trays, used valentines, a phone book, corn. Unopened and unsent Christmas gifts, too, not to mention the makings of gifts: ribbons, wrapping paper, tape, scissors. The large items—first the durable goods he could no longer endure—then the small, until the initial outflow thinned to a drool, until the last drips—unused stamps, paper clips, floss—left the spigot. Every bit, then the bits of every bit, tagged and banded like birds urged back into the wild in the vain hope that they might prosper again. Just to see what would happen, he said. A lark, writ large. All in fungible. To see what he was worth.

In "Funes the Memorious," John Luis Borges wrote of a man who was incapable of forgetting anything. His mind was a storage battery set on permanent binge, a hard drive from which not one sliver of input was ever deleted. Ultimately, the sludge of data became too much for him, and he died of congestion. Although the sale is not recorded, I would not be surprised to discover that the knock-off entrepreneur from Iowa had pinned cautionary passages from that tale to his bulletin board—temporarily, that is, his having undoubtedly sold off that ballast with the rest.

Hypothetically speaking, there is no limit to the ways in which one can confiscate himself. Having cleansed the premises, one can systematically subtract one's own body from them. Just as Howard Hughes stored his effluvia in jars, this guy might likewise have tried to discharge himself, for a price. And so I further imagine this guy shaving his head and offering the hair, looking into the going rate for plasma and (when the price peaked) hooking himself up, sawing off digits to deliver to the highest bidder, and finally scraping by on sales from scrapings from his own cells. In a moment of largesse, perhaps, he might drop off the odd kidney in the poor box. Extract, divorce, amputate, shrink, dismember. Shrivel to the most compact package possible, then barter that. Boil presence down to the lessness of a Beckett play, the last gasp signaling dissolve.

As it turned out, his family got wind of his emissions and bought up the lot. For about $160 they reclaimed all of it, gathered his jettisons and by-products, his would-be recyclables and scabs, taking him up. Then they packaged everything and gave it back to him. Whether it was delivered as a reproach or as a present is not clear. However, he did leave a last post on the website announcing the successful conclusion of his "experiment," explaining that he'd figured he "had nothing to lose by trying," and thanking everyone involved for participating.

You may be surprised to learn that the black granite came from Bangalore, India. Polished to a reflective sheen, the blocks absorb the faces that face them, as if the dead were taking their measure and turning them to stone. No Medusa could ever act so efficiently or do in so many.

At the 1982 dedication ceremony, Maya Ying Lin said that in designing the Vietnam War Memorial, she had intended to separate the sacrifice of the American soldiers from United States policy and, indeed, from any recognizable partisanship. (This may be the reason that the proposal to place a flagpole at the intersection of the walls was overruled.) She had meant "to make no political statement whatsoever," she said.

To be sure, the overwhelming impact of the Wall is silence. (We have come to refer to her work as "The Wall," but in fact the memorial is composed of two walls. They are 75.21 meters long, and like a pair of enormous, Euclidean wings, they stretch toward the Lincoln Memorial and the Washington Monument, respectively, and connect at the central "spine" to create the piece's maximum height of 3.12 meters.) Approaching, you may hear the soft scrabble of shoes against the gravel verge, like an outfield warning track. Perhaps you hear weeping, perhaps some private consolation among family members, although that tends to be indecipherable, and it would be rude to listen in. The line moves along. A few may break from the procession to insert a flower or to take a rubbing from the specific name that implicates them, but protocol dictates that you continue at a regular, moderate pace, which clocks at about the speed of the passage of graduates, and quietly. The density of the Wall (3364 kilograms per cubic meter, supported by a foundation of 140 concrete pilings driven approximately 35 feet down to bedrock) imposes quiet, a solid hush.

Statistical weight serves as its own consecration. The Wall cost $4,284,000 to construct. There are 70 inscribed panels for each of the two sections, plus two blank ones at each end, which are said to represent an aesthetic decision, rather than an expectation of adding to the list. Each panel is 101.6 centimeters wide, 7.6 centimeters thick, and between 20.3 centimeters and 3.12 meters tall, depending on where it is situated. Precision is something we have to steady us, something to go on. The height of each letter is 1.35 centimeters. The depth of each letter is .038 centimeters. Precision is the least we can do.

"If you can't accept death, you'll never get over it," Maya Ying Lin told PBS. "So what the memorial is about is honesty. You have to accept, and admit that this pain has occurred, in order for it to be cathartic." That is part of the reason for the sheer size of the Wall: it forces acceptance upon us. Heavy and definite, it settles accounts. It gives good weight.

Up close, the Wall is a glossary of loss. From a distance, it is an open grave, as though the earth had shrugged at the tonnage, trying to shift the burden like Atlas shouldering the world, and in doing so heaved up the ranking dead.

First and foremost, we picture the Wall, but the Vietnam Veterans Memorial is actually a complex that includes three other components. The Three Servicemen Statue (designed by Frederick Hart and dedicated in 1984) consists of a trio of bronze soldiers halted while humping it through something. There is a flagpole, also bronze, installed in deference to veterans who had been disappointed by its exclusion from the Wall itself; it bears a brief description of the principles and circumstances they served under. Then there is the Vietnam Women's Memorial (designed by Glenna Goodacre and dedicated in 1993), a spread of red granite paving stones and eight yellowwood trees representing the eight female nurses killed in the war. Each of these comes complete with its own statistical briefing, which may be conveniently accessed on "The Virtual Wall," a searchable Internet site.

~

What with the price of hotels and plane fares, the difficulty of maintaining family chemistry in its post-nuclear age, and the fact that no activity advertised as "fun for the whole family" has ever been anything your whole family would tolerate, I hereby propose a means of preempting the inevitable addiction to all things Disney that will sooner than you'd ever anticipate afflict your child and, by extension, you. Rather than dedicate yourself to some hazy and doomed determination to shield your child from Disney—so insidiously and cleverly engineered is their campaign of universal saturation and infiltration that I almost believe the rumor that a kid abandoned to a Bavarian forest and raised by wolves was reported by campers who happened upon him to be humming the soundtrack from *Aladdin* to the indigenous fauna—consider this strategy. In your baby's infancy, as you change her diaper or coo in duet over a spill of Cheerios, remind her of the good times you had together at Disneyworld—a vacation, remember, that you and she have never taken and, if you follow these instructions unflinchingly, will never have to. "Remember when we rode the monorail? Remember the big parade with all the characters from the Disney movies? Remember when Goofy came over and gave Mommy a hug? Wasn't that funny?" Because kids exist on the charmed periphery of truth (and that's crediting them generously, as any day care worker who has had to arbitrate among restless toddlers will attest), your child will be susceptible.

Trust me: she trusts you. At least, for the time being, before hormones lay waste to your parental labors, she does. So you must press the false memory upon her while the clay is still malleable. (In childcare as in cooking, ingredients must be added before the batter hardens.) If you steadfastly sell the episode, and presuming both parents and sets of in-laws stick religiously to the story, your child will remember, distinctly and in considerable detail, something that never happened.

Listen, hypocrite, when the volume rises during the fight about how the credit cards are overextended or the dinner's underdone, you bowdlerize the story for your baby boy or girl, don't you? Then you stage kisses for her benefit, with each of you feeling about as sincere as the Israeli Prime Minister enduring the clasp of Arafat. You do not hesitate to defer the truth about sexual hydraulics or the history of race in America for the time being, withholding the profounder facts like an allowance she hasn't earned yet. You are perfectly willing to plant your sweetheart in some part-time Santa's lap, coddle her with God like the promise of a Popsicle after the DPT shot, or assure her as you tuck her in that, despite your bad HDL-to-LDL ratio and the actuarial odds against it, you'll be with her to love her always. For all the axioms you grind about being honest with kids, you do your level best to deflect the news, which, face it, is positively filled with luscious slaughter and blood enough to brim the *Iliad*. Don't you? For all your sophistication, you get between her line of sight and the television when something vulgar blooms from the screen, then soothe her with fables about perfectibility and a peaceable kingdom, all runny with sunshine. So don't bluster about your unbending ethics—raising a child is too consequential to waste time pretending that you don't pretend. Follow my advice, and you won't have to fudge the budget or begrudge her happiness, which, believe me, a genuine pilgrimage to Disneyworld would end up doing. And give the kid a little credit: properly nurtured, imagination is its own E ticket, anyway.

⌖

In his documentary about Auschwitz, *Night and Fog* (1955), director Alain Resnais employs a simple and devastating editing technique: he shifts back and forth between the hideous black and white archival footage of the extermination camps and imagery of the postwar landscape, caressed in verdant colors. In this way, for example, a shot of a line of doomed revenants is duplicated in the context of what has become a monument and tourist site; suddenly, the shot rediscovers the line of prisoners, as if the camera itself were so traumatized by nightmare that it cannot keep its grip on the present day. All the while, the narrator, Michel Bouquet, maintains his dispassionate tone, deadpanning the panning of the dead. The result is both to make us crave the reprieve from dread and to distrust it when it comes.

Although it seems to run much longer, the film lasts only thirty-one minutes. It provides no compromise with the past whatsoever, wins nothing by negotiation. (Any convalescence is defined by disease.) If you want to be rescued, Resnais seems to be saying, look to something other than art.

Night and Fog concludes in the midst of a final color sequence. Silence accumulates and abides, but so does our suspicion, as the camera scavenges among the ruins of the crematorium. Conducting the solemn, dubious stations of witness, the camera observes the broken watchtowers, picks through twisted wires, slowly tracks past cracked concrete blocks. The atmosphere is reverent, perplexed, haunted. We pass like vapor. Then a voice finds us: "The crematorium is no longer in use. The devices of the Nazis are out of date. Nine million dead haunt this landscape." It is the narrator, speaking of the dead, for them. "Who is on the lookout from this strange tower to warn us of the coming of new executioners? Are their faces really different from our own?" We detect the slightest rise in pitch. Urbanity can hold out only so long. Aesthetics won't save us or let us off. The voice goes on to tell us that some of the perpetrators remain among us, if not prosperous, alive, among and—in a sense, our very heritage—within us. "And there are those of us who sincerely look upon the ruins today, as if the old concentration camp monster were dead and buried beneath them. Those who pretend to take hope again as the image fades, as though there were a cure for the plague of these camps. Those of us who pretend to believe that all this happened only once, at a certain time and in a certain place, and those who refuse to see, who do not heed the cry to the end of time. . . ."

All the while the camera tracks relentlessly the slow length of catastrophe. Nothing is more hopeless than the death march of linear plots, but we cannot imagine any way out.

The camera halts. What do we see? It is a slab of concrete, a platform or pedestal, possibly, we can't be sure, but clearly shaped by some intention. On it, a rusted bramble of metal—the moorings for some malign contraption or other, perhaps, or possibly shards of the contraption itself. Perhaps a blasted tabernacle. Who can say? Nothing is obvious about Auschwitz. The film has inflicted the evidence of so many torments that we are prepared for the brunt of another horror—as prepared as we can be, having endured the documentary—but in fact, this one defies conjecture. What but design of darkness to appall, right? Of course, the context refuses to let it be innocuous. We cannot tell what we are looking at, but we cannot help but look. Whatever it is, the camera cannot let go of it, cannot penetrate or understand or forget anything about it.

It is spring. We surmise a breeze. In the documentary shots, daylight hung in the air like dust beaten from a rug. Now, instead of the scalped, hollow surroundings we anticipate in the wake of the Holocaust, Auschwitz, incredibly, is cupped in sun. "Round the decay / Of that colossal Wreck, boundless and bare / The lone and level sands stretch far away."

Meanwhile, off-screen, so we may suppose, every temple tapers upward, targeting the infinite, zeroing in. The architecture suggests longing. Every temple reaches after a grand idea, grazes heaven, summons thrust.

From that perspective, any church or mosque is more or less a missile silo. And what is the Parthenon if not a ravaged launch pad?

Where we worship, great tusks of light stab through the stained glass, making each of us a magician's assistant in a box run through with swords.

The camera strands us. What is missing is wherever we are.

༌

In her book *Holy Personal,* Laura Chester roams America to uncover some of the idiosyncratic ways in which we customize private environments to contain our devotions. She visits people who have made chapels out of car tires, propane gas tanks, and wine casks. She finds ziggurats of plastic liter pop bottles, cardboard cloisters beneath highway overpasses, and altars contrived inside root cellars, grottos, caves, culverts, and cedar closets. Someone gutted a cypress in the Louisiana bayou to situate his spirit in; a family in Worcester, Massachusetts, rigged their garage for worship; a farmer in LaCrosse, Wisconsin, consigned his soul to the hayloft. Apparently, when the need to remember and adore comes profoundly upon us, any culvert, declivity, divot, or ditch might do.

As might the paragraph that says so. If you take a linguist at his word, that word and every other is a memorial, a signifier scratched into the ear or page to commemorate the missing thing it christens like a ship that escaped the dock. Furthermore, the words we rouse for a given day's employment get out of deep beds of derivation to go to work for us. On certain especially self-conscious days, each one seems to drag its etymology by me like a bridal train. I have many friends, but I reserve "companion" for someone who shares my bread. I hesitate to flatter the woman whose amethyst pendant bobs expensively about in her décolletage because

I recall that "amethyst" began as a preventative against drunkenness. While others congratulate the hostess on her porcelain, I pause before its origin as a sow's vulva and, as politely and inconspicuously as possible, refuse whatever delicacy it contains (my enduring penchant for candy notwithstanding). And because a sarcophagus literally eats flesh, I cannot help but see the cemetery as a cafeteria: the cadavers are served up on coffins, the flowers the mourners drop onto their dead are garnishes, and the shoveled dirt is the condiment essential to making the meal go down easier.

Woe to those like my Aunt Dorothy who hardly even designate anymore. They gauge in vain the escape velocity of objects that sit still for others, that nestle dependably in the same names we left them in.

Words burn brightly on the page, or so we hope. Readers feed the drippings back into the molten bowl beneath each flame. I like to think that wherever we pause, whether it is at a substantial passage or before the porch of spirits lingering, that is the very least we do.

A Few Paces from Hemingway

There he sits, sunk in his idiom like a stone in a river-bed.

If I were able to dream myself an entry to some post-humous function where bygone literati were gathered, I don't imagine that the heavenly hosts would seat me next to Ernest Hemingway. This is not just a matter of insufficient eminence on my part. True, nothing I have ever written has been tagged with the phrase "eagerly awaited." No code could conceivably be contrived from my idiosyncrasies to compel a generation, and there will never be a campaign to award an "esque" to make a modifier of me. (Some of us are named for our accomplishments, others for our longings.) And frankly, "Grace Under Pressure" always sounded to me less like an existential tenet than like the title of an adolescent novel about a plucky girl detective. No, I predict rejection based on the fraternity of Hemingway heroes, to whose rush I would never be invited.

And they would be right to refuse me. What kinship could I claim, anyway? For them, the boxing ring, the bullring, and the battlefield are sacred settings designed for the exercise of personal command and mettle; for me, they are variations on butchery. Hemingway's chosen few are fully versed in the arcana of alcohol, always able to penetrate the pleasures of absinthe and, however much they've drunk, to pronounce "pernod" without error. Whereas in my case, it wasn't until I went off to college that I first saw a beer in a fridge.

Who is more secure in his knowledge than a Hemingway hero about executing a foreign city, a right cross, or a perfect cast? Who else interprets his environment so assuredly? Who so rapidly masters the local dialects and protocols? Here is someone who can be dropped down into any circumstance whatsoever and make a living with his hands. And on those rare occasions when he is confounded, he is stoic as a tombstone about it. Meanwhile, I still get lost in the town I've lived in for twenty years, and I start fretting over tax receipts months in advance of April 15.

Hemingway is wearing his safari jacket and pith helmet, and there is an iconic bottle before him. (Gods grown large contain themselves as well as their parodies, I suppose.) If I were to approach him, would he speak in the same collapsed vein he writes in?

Given Hemingway's notorious dedication to the clean, considered minimum, there is no telling what he'd make of the baffle of whispered Yiddish that surrounded my youth and that occasionally flavors my conversations even now. For a Jake Barnes, a Robert Jordan, or a Robert Wilson—no one in my neighborhood had names or priorities like theirs!—words are a questionable expenditure at best, dry rot at worst. No one in American literature is as allergic to varnish as Ernest Hemingway is, and you'd usually have to use a razor to get one of his protagonists to open up. By contrast, there is nothing that the families I knew did not take out in talk. What would he have made of a Chanukah get-together, featuring regular crushes of Polish consonants like bundled commuters shoving through a subway? I try in vain to picture Robert Jordan pinned down in the crossfire between Jewish uncles declaiming the merits of mutual funds or trying to withstand a bout of parental career counseling. How long before someone's Bubbie bled the starch out of Robert Wilson with her brisket and solicitude? How long before diligent aunts broke Jake Barnes down with questions about the pretty *shiksa* he'd been seen with or unmanned him by cooing and condoling over the wreckage in his crotch?

He has me in his sights now, he is sizing me up in a single glance from that furred, disdainful brow, but he does not fire. Instead, he bears back down upon the bare spot between his glass and his chest, trying, so it seems to me, to hatch another immaculate noun. Stern, furious, crabbed, intractable, wretched Hemingway presides over a closed ceremony or private reproach he alone is paying for, in full. For the moment, not a single word escapes him.

Perhaps the maitre-d could pass along a message on my behalf. I would like to let Hemingway know that, however distinct our statures and affinities, there are a few instances in his otherwise alien and—face it—occasionally offensive output that, were we by some divine mischief seated at the same table, might keep things civil between us. One has to do with Jake Barnes's declaration only a page into *The Sun Also Rises:*

"I mistrust all frank and simple people, especially when their stories hold together." Admittedly, this comes at the expense of Robert Cohn and, hence, could be said to represent the book's initial anti-Semitic burst. (I'm no lover of the insufferably suffering Cohn either, but blood is blood, and even the abuse of a moony Princeton Jew abuses me.) Yet Jake's sentiment is one I tend to share. Coherence, finality, and the streamlined thesis are dreams I would not believe in even if they manifested in my lap. If there is one thing that all criminals share, it's conviction.

Whenever someone crafts an answer that, like a smooth Brancusi sculpture, betrays no seam, I cannot help but remember one afternoon when I found myself driving behind a trucker who was transporting bales of hay. As he sped heedlessly down the highway, his massive packages threw numberless quills against my windshield. The faster he went, the more he cost himself. He kept shedding wisps and whiskers as if the wind were some invisible depilatory. Unlike Monet's ghostly haycocks, which weathered without diminishment season after season of the artist's concern, these bales were losing propositions. The flurries ended only after he turned off the interstate. With my field of vision restored, I could relax into the trip again and contemplate how surprised that farmer would be when he stopped to inspect his cargo and discovered just how much of all he'd meant to convey did not cohere after all.

I'd like to send word of that episode over to Hemingway's table, but I see that he is busy inscribing sentences and is not to be disturbed. He uses the same dread meticulousness he reportedly applies to the tying of flies. He glowers at an overstuffed clause, and I imagine him lasering away spots of purple like ragged-edged moles.

Another instance when we converge occurs in the middle of that same novel. Jake Barnes, Bill Gorton, and the hapless Robert Cohn (the clinging Jew Jake regularly, uselessly abjures) are heading by bus toward Pamplona through an unspoiled terrain, free for the time being of all ambiguity. There are only natural resources and simple conjunctions. "I was up in front with the driver and I turned around," Barnes says. "Robert Cohn was asleep, but Bill looked and nodded his head." Now I am no aficionado. Where others are clued in and omni-competent, I am incurably green. A toreador could carve a bull apart any which way and my gorge would rise regardless. Take me into the woods with you, and I'd clump and blunder about so badly that I'd spook anything shootable. You could fish with floss and chewing gum, then pack your trout in your trousers for all I care—I'd never recognize a breach of proper method. You could run down your next lion with your Lincoln Town Car and I'd deem him just as justly dead. But where Hemingway and I concur is on the matter of that simple nod of acknowledgment through which Bill and Jake quietly, modestly confide.

True, the only bulls I have ever seen run are the Chicago Bulls, but when they reigned over the NBA, I had plenty of opportunity to see that nod. While the crowd cheered insanely over a Michael Jordan jam, he would discreetly relay his appreciation to Scottie Pippen for the pass that caught him at the perihelion. Not a protracted celebration but the merest lift of his chin as he loped back on defense with further work to do. An almost imperceptible little point of his finger instead of an exclamation. To those in the know, nothing else is required, and anything more, like a drool of sequins or too much rouge, would ruin the effect.

So these are our connections—modest as a couple of the Master's clasping "ands," but marks of integrity nonetheless. I check Hemingway again, and he's cleaning his rifle, as focused as a Buddhist or a reptile, so focused in fact that he never detects my stammering heart, with its "unlesses" and "what ifs" swishing and shivering like little fish through it—fish he'd throw back. The scourge of sophistry and the subordinate clause, Hemingway makes a solid hill of himself, a human bunker or sentient hump, and continues to work the problem that proves no problem for him.

For some reason that will stay a secret, blood is running down his leg.

I want to tell him about my own pleasures of concentration—the luxury of peeling an orange or of sifting a ragged hemisphere of beach in cupped hands— but it would offend his concentration to do so. I admit that I cannot match the man for moral gravity, and I cannot sustain for more than a minute or so the requisite mien. Nevertheless, in some essential ways, we still inhabit the same sense of the same world.

So how should I presume?

Only now, some vaguely authoritative types have bracketed me and latched on with weathered hands. They are taking me out like a bad adjective. They know that I have had no old days with Hemingway to reminisce with him about in muffled Spanish. Loyalists, they are determined to prevent me from disrupting his regimen. "Please?" I plead. "That's better," they say. "Please is much better," but they continue to usher me toward the door.

I send Hemingway one departing glance—obvious and romantic of me, I know, and patently unworthy. He stirs, preparing to make his way among clenched sentences like a colonel inspecting the ranks. Was there a gesture meant for me? The briefest wave or moment's recognition? But before I can decide whether he senses a resonance between us or whether I am simply saying good-by to a statue, I am already out on the street. And there is no time to wonder anymore about it because it is raining a drenching, mythic, predictable, uneditable rain, and, wherever I may think I am right now, I have to walk all the way back in it.

Don't Breathe a Word

> What should I say? That the term itself—my
> life—is a desperate overstatement.
> —Don DeLillo, *Valparaiso*

I can make it happen. Just by concentrating, I can ignite the symptoms. A web catches in my chest. Something burbles in there, some viscid carbonation. Something syncopated, like toads colluding in a dark tree.
A false fever—false because it does not register on the
thermometer—spreads over my skin like a gas fire. I
can do nothing to stop it, but just by thinking about it,
I can set it off.

Beneath Doctor K.'s fingers, my ribs feel exotic as a
crop circle. All that intimate delving he does—he's as
earnest as a D.A.R.E. cop at a junior high assembly. By
reflex I seize up—he's violating my air space, my Fair
Use laws—and it takes an act of will to unclench for
him. Ultimately, I give him every access to my every
access. I cede my entire inscape to Doctor K. And I am
heartened and dismayed when after a series of expensive assaults, he pronounces me fit.

"There is nothing wrong with you that I can see.
Medically, you're normal." This is like telling a corpse
who's been dressed in his best clothes for the coffin

that sartorially, he's looking good. I actually have the presence of mind to say this to Doctor K., who does not react. Melodrama and analogy: favored habitats of patients who cannot find themselves indexed anywhere in the manual or accounted for on-line.

As I see it, as I sense it, the problem is, I can't seem to get my respiration in line. Some laundry has balled and blocked the chute. And that sets off everything else. Mutinous grumbling begins in all my body's colonies. A quaking spreads through my shoulders. Something akin to a slipped clutch in my stomach. (Oh, God. My somnolent, impervious guts!) A shudder in the loins engendered there, wherever "there" is. Etiology is on the move like a floating crap game. ("Floating crap" says it just about as well as any other phrase could.) I have to try to talk down my tremors from the ledge and bargain with my blood, vow an extra hour's sleep each night (video rentals and student papers be damned!), but my symptoms have all the spirit of compromise of a zoning committee. Mine's an entire system immune to counsel.

How can I make myself more penetrable than I already feel, naked and compliant and culpable as I am? Shameful to be so ambiguously sick. Shameful, in the context of this detoxified office (whose sanitation no microbe could survive) and Doctor K.'s rigid solicitude, to be sick at all.

It's basically a bait-and-switch scam, being born. How many durable goods endure according to their original design? You never stop buying the house you've bought; every termite trail and patch of rust, every leak, creak, and crevice that appears after your realtor has turned the corner on you is as much yours as the house itself. Your car dealer has dealt you a hand you have to keep drawing to forever, with no alternative but to meet each raise. Your refrigerator, your furnace, your central air—all are humming blithely away, each concealing some mortal coil or other. Entropy is at the core of every contract. Just so, the body you inhabit is from the beginning a breakdown waiting to happen.

But I don't want to get ahead of myself. Frantic gets you nowhere but frantic. I tell the doctor that it feels as though my lungs are plugged. "'Plugged' as in stopped up or as in perforated?" he asks. He wants to be clear. Either, I tell him. Both. Maybe that's it: I might have swallowed a contronym. I've come down with a figure of speech. It seems as if my lungs—here, I say, indicating with all ten fingers perched on my chest—are chockablock (but the X-rays show nothing) or chewed (again, nothing shows up). But not exactly. I want to be clear.

"Too bad you don't smoke," he says. "That would give you something to give up, right? A condition you would know how to be better off than." I've played racquetball with this man, which I suppose grants him the license to talk to me like this. I've been naked before him in another venue.

Easy for him. Just *look* at that man *breathe*. In, out, in, out. Now *that's breathing!* A Platonic template for respiration, beautiful to behold. He should put out a damn video.

He jests at cigars that never felt a fume.

150

Literally, I have disease. Dis-ease. My ease has been dissed. For lack of more precise terminology, mine is one unidentifiable brand of invisible afflictions commonly known as anxiety disorders. This is not to say that my anxiety is not functioning; in fact, its practice is thriving, so much so that it is considering opening up branch neuroses in other aspects of my daily life. "Of course, telling someone to cut down on his stress usually increases it, doesn't it? What good does that do? Why not tell me to get taller while you're at it?"

Doctor K., ruthlessly professional, ignores this. Doctor K. is the most proper noun I know. He continues instead to interview my illness directly, teasing out its conditions and qualities, identifying them like the stratified notes of a sophisticated perfume.

"Disorder" implies order—respiratory propriety and a regimental heart. Once we figure out what template my body has strayed from, it might be urged back to normal. Unfortunately for us, this disorder prefers to travel incognito. It forges its signature, masquerades as other maladies—some contradictory, some overlapping—and flouts his medical abilities and my metaphorical ones. Call me a clumsy function of the *Physician's Desk Reference.* He'll have to red-shirt his diagnosis for now, junk the a priori, and just keep probing.

Just thinking about it makes it happen, so it is a risk trying to define it. Before I convinced myself to make the appointment, I determined that thinking the worst was a viable defensive strategy against the eventuality: first, fastidiously docket every inner fillip and glitch, then subtract my fears one at a time. That was the plan—to lay in logic brick by irrefutable brick like a retaining wall. But I'd be hit by an indigestible image out of tenth grade—the Tinker Toy scaffolding covering all of Mr. Welch's chalkboard to depict chemical reactions—and the thought of trying to swallow down a double helix did my jerry-rigged serenity in. Down went the wall. Down I'd toboggan down the slippery slope to a vague, fantastic doom.

So here I am thinking about it, and thinking only stirs it up. The sleeping animal catches my scent. Then, a fit of esophageal juking: gasp and misgiving, gasp and misgiving—one embalmed breath after another. And so it goes, or just barely does, only just so fur and no further, as Huck Finn might say. You can't breathe a lie—I found that out.

My limbs have gone Jello-y. As Doctor K. looks me over like a used car he's considering, I wax nostalgic over the notion of perfect fitness I probably never had. I resume old negotiations, promising God I'll lay off processed sugar and sleepless nights, get off caffeine and on the treadmill, if only He'll restore my buffed, unblemished presence, the immaculate preserve of my physiology. Lead me to the Promised Land of impeccable health, restore my constitution to Canaan's clement inner weather—I'll lay off milk, I'll lay off honey—and I am Yours.

He slides the test results out of the massive manila envelope, along with the X-rays they interpret, which look like siding samples to renovate a house in a ghost story. The hospital visit did not help, did not find anything that needed helping. I had come in with arrhyth-

mia to light up the switchboard and, like a savvy dab-
bler in the stock market, got out while the numbers
were still high. Making my way out of the hospital, I
passed a post-surgical patient who hugged the walls as
he went. He progressed by hunching forward as if his
body were a machine he had to learn to operate like
someone else's car—the gears were positioned differently, or they slipped at unexpected stages; the shifts
felt funny, and it would take time to accustom himself
to the diminished dash. Is it possible to *walk* amok? He
was walking amok.

Leaving the hospital, I felt like those students who
know they've blown the midterm. "He never *said* this
would be on the test!" they complain as they slink away,
amok. Lowing the last-ditch lament of the done-for.

"I'll give you two choices, Doctor." I could call him
David, claiming a right of familiarity earned in the
locker room and secured by my having taken two of
three from him in last week's match, but I want to be
reassured from a higher elevation than "David" looks
down from. "I want you to chuckle over my chart and
tell me how obvious and easily corrected the thing
is. Otherwise, I want you to tell me there is nothing
whatsoever wrong with me and to stop acting crazy.
Let me in on my outcomes, Doc. Bring that certain
slant of light of yours to bear. Give me one of those
grooved commentaries doctors give to hypochondriacs
and hinky kids afraid of the needle. Tell me I'm boring
you with symptoms you've seen half a dozen times this
week alone. Say my organs are naughty and that you'll
put them in detention until they've learned their lesson.

Say that there's some minor insurgency in my lymph system, wherever that is, whatever that is, that you can put down without bothering to alert the media or to call up the National Guard. Say that some corpuscles that should be pounding a beat near my heart are slumming by the lungs, and that you'll have a squad car do a drive-by to clear out the neighborhood. GIVE ME A PILL! Is that asking too much?"

The air enters in cellophane and departs in parentheses. It's as if the oxygen has been in someone else's mouth before mine. Like that, only not quite. Better Communication Means a Better Haircut. I noticed that sign the last time I got a trim and scoffed: everyone's a professional these days. At Jiffy Lube you see a consultant, who sits down with you on the waiting room couch to brace you through the bad news. ("Are you here for the Chevy Impala? I'm afraid it's the transmission. All we can do now is make her comfortable. Is there anyone you need to call?") At Subway you are served by a sandwich artist. ("He has worked almost exclusively in oils, of course, but he has taken the occasional aesthetic risk with shredded lettuce.") All that soothing euphemism and sunny expertise. Meanwhile, Doctor K. looms and hedges and sidles like a bandit. The others are salesmen, you tell yourself, whose mission is to make you want what you do not want. Then it occurs to you: the doctor, ticking off your body's delinquencies in the file you cannot see, is no different.

About as congenial as a gauge, is Doctor K.

But just as your car won't make the noise for the mechanic that it makes for you, the sensation you've raved about doesn't show up. "Fresh air, and it's as if I have to gulp the stuff like slag, like someone's shoved mulch in there." But it isn't mulch or slag exactly, and I'd rather he'd said it for himself. It's not necessarily even a specific organ that needs tuning so much as a queasiness in the pit of my being, wherever that is. A yin-yang yo-yoing, in a manner of speaking, which is what I fall back on.

"When it's happening, I think, What I wouldn't trade for a few unobstructed, unconflicted breaths right about now." He eavesdrops once again on my heart and lungs from every conceivable angle.

"Something slimy and sliding about in there, it feels like?" I offer. Some viscera bidding oily valediction, say. He tracks my pulse at several points and surveys the bends and intersections of moving blood, monitoring my internal traffic, anticipating gridlock. I am trembling before the conjecture to come like bait on a hook. I intuit bruises within me, bruises due to some unrecalled damage I've done or some forgotten wrong done me. I gird myself for the unstinting, irresolvable, inconvenient results, which he will undoubtedly have to shove down my uncooperative gullet like wadding down the barrel of a gun. But nothing shows up.

"Just concentrate on breathing naturally," he tells me, implying that this requires no special talent or dispensation, even for somebody with a roll of bubble wrap wedged in his chest. Nor am I in my own practice above resorting to paradox on occasion to parry objections: "If you *knew* it was going to be on the test, it wouldn't really have *been* a test, now would it?"

155

"You know how you build a hesitation into the titles of each of your articles?" I said to Pat. She had been good enough to agree to cover a class for me during my doctor's appointment, so I owed her specifics. "You know: silly title, colon, real title? Take a look at your vita—seven published articles plus nine conference papers equal sixteen colons. Your publication list reads like the proceedings of a urologists' convention. 'Scribbling in the Margin *colon* The Refiguration of the Female in *Aurora Leigh*.' 'Clocking Out *colon* The Challenge of the Temporal in Victorian Women's Fiction.' Or how about all of that stick-and-move business in the title of your Bronte article, all that punctuational scaffolding? 'Infer/in fear-I/or-icity,' or something like that. It's like Duchamps's 'Critic Descending a Staircase.'"

"Well?" Already I was losing her.

"Well, that's what it feels like. More or less. It's more or lessness."

"You don't like the titles?"

Some disabilities are poignant and grand, compelling telethons and ready tears. Others are just plain irritating. "On the contrary. I like your titles just fine. I just don't like feeling as if I've swallowed one."

Demoralizing, all the blunted, blighted breaths. When it's under way, for anywhere from twenty minutes to an hour, I can't manage one uninspected breath. Not one breath that is unselfconscious, that is less formal than a transaction with the atmosphere. (And just how many consecutive sentences will have my bad breath on them?) The main channel's on the fritz. The fittings have slipped. I'm misfit. You know O'Connor's

Misfit? "Look up it was a ceiling, look down it was a floor." Preached at all his life, he couldn't get past the fact that he existed utterly in his own body, whose walls kept pressing in. A confinement and claustrophobia to last a lifetime. Who could be expected to breathe naturally in there?

"When it comes, the Landscape listens—/ Shadows—hold their breath." With every inhalation, I think nope. Nope, nope. Not that one. Not that one either. How I crave good old-fashioned breathing, pastoral breathing, Wordsworthian inspiration, its natural legato, its unruffled intake and downy flowing out! During an episode I dream of being unobsessed. As well as my panting allows me to, I plead with the empty air. Grant me one really good one, one really deep one. I fantasize about one voluptuous breath the way others long for chocolate or guilt-free sex. Let me smuggle just one past. But until it subsides—always unpredictably and of its own mysterious accord—my breaths are all ungovernable. They pack my throat like subway passengers. "When it goes, 'tis like the Distance / On the look of Death."

Inebriate of Air am I, too, Emily, unless it's simply hyperventilation that makes me woozy.

Doctor K. ticks off the odds against various gruesome ends I've imagined. Although the instruments insist there's nothing there, half the time I'm gagging on the very air. I start drowning in my own office chair. That something undetectable sticks in my craw sticks in my craw, wherever that is. My chest feels like it's shut up in a chafing dish, Doc, or it's playing the part of the witches' cauldron in *Macbeth*. (You must know the play.) I'm a paper bag choked at the throat. Trying to catch my breath is like trying to catch the puppy when it's got hold of the sleeve of your only clean shirt.

It's a tangible attack force on the move in there. Just because your figures can't touch it . . .

Doctor K. listens in again. It's like trying to pass counterfeit twenties, my breathing. So go droll. Go oblivious. Go numb.

"So? How am I doing? How do your data like me so far?"

"Quiet," he says. Is he admonishing or reporting?

For English teachers, too, interpretation can get pretty frustrating; it certainly puts off the non-majors in the class. I wonder what is worse: being obviously afflicted, plagued by cliché, or elliptically so. On the one hand, I have to brace myself against the implacable judgment of finally recognized disease, replete with fatal stats drawn from funded studies; on the other hand, I have to withstand the inscrutable. For now, because Doctor K. has to explicate me, because he cannot digest my meanings at a glance, appraise my cadences or fully appreciate my read-outs after a single reading, because he cannot take my face at face value, I am a poem to him.

And in short, I was afraid.

"It *is* a strange set of symptoms, I admit," concludes Doctor K., but he does not speculate further.

"Great. At least I'm not trite." Presuming I need not breathe iambically to impress him. Presuming I need not be comparable to survive.

"That's right," he says. "It helps to joke about it. After all, whatever it is, if it's anything—and I'm not saying it is yet—it isn't going to kill you, no matter how rotten you feel during." He is undeterred and never, never betrays anything. I particularly like the picture of him in the local Yellow Pages. Whereas every other physician settles for a head shot or the typical swat team of consonants announcing his credentials, Doctor K. is revealed down to the waist. His arms are folded, his shoulders are judiciously set, and his expression reads dismissiveness. It says, "Illness? Hah! I *dare* any body to defy my erudition." It is only a matter of time before he puts a name to the perpetrator hiding inside me—probably using a Latin alias, clever bastard—and brings it to justice.

Doctor K. absolutely seethes composure. And yet, he's been vetting my essence for a high-priced half an hour, and all he has to say for himself—for myself, that is—is that I'm enigmatic. Do chicks dig enigma?

"They didn't have any answers for me in the emergency room, either. Four of them watched the monitor play my outtakes for twenty minutes, then they said I should see you. I guess I'm a passed buck, huh?"

Still nothing registering on Doctor K.'s face or in his posture. What a poker player he'd be. Hook *him* up to that hospital monitor: would there be any readout at all? Hard to believe at this moment that we've competed on the court together. We have showered at adjacent spigots and shared the same bar of soap without flinching or flicking off imbedded hairs. "Hey, could you plumb me, buddy?" That's all it should take. Just us guys giving each other a game. And when a ball gets away, it's just common courtesy to retrieve it and flip it back into play. That's all I'm asking for: the medical equivalent of "Ball up!"

We are a couple of carbon-based life forms. So if I tell him, earthling to earthling, that while he's smoothly ingesting the proper molecules, my portion is riddled with little bones . . . surely we are not so different that we should be incapable of communicating.

But Doctor K. is as charismatic as a clipboard, and about as forthcoming.

"Do you feel anything now?"

Every breath pinched like a criminal, snagged like a duffel off the conveyor at baggage claim. My body's involuntary actions are devolving. I would insist on other imagery. I wish to be put on other terms. I'm dealing with a kinked pipe here, a throttled progress, a glottal stop. Something's clogging the ducts, Doc, no matter what your dials say. You'd think I'd gulped one of those rubber gloves. Well, I don't feel it now—the flue flutters shut, then it opens up again—but when I do, it's like a delta of mucous has developed all of a sudden. A mucky undertow. I. can't. get. a. damn. sentence. out! Got it? It's like a cotton crop. Hostages are bound and squatting down there, whatever they are, wherever that is. My wind's been waylaid. Something vital's been headed off at the pass, knocked cold and stuffed in a culvert.

"How about now?"

I expect another internal putsch any time now. Armed guards escort each targeted breath out of the compound.

All right. That's the lot of it. I've forked over all the analogy I've got.

I imagine that if he could just slide some sort of snake down my gullet or drop a pharmaceutical depth charge, he could unblock the whole business like a sinus. "Hey, could it be sinuses? I mean, how far do they reach, anyway? Maybe histamine's behind it all?"

Samuel Beckett's *Breath* is a play that lasts all of fifteen seconds. There is an amplified inhaling offstage, during which the light comes up on debris; the light subsides as the breath is released. Fade in, fade out: a dismal circuit bracketed by screams. It could have been any breath anywhere in Beckett, I bet. The same suffocation pervades everything he does.

"Strictly speaking, it's not a breathing problem at all, you see? Don't get me wrong. The anxiety manifests that way, but the cause—causes, most likely—lie elsewhere. Which is to say that an inhaler probably isn't the answer." The epicenter of my suffering is somewhere else. Unidentifiable leaks in unlocatable gaskets. Yet there's no denying my misguided experience of whatever it really is that's the matter. All the blocked and blunted breaths, making their ragged way like wounded soldiers returning from the front. All the stippled, shredded, stifled, stymied breaths.

"Is it nerves, then?" What a disappointment. What an old lady's malady. Nerves are what the members of Aunt Bea's flower committee suffer from. Nerves are what they secretly subdue with elderberry wine, kept in a nippy bottle under the porch swing. "I don't *feel* anxious. I mean, once I feel it coming on, *then* I feel anxious, but not before."

He regards me as if he's caught me at some mischief, as if he's recognized the kid who spray-painted obscenities on his garage door. "Nerves aren't the problem, either, although nerves do make it worse." In any event, he'll prescribe something to comb out the tangled dendrites. Replace the synaptic spark plugs. Whatever.

"Don't get *me* wrong, Doctor."

He is at least a little worried about me. Rather, he is worried that I am worried about me, which triggers and intensifies the anxiety, if it is anxiety, that is. He asks about my appetites for food, work, company, exercise, sex, checking for impending panic or trying to define it by its wake. It strikes me that the signs of suicidal tendencies and signs of recovery from them are frequently identical. Such as losing weight, making amends with those you've flummoxed or offended, clearing your desk. Getting out from under: the effort is either suspicious or sound. The peeling off and away from the past, the stripping of bones. "There are moments a man turns from us / Whom we have all known until now," writes James Dickey in "Drowning with Others." "Upgathered, we watch him grow, / Unshipping his shoulder bones // Like human, everyday wings / That he has not ever used." Peculiar or inspiring, the dispossession that allows one to soar, or at least enjoy a little more altitude for a change, for a while.

When I'm sick, or think I am—the results are ambiguous—the world implodes. I go stertorous, gag like a lawnmower fed the wrong fuel, and the whole species seems endangered. Existence is suddenly up to me. Existence suddenly comes down to me.

"I wouldn't worry about it," says Doctor K, leaning back.

"Okay. Should *I?*"

I went around my department confiding my predicament and appearing, I suppose, like a hit-and-run victim trying to gather witnesses. When I told Jeff about my physical situation, he offered uplifting quotations to me—bromides from better breathers. Jeff is a fan of human potential. Jeff is a fan of the power of positive thinking. ("Do you have to work tonight?" I asked him one afternoon. "No, I *get* to work tonight," he corrected me.) Telling Jeff was a mistake. So was telling Pat, but I needed someone to cover. Like in every other war picture: "Cover me. I'm going in."

At the very least, I expect Doctor K. to give me several multi-syllabic prescriptions, accompanied by the suggestion that I'm lacking half the alphabet's worth of vitamins. Instead, he sets me up with just the one tranquilizer—nothing far-flung or newfangled about it, either—and tells me to check back with him in a few weeks. He has other patients stashed in other examining rooms, so as I ease off the table to fasten my pants, he lifts a couple of elegant fingers in lieu of a handshake in the manner of Michelangelo's Lord bidding Adam rouse himself and get on with Genesis.

"What about meditation, Doctor? Maybe I should try that?"

"Why not? No harm in it." Not surprising that Doctor K. is inveterately Western- hemisphere in his orientation. "So," he says, ungloving, "is there anything else on your mind today?"

"You mean, as in 'Apart from that, Mrs. Lincoln, how did you like the play?' No, there's nothing else on my mind. That's the problem."

At the pharmacy I'll look up the drug I've begun and discover that there are only two sorts of problems associated with it. One is related to what could happen when it doesn't work the way it is designed to; the other is related to what could happen when it does.

"Tell me, what is it you plan to do / with your one wild and precious life?" asks Mary Oliver in "The Summer Day." With my one wild life, I plan my routines. With my one precious life, I plan to keep my appointments and to stay on my medication. I plan to keep writing although writing can make it happen. I plan to breathe in, breathe out, then do it again until I've got it right. Then do it again.

Here is where doctor and muse conspire: they issue consecutive life sentences. *Conspire:* literally, to breathe together. I'm told it helps to joke about it. A man walks into a doctor's office. "Doctor," he says, "it hurts when I do this." "Don't do that," the doctor replies. "Next?"

In this one wild and precious life, the poet is right to find loveliness while I labor at my ease, although I cannot say for certain which of us is distracted, she in her inspiration or me in mine. (There it goes.) She raises her arms to pray and to praise, to take it all in; I raise mine when I feel myself going under. (There it goes.) You can see how we make similar gestures.

Until it ends, we haven't much more than words to go on.

Savages

When we were kids, daring was basically something you did with your body. Once you got beyond gender distinctions, there was no difference more significant than the one between those who accepted, even sought out, prospects for personal damage and those who preferred to go the long way around. There were those who thoughtlessly jumped ditches on their Stingray bikes, hoisting the handlebars abruptly at each precipice as if they had horses bucking under them, and those who pulled up short on broken colts. There were those who did not hesitate to lay out parallel to the ground to stab at bad throws, performing as recklessly and unpredictably as the throws themselves and diving no matter if the game was played on pavement; and there were those who held back, figuring that no completion was worth the hurt. You either stepped forward to be counted, or you retreated, abashed, into contemplation of those who did.

Back then, real risk was physical. It was left to the grown-ups to know the numbers of their group insurance plans while their intrepid beneficiaries heedlessly launched themselves from the playground apparatus. We had heard that discretion was the better part of valor when, in fact, it was only the loser's portion. The

166

saying was a salve for patrol boys, spelling mavens, and the meek who inherited an earth that never earned a spot on any highlight reel. In other words, the parable bespoke a coward's politics, for weren't politics the province of cowards in any case? Meanwhile, it took a lion to claim the lion's share, as even our primitive understanding of natural selection made clear.

In "Autumn Begins in Martins Ferry, Ohio," James Wright mourns the transitory capacity of high school football players to "gallop terribly against each other's bodies." They hammer and thrust before the gazes of their shamefaced, domesticated fathers and the shadow of mortality. There will be time enough for treating living like an intransitive verb; a sobering, inevitable future of cost-consciousness and fastened seatbelts awaits them. Here and now, however, action is drastic, and Wright's footballers view themselves as wondrous brunts to be borne. For the sake of a game, they aim themselves like missiles; in time, age and ordinary Ohio will disarm them. Wright calls them "suicidally beautiful," the town's urgent, negligent sons, who, unlike parents and poets, never seem to stop to consider, never flinch.

"Let's see what you're made of"—no child I'd ever met confused this with a request to see his medical records or report card. And weren't some of us yearning for arenas in which to prove ourselves? Didn't the regularly self-flung among us fling ourselves after passes we had no hope of putting a finger on or, when a series of true tosses grew monotonous, add a tumble like a jazz riff to ones we could reach with ease? Do not question what hormonal excesses propelled us. Reason not the need to be unreasonable. As Tom Sawyer put it, "Well, that *is* a question, I must say, and *just* like women! Why, I wanted the *adventure* of it: and I'd a waded neck-deep in blood to—goodness alive, AUNT POLLY!" If you have to ask—and it's only the sticklers and the scolds, the incurable hall monitors in our midst who did or ever do—you probably wouldn't understand anyway. Go help Aunt Polly count her silverware in the kitchen.

To be sure, testing your mettle meant determining how much *metal* went into your make-up. This was no diction glitch kids fell for but fundamental dogma. The template for what we dreamed of being was the imposing definition of any comic book superhero, sublimely muscled and aerodynamically cut like a new sports car. The Justice League of America gleamed at the conference table like the pre-race line-up revving at Indy.

If there were such a thing as Truth, we would know it not by vague beatitudes but by the bruises it left.

It was not until high school biology that we *did* see for certain that what we were actually made of was slop. Our bodies turned out to be kettles chock-full of oily, ambiguous globs like the ingredients of leftover stew, all gone soft and covered with scum. After such knowledge, girding oneself for a challenge seemed as unlikely and as useless as stacking fish. And when it came to dousing the erstwhile Hotspurs in the group, science and religion suspended their ongoing grudge match and took up the hoses together. Both disciplines preached discipline and warned us about the susceptibilities of the flesh. Appearances deceived: during the week, science class spread the rumor that germs lurked everywhere and showed us that we were flimsy-skinned and delicate down to the bones. Then in Sunday School they confiscated our comic books and replaced them with homilies designed to make us docile. Although we attacked each recess like a pack of wolves, the Bible alleged that we were sheep beneath. We were souls impressed to serve on frail vessels. We were chalices brimming with precious liquid that might at any moment, with the slightest jounce, spill. Thus the forced march of decorum was conducted for our own good.

And so we grew to think, and in time thought better of ourselves. We put away our mischief and tucked in the blanket when we left the bed. We reserved our courage for the PTA or department meetings, where Robert's Rules of Order reigned. We found ourselves clucking our tongues at unsponsored children who hurtled roughshod through the neighborhood, and we refined cautionary tales they'd never attend to, at least not until, like us, they'd lost their dash. We counted our fat grams and cholesterol. We cowered in our sullen, vulnerable bodies. And we congratulated ourselves on being mature.

From the sidelines, fathers clutch themselves against the November wind and vaguely promise themselves to start working out again. When did play become work? Mention "guts" to them, and they do not think of boldness but of the body's betrayal—their bellies swelling under their coats, succumbing to genetics, gravity, and years of improvident digestion. (Some of the men are so

distended that even excretion can be a tough negotiation or one more thing they have to take on faith; the
truth is they cannot tell if they've got a decent stream
going until it strikes the bowl.)

In *The Sound and the Fury,* Faulkner describes
Dilsey's "somnolent and impervious guts," which are
the repository of demise. "I'll lug the guts into the
neighbour room," grunts Hamlet, dragging his dead
load of Polonius. These quotations come from books
they pressed upon us when we could hardly keep in our
seats, much less muster the patience for prosody.

Once their sons would brag on their dads, routinely
threatening to pit them against the dads of other sons.
"Make a muscle, Dad," they'd say, and the sight was
more consoling than any college fund could be. "Now
feel mine." And all across the country fathers and sons
would flex together in the bathroom mirror. "Some
day you'll be as formidable as your old man," each man
assured, as his boy kept straining optimistically under
the reflection of his dad, who loomed over him like a
destiny.

Now, of course, the sons have taken the field themselves, preparing for scrimmage in postures of brutal
devotion, their hearts set like bombs to go off.

Meanwhile, their moms, who used to cringe at every
hit their darlings delivered or endured, have stopped
going to the games altogether. Each would scour the
savagery out of her son like mildew out of grout if she
could. She would culture her pearl. She would try to
entice him with gardening, ply him with birding and
Bach. She plots haircuts and Ritalin prescriptions. She

believes in piano lessons the way her own grandparents believed in the president, penicillin, and the benefits of fresh air. (Conveniently, she has forgotten how as a toddler he treated any object that he could get his hand around like a gun. "Bang," went the washable marker. "Bang," went the bunny.) She would restore the gentle child she sometimes has to struggle to remember.

Yet however fervently mothers might deny it, their babies are only a plane crash away from turning feral and *Lord of the Flies*.

The boys don't have the words for it—they do not need the words—but buried in the reptilian core of every player's brain the same single impulse hums: Apocalypse? Cool. Bring it on. Could technology eavesdrop on the fetus, it would discover a muffled but insistent "vroom."

Fathers look on. One of them recalls how yesterday his wife's frown forced him back to the bedroom to find a different tie before company showed up. Another thinks about the day he pulled the Chevy over to break up a clot of neighborhood kids who were burning ants with matches, delighting in watching them implode into tiny periods, delighting in fire. "Don't you boys have anything better to do?" he'd chided them. A third one wonders about what the night has in store for him. Might his bride of twenty years—goodness, has it been that long?—be willing tonight? It's been a while. When was the last time at the office he drew a strand of woman's hair from his mouth and his concentration came apart like a seam?

Eventually, there is nothing that doesn't become a job.

Not so long ago, Jonathan contemplated what a firecracker in her mouth would do to the favorite Barbie doll his sister hid under her bed or, come to think of it, to the family dog. Richard considered flipping kitchen knives at the throw pillows to get them to stick or, while Dad was distracted and Mom was in the shower, prying off the back of the television set, just to see. Gregory made mental notes to study what it was about the wine that consigned it to the top shelf in the cabinet and resolved to bide his time, more patient than he'd ever been in church. Mark, Kevin, Luke, and Chris all fantasized about BB guns like their first pornography.

The boys wear jerseys that proclaim them Wildcats and Braves. The stains are deep and indelible, and they do not care.

Their mothers create a salve and sacrament on the stove while the talk show in the background tells them to trust in the lasting effects of "quality time."

Their fathers, hugged by flesh that still surprises them, flesh they've never gotten used to, ask themselves when they might work out, or whether they can at all.

All across the country, the games go on. We grit our teeth and learn to take it.

Cast Irony

The Crayon World is just a broad-stroked test.
The test of how to enter it, and walk back out in-
tact.
　　　　　　—-Richard Powers, *Plowing the Dark*

"Everybody is *really*," said Pooh.
　　　　　　—-A. A. Milne, *Winnie-the Pooh*

Some people say there are two kinds of people: people who think that there are two kinds of people, and
people who don't. Those who do content themselves
with binaries; their world cleaves evenly and predictably into 0's and 1's like so many idealized eggs broken
against a digital computer. Those who don't, don't despair. They simply organize the species via more complicated schemes.

Leslie, for instance, is convinced that people can be
parceled according to types provided by A. A. Milne.
She is not the first to mine his children's stories for
more than children's entertainment. Author Benjamin
Huff devoted a book to the spiritual wisdom of Winnie-the-Pooh. Claiming allegorical stature for Pooh's
dazed behavior, Huff rebuilt an entire Eastern philosophy on the back of that "most *effortless* bear." Basically,

he deferred to Pooh's simple, clean genius for being in the world by throwing in the Tao.

Leslie takes an even more complicated tack. Instead of contending with the alchemists that each of us is a uniquely bottled concoction of four fundamental humors—Black Bile, Yellow Bile, Choler, and Phlegm, sounding like a law firm out of Charles Dickens—she insists that Winnie-the-Pooh and Company provide all the ingredients needed to explain any personality she has ever met. Consider Pooh, who has half a mind to try anything, but only just, and who wins us over with winsomeness and woozy cheer; Owl, puffed with his penchant for compartments, his downy pedantry and feathery bluster; and Rabbit, fidgety and jittering in his hutch, who wakes with an alarm that stays with him throughout the day. Consider the patient presidency of Christopher Robin, who gladly casts his lot with less dignified cartoons; the watchful, incorruptible repose of Kanga as Roo tumbles in blessed contentment beneath her; the eternal, antic spring of Tigger, whose bumbling verve is at once an affront and an apology for it; and the sweet naiveté of Piglet, unaccountably sunny as a Cub fan, yet, secretly, a Pooh wannabe.

And how could any deconstruction of human character be sustained without Eeyore's unswayable gloom? Eeyore, who knows better by always knowing worse, may seem out of place in the elaborate lullaby of the Hundred Acre Wood, stuck like a rusty wrench in the dreamworks. However, with so many of us trawling for Prozac in the shallows of the new century, with seeming legions of Eeyore lugging themselves through of-

fice halls and city streets, that gray, eminent complain-
er may be as essential to any modern recipe of self as
garlic to a stew.

Freud's id, ego, and superego cannot constitute
so intricate and distinctive a play of traits as Leslie's
pixilated infantry can. Indeed, Leslie finds herself surrounded by compounds. In her eyes, every acquaintance parses out neatly as cold cuts on a platter. For
example, she concludes that her boss is a martini made
from six parts Owl and one part Pooh. Her husband
was born under the sign of Christopher Robin, on the
cusp of Tigger. Her mother is Kanga—what mother
worth her nurturing assaults isn't?—with Rabbit rising. It took Leslie just ten minutes to pin down her
landlord's tag-team of Rabbit and Owl to the mat; she
still marvels at the man's isometric essence, like Chang
and Eng bundled into a single trunk. Meanwhile, she
deems herself Tigger burning bright, with perhaps a
hint of Piglet, a dash of Pooh, but she admits that it
is harder to know ourselves than to anatomize anyone
else.

When I question her interpretation of a given friend's
or family member's psychic compacts and compensations, my skepticism marks me as an Eeyore, which
distinguishes me not one whit from any other English
professor who trundles, Roo-less and rueful, in clumsy
perturbation through the dust with me. Or so I say,
and in saying so steep myself all the deeper in that designation. One may be full of Roo or full of rue, you
see, or so I see it, as would any Eeyore, a cartoon who
affirms nothing but negatives and despite that status

balks at animation. Or so I am destined to see it, if Leslie's alternative zodiac is as fixed as a chosen swatch of stars might constellate me, barely holding my snout above the ground and attached to my sad tail, dragging it after.

Frankly, I believe that a more detailed chart would show that I am no pure-bred donkey after all. I place my idiosyncrasies in evidence to argue that only in bad fiction does someone act out of character. Incurably extratextual, we cannot. The self is expansive, a cocktail of possibilities. If your wife says you aren't the man she married, tell her that in fact you are—she just didn't know so much of you back then. Like each of the five philosophers in the fable, she merely caught the first part that dangled as the elephant passed. She merely fixed her sights on the first characteristic that got separated from the herd, and the herd persists beyond her scope, always on the move. To everything there is more than one season. Your soul is its own society, a divine majority organic and incremental. One can barely predict one's own weather from one hour to the next. Take an umbrella. Take a sweater.

Expert opinion to the contrary, *this* Eeyore often spreads the day's stale bread with relish. I indulge the offensive habit of picking at contradictions so they will not heal. I tell the waiter to leave behind the contentions that lie on my plate so I can suck the bones. No, I am not defeated when schemes of being collide. I have a well-developed both-and aptitude, which leads me, teacherly, to intercede between contesting sides with the suggestion "You're both right, but neither one entirely." That's the Christopher Robin in me barging out, I guess, unless you find my being so sure of uncertainty Owlish (as if my choice of profession and penchant for semicolons weren't proof enough) and decide that the way I cope is that thing with feathers.

If "cope" is the word I've ever been after. I grew up with the *Chicago Sun-Times,* a newspaper that exercises its own both-and strategy in the midst of its large, windy readership by including *two* astrologists among its columnists. Their competing visionary gleams, published as Ask Jillian (along with a picture of its brisk, pretty seer) and Ask Omarr (accompanied by the sterner gaze of that stargazer), are printed side by side. Most of the time, by virtue of the conventional vagaries provided by the horoscope trade, their predictions are models of cosmic reciprocity. But occasionally, Jillian and Omarr will tease radically different readings out of the Rorschach sky. Jillian will announce that the runway for some unnamed upcoming trip is clear, but Omarr will pick up a storm front and restrict the reader to domestic activities. Jillian will forecast impending love for February, but Omarr will maintain that May is the likelier month to empty the heart's day-planner in preparation for its visit. Jillian will tell Libra to trust the counsel of Aquarians, while Omarr will tip the scales in favor of Pisces when it comes to handling investments. Jillian will rate Taurus's Thursday a five-star success, but Omarr will call that bull and handicap the day differently, giving the Goat the nod. But even an obvious conflict has no appreciable impact on the cosmos, and apparently no one is troubled at the *Sun-Times* either.

Certainly the two astrologists betray nothing in the wake of contradiction: having bet red, Jillian looks just as unassailably sure of heaven as ever; nor does a single drop of sweat moisten a crease of redoubtable brow of Omarr, who placed his stack on black.

I now live a state and a half away from Chicago and far from the threat of getting a major newspaper, but leave it to an Eeyore to keep the subject sore. Our local Szechuan restaurant features paper place mats that complicate the issue by introducing a Chinese classification of time. Its logic is solar rather than lunar, and it offers a different bestiary than the *Sun-Times* or A. A. Milne does to bear the sense of homo sapiens. So although Jillian and Omarr agree that I am a Lion, Grand Fortuna recognizes me as a Snake (a diagnosis, incidentally, that my ex-wife immediately agrees with). It may take more contortion to reconcile those creatures than even a Tigger might manage, but I try to take a cue from my little girl. Another Leo, she simply accepts the ambiguity—a good deal more Kanga in that kid than me, not to mention considerable Piglet deep in her chromosomes—and she busies herself with her lo mein noodles. The task for her own personality is to merge a lion with a horse, but negotiating two chopsticks causes her greater consternation than getting those two inimical animals to cooperate.

Although she is not the sort to linger over the make-up counter, I wonder if my daughter may one day be seduced by the divisions stipulated by *Color Me Beautiful,* which does for clothes and cosmetics what Northrop Frye did for literary criticism. According to that book, program, and buyer's guide, one is born a Spring, a Summer, a Fall, or a Winter, as determined by such factors as eye color, hair color, and complexion. Discovering one's true identity is the advent of professional advancement, social confidence, and even sexual conquest, for, as Northrop Frye himself and any literary critic would undoubtedly concur, heroism largely consists of learning who one authentically is.

Did you catch a whiff of suspicion just now? That's Eeyore you're detecting, hoisting himself out of the gorge. If I am sometimes too stubborn to enjoy the ointment for the fly, forgive me. Eeyore is the chronic anthropologist at the party. Even in the company of others, I confess my solitude, but I am not alone in this.

Huff is pretty dismissive about Eeyore's severities. He sums up the "Eeyore Attitude" as shortsighted, loveless, and "really not so awfully much *fun*." But if you believe an Eeyore can be drawn one way only and never on to pleasures, you really ought to see me get a haircut some day. I think of the barber shop as a massage parlor for the faint of heart because its principal appeal is not the improvement in my looks, which is indiscernible anyway, but the delicious rhythms of grooming. Do not be surprised: a Lion will lie still to be curried; a Snake will eagerly trade ministrations with the first woman he encounters; even Eeyore will endure a couple of patronizing pats when someone re-tacks his fallen tail to his ass. And so, in the absence of a lover's touch, I rely on those delectable surrenders legally and cheaply available at the barbershop.

179

Watch the way I laze during my haircut if you want to witness a less selfish, more reconcilable version of the lover who lets his partner exert all the exotic effort. In fact, as the utterly ductile, willingly subdued customer, I am no lover at all, "lover" implying more transitiveness than I manage as I deliquesce, relieved, beneath her casual expertise. (For Eeyores are seldom casual, less often expert.) Like a spoon into pudding I sink, until I am the sunken pudding myself, the mute, convalescent clay to be shaved, scented, and preened, to be restored, reformed, and redeemed. Every six weeks I budget a twenty-minute session at one of the drop-in parlors, Pro-Cuts or Super-Klips, typically—it does not matter, so long as it is a woman into whose hands I deliver my drab, disheveled head, my dull skull. It is my scheduled swoon. I never speak during the procedure but nod off and dream myself briefly elsewhere and other than the Eeyore I am. I wake to the swoosh of the drop sheet, startled to be left intact like china on the dining table after the magician has with a flourish snapped away the cloth. There is so much to savor at that moment: the tingling straight across the base of my neck as though I'd been nibbled by rational insects; the wisp of scissors still in my ears; the agreeable sting of aftershave on freshly cultivated skin; and best of all, when the chair dampens back down to floor level with oily, hydraulic ease, the post-coital, Pooh-woozy sensation of well-being that, I imagine, astronauts experience upon regaining the earth.

So what am I to make of myself now? Does my exercising this conventional release with such unconventional delight pop the seams of my hide-bound confinement? Would Jillian judge me otherwise and re-consult the stars on my behalf if she knew? Would Omarr begrudge me parole?

I hereby promote myself as both-and and more. How many persistent roomers crowd my boarding house of a body, Omarr? Jillian, trick me out as a traffic tie-up. As a one-man gang I mingle and blur before the door so census takers quail before me. I am all of Shakespeare's index set on puree. Heaven save me from being compressed or colored in altogether, even if there's beauty in the bargain.

Ah, just like an Eeyore to deny his sole self like that, Leslie counters. Just like an Eeyore to insist that like some gimpy Whitman he contains multitudes just because his collar chafes, just because he can with effort crane his neck to glimpse a bit of sky. And just like him to bray that he does not bray when he brays.

And yet, I have to admit that it's tempting to succumb to her understanding and simply commit us all to graph paper. While waiting for their turn in the barber chair, Rabbits are churning and checking their watches while Poohs doze over month-old magazines. A little boy has set up camp under one of the chairs and is improvising battles among trendy monsters, and I think to myself, There's unadulterated Roo.

His father keeps sleeping in the very chair his son fumbles under. Sleep can be a tough undertaking for adults—Roos will become Kangas soon enough, of course—so you take it where you can get it. I think of how it takes all three Stooges to complete the circuit of a snore: Moe gnawing at the air as if, even unconscious, he knows he needs special reserves of oxygen to keep his rancor blazing; Larry whistling out the spent gulp like a bad taste that his face forever registers anyway; and Curly bidding the breath farewell with his signature bird call—his oral ellipsis. And I think, would Three Stooges do to account for the human community? A friend of mine from high school, one of those inveterate binarists I spoke of earlier, used to say that there are two kinds of people: people who find the Three Stooges funny and people in comas. Would those who might treat them as the core of an entire human genome project represent a third category or just the logical extension of the first?

There must be dozens of other programs to channel. Maybe we could effectively compost down into four Marx Brothers or have L. Frank Baum bard us with figures ripped from Oz. (Scarecrow, Tin Man, and Lion, already well-established emblems for the brain, the heart, and the nervous system, respectively, could constitute a solid physiological basis for human prospects.) Or size the phylum down to the Seven Dwarfs, and will all our sins, savageries, and saving graces be covered?

There are two kinds of people, I suppose: those who think so, and those who don't. Both have work to do.

Oh, bother!

Prosthetic Devices

An act of substitution, as maybe love always was.
—Lorrie Moore, *Who Will
Run the Frog Hospital?*

The feel, in his palm, of the thudding rubber ap-
peased him, slightly.
—Samuel Beckett, *Watt*

It makes perfect sense in retrospect, as things most
often do. The man who was charged with egregious in-
fractions against decency—I never did hear the specific
wording of the indictment, but that was the gist—was a
junior high health teacher. He had been pulled over for
speeding through a school zone, an irony that, if it was
not lost on the arresting officer, obviously did nothing to forestall him. Whether in their classrooms or in
their cars, teachers are role models twenty-four hours a
day, and even if they cannot refrain from frequenting
the liquor store or downloading celebrity nudes, they
are expected, like ministers and politicians, to exercise
their penchants in seclusion or suffer the public conse-
quences. When a teacher speeds, he threatens the wel-
fare of his students as surely as if they'd been actual
passengers, trusting and unbuckled in the back seat.

What *did* occupy this teacher's back seat was a polyurethane torso, decapitated and flensed down its left flank, whose skinned head and bundled guts were tucked together on the floor. There was also a large cardboard box containing a massive plastic ear and a giant's eye—two pieces of Bunyanesque sensory apparatus, each brightly painted and covered with numbers to indicate their respective component parts. A cannibal's trophy case, darkly comical out of context, which impressed the cop as profoundly as if he had come upon the remnants of Jeffrey Dahmer's prom date.

Of course, such clinical, bloodless butchery suggested subtler purposes—disturbing, perhaps, but hardly actionable. No one knows better than the police that there are more things in heaven and earth, and so on. Investigate any neighborhood, and you'll find odder hobbies and more nefarious appetites than this. Unless you cultivate equanimity pretty quickly in this job, they say, you'll never reach your pension. No, what set the officer off was not the meticulous slaughter in the back seat but the open black case next to the driver. A plush casket, expensively lined and specially contoured to hug its explicit cargo: demo genitalia. A detached phallus and set of testicles, tastefully, chastely imbedded beside a gleaming vaginal tract, whose fallopian assembly was spread like a delicate set of antlers or, more aptly, like a lover's hair upon a pillow.

Now ordinarily, most of us are ordinary enough, a point that retrospect tends to clarify. In this case, because our harried teacher had overslept, he hadn't had time to pack neatly and inconspicuously away in his trunk the things that were too valuable to leave in his classroom overnight, what with vandalism being what it is, and the times, and so on. Which was why he was speeding and why those parts of the fully delineated, expertly massacred body were splayed throughout the cabin of his car, as well as why the Sadean sample case wasn't shut, because, never having been placed flush in their sculpted crotch in the first place when he'd roared off to work that morning, they'd jounced free, so that, like a teenaged masher cruising Main with his well-lubricated date, he'd been trying to manipulate the restless genitals while keeping one hand on the wheel, which also contributed to his losing sight of his speedometer. Not at all mysterious to one who would make an effort to put it all together. However, deciding to err on the side of seemliness, the cop took him in anyway, confiscating his carnal booty for further study.

Conducted through the station, the suspect felt like a fly skimming a gauntlet of frogs. Nothing in a police station is ever safely beyond reproach; perpetrators and victims alike are prisoners of context, and they more or less equally exasperate law enforcement. Any man collapsed at the detective's desk, his face looking like a paper bag that had been buffeted about the interstate . . . whether perpetrator or perpetrated against, he is warned to keep his elbows off the papers. Hoping not to contract anything or to give offense, our teacher reflexively folded in on himself as well. Reason not the rationale: whatever one's case or business in a police station, penitence feels like the proper response.

In the end, once the whole story came out, it made perfect, unremarkable sense. Pending allegations more or less melted away, and although the arresting officer's glare was still set on Annihilate even after the teacher had entered his statement, they let the teacher go. With a warning.

If literature teaches us anything about love—a debatable premise, no doubt, but let it stand—it is that love is predicated on substitution. Elaborate substitution. Unconscious substitution. Subtle, startling, rueful substitution. Slickness of phrase, sleight of heart. When we fall in love, we plummet. The bait-and-switch of romance ambushes the erstwhile Sleeping Beauty, bringing her up short as she changes the sheets the morning after, as she wonders what rough beast slouches toward the bedroom to be borne again tonight.

Love is a mugging in the mist.

My point being that, the teacher's explanation notwithstanding, perhaps the cop had the right guy anyway. (Objections in the mirror are closer than they appear.) That if that junior high science teacher was telling the truth, he wasn't telling all of it. Don't talk to me about innocence when the subject is love. Context has him as surely as it does the rest of us, bringing him down like a fat buck caught in the crosshairs. As I say, the proper reflex is recoil; the proper posture, penitent.

Nor do the authorities themselves escape entailment. Imagine spores of suspicion clinging to the arresting officer, invading his fibers, following him home. They release in his own relationship, attach to his attachment to his wife, who, after hearing about his day, finds herself glossing his grunts when she lets him have her as the dinner dishes soak. ("Those other women were only dry runs," he'd gushed the first time they made it together, his lust homing in.) Will she sit up in the middle of the night tonight, resentful that her interest in whether he'd remarry in the event of her death doesn't wake him? Will he one day have the indecency to commit his indecencies beneath different sheets? Will his hypothetical slut stay their shared treachery even long enough to have him explain the marital stains on the mattress away? She watches him twist in sleep and asks herself who is filling his dream.

Thus do we ever spend ourselves in surrogacy. The lover loves her projections because she made them; she cozies up to her inventions like a child drawing her stuffed bear close to ride out the night with. (Who would be so callous as to tell her that her security's absurd just because Teddy's stuffing is bleeding through the stitching?) My mistress' eyes are nothing like the sun, thank goodness, so I can see myself swimming in their vitreous humor. One might as well take oneself out to dinner, then congratulate oneself on how much one has in common.

Ask a room full of grade school children about their marriage plans—I've done it, actually—and you may be surprised to discover just how many kids already have them. Oh, they have not yet selected the church, the cake, or the other half of the couple to come, but many have married the idea of marriage. Puberty may still be nothing other than a rumor for them, but marriage is a destination as real as the family trip to Yellowstone next summer. I tested this premise out on my own daughter while she was attending first grade and received an early wedding announcement: she would marry when she was twenty-nine. Her plan was to settle down with her husband and five dogs in California (yes, closer to Disneyland, making it less of an ordeal in the future for her to visit there). This news contradicted both her current revulsion toward boys—insufficiently beguiled by Barbie dolls and too fascinated by farting sounds and football scores, all the boys she knew seemed ill-equipped to become suitors any time soon—and the fact that cramped quarters and rampant allergies had always rendered the pet question moot. For now, she made do with videos of *Cinderella, Snow White, The Little Mermaid*—a starter's kit of conventionally animated ever afters, Disney's wedded blitz—and a zoo's worth of stuffed animals. Meanwhile, the twenty-three year countdown continues.

And if love is an act of substitution, substitution may be an act of love. Listen to Carrie, whose husband left her after twenty years of marriage. She since determined not only that he did not love her anymore, but that he *never* loved her. Through an elaborate Orwellian finesse on the order of the willful revision of history in *1984,* she edited and supplanted, she impounded and purged their past. She boxed up the souvenirs from vacations she'll disremember; she overdubbed his voice on the answering machine; she excised his face from every family photo; she bestowed upon Goodwill every item of clothing that carried his stink; she consigned cards and letters to the fire. So the truth, which had been buried beneath birthday gifts, valentines, and late-night trips to the pharmacist, finally came out: their past was not a prologue but a pretense. "Love . . . will not let him be / The Judas that she found him," wrote Edwin Arlington Robinson in "Eros Turannos," disclosing the politics of affection; in Carrie's case, Love's departure unmasked the Judas who'd used her.

Meanwhile, a coven of female friends closed ranks around Carrie, buttressing her recuperation with cooing, baked goods, alcohol, and object lessons about the inherent uselessness of men outside of the rudiments of procreation. Like Maenads they decried the species' lesser gender; they came together in a cloud of estrogen and indignation for lingering lunches and assaults on the mall. Beware, you errant knights, you clumsy waiters and trawlers of bars: a single gelid glance from any one of them would have rooted out the prodigal husband and incinerated the sinner, would have retracted the telltale testicles and shriveled the will. Yes, they mournfully agreed, intelligent single women would not find much to inspire them in the local landscape. Why was it so much to ask to find someone unencumbered, heterosexual, and employed, whose neuroses (if he must have them) were, if not negligible, held in relative check, who showered regularly, shunned right-wing politics, and had at least once in his life read a hardcover book? Was there really not one single guy within the sound of their collective keening who had matured past the age of fourteen? Alas, they decreed that there were about as many righteous men as there were right angles in nature, give or take the odd Samaritan.

Nevertheless, Carrie was urged and prompted. Take a dip in the Personals, they advised her. Try the chat rooms for a bit of dot camaraderie—what could it hurt? What's to lose that you haven't already lost? Dye your hair. Join the Y.

And if some day some princely facsimile cantered past, wouldn't Carrie nurse some kernel of doubt to give him the benefit of? If he saw something in her as he sidled by to ask to see again, wouldn't his discernment earn him a second chance? And so she and her companions in retrospect relented. After all, she was too young to let dwindle, too vibrant to let dry out like laundry left on a line. Unattached, Carrie would drift; a man's ballast would, if nothing else, give her blood reason to run, not to mention level out the bed. There's the rub: having so much to offer, she needed to offer it to someone.

Which brings me to the latest bulletin: Carrie has managed to defy the long odds and romantic dead ends and has gotten engaged! He's a genial fellow, too, by all accounts, meeting with a consensus of approval from the voting membership (abstentions being counted in with the majority, as rules of order dictate). If he's not necessarily exemplary, less Lancelot or Kennedy than modest companion, he's kind to her child and solid as a dock. He'll do.

In short, the majority supports her, knowing that loneliness is everything it's cracked up to be; certainly everyone welcomes the improvement in her mood. The official report is that she has finally found true love.

When the Mississippi River flooded several summers ago, finding its current course, subsequent cartography confirmed the result without documenting a prior bed. We might all be happier were we to follow that lead. Othello called his love false as water because Desdemona did not lie where he left her. He might have fared better had he learned to go with the flow.

Well, there's retrospect for you. Having neglected to bring the umbrella, we blot with towels as best we can.

I mentioned the majority opinion on Carrie's behalf. Steve has remained a stubborn holdout on the matter. He wants his skepticism on the record, although he hastens to add that he wishes the happy couple well— well, as well as can be expected. The man has a heart; he just prefers to keep it caged, the way anatomy intends. "The fountain from the which my current runs / Or else dries up—to be discarded thence! / Or keep it as a cistern for foul toads / To knot and gender in!" So moaned that Othello fellow again. To put it mildly, the man had issues.

Now Steve is not one to resort to pentameter to make his case, nor will he boycott the wedding. The source of his dissent is the reliance on romance—by his lights, a mass delusion. In particular, he abjures the language that dresses up love in so much crinoline it can't get through the door. Oh, he'll allow that love is more than just a function of maverick glands. Only don't try to get poetry past him. "It's unmitigated crap," he told me once, not bothering to pull his punch in deference to my personal and professional devotion to it. When I pointed out (secretly adducing the aid of Marianne Moore) that once you get past the fiddle section there might very well be something genuine swelling upstage, he said, "Okay, okay, so maybe it's mitigated crap." Steve is a financial consultant, by the way, and isn't typically given to retrospect, which he deems about as useful as last hour's stock quotes.

But if spring was the sentimentality in Carrie, it was the mischief in me, and I persisted. "Come on, Steve. Can't you find a single moment in the whole multi-volume Norton anthology to make you go 'Ah,' or do you reserve that exclusively for the dentist? Don't you ever wonder whether among its garble of options we are the universe's priority or pun? I mean, man's reach must exceed his grasp, or what's a metaphor?"

But he didn't want to play. He never does—not that game, at any rate. Figures of speech regularly figure in my faith, but in his mind they never figure anything out. So while he goes back to his clientele, I have to imagine his rejoinder for him: "Similes are too skittish to bank on; like junkies, they aren't to be trusted to testify in crucial cases. We're in a war for reality, boy, and we have to make an example of the sedition perpetrated by like-minded men. Now, you're a friend of mine, so I give you fair warning. You can clack about further on hyperbole like a clown on stilts if you want to, but I have people's futures to see to, and it would be irresponsible of me to wait around for the crash." Or words to that effect.

And it *is* a war of sorts we're in. From behind the stronghold of his mahogany desk Steve launches sleek, aerodynamic sentences like sorties over hostile territory. He believes that like any wise fighter pilot each word should drop its payload of signification on its intended target, then peel off and get out of harm's way. As for what Wallace Stevens calls "the intricate evasions of as," well, they convene military tribunals to deal with spies, don't they? In time of war, one may rightly be shot for dealing in false compare.

The trouble is that a strict interpretation of linguistic evidence could make every word subject to court martial. For all words are mercenaries, Steve, when it comes down to it, double agents and wily behind the eyes. It's not only that "words are no good; that words don't ever fit even what they are trying to say at," as Faulkner's Addie Bundren complains. It's that they're soldiers stuffed with straw—scarecrows in uniform we lean against the parapets to try to slow reality's assault. In other words—more hollow men, more shapes to fill a lack—words are always prosthetic devices. A sentence extends from experience like an artificial limb. After one glance, any cop worth his badge (better to err on the side of seemliness) would run it in.

"That novels should be made of words, and merely words, is shocking, really," writes William Gass. "It's as though you had discovered that your wife were made of rubber: the bliss of all those years, the fears . . . from sponge." Now there's no law against bedding down with a sentence; caressing its consonants and mouthing its vowels violates no propriety, so long as the bills have been seen to and the wash is done. What wife would worry if her husband remarked that he was taking Austen to bed with him? Not even the most chaste and ardent Janeite would shudder to hear it, much less dial the hotline. What husband, blundering upon his wife under F. Scott Fitzgerald's covers, would the next morning make an appointment with his attorney to revise his will? For the lives in fiction are fiction, not life, as even the weepiest reader will avow. Romance addicts pine for placebos, not persons; whether they realize it or not, a flash of phrasing, not the sight of an exposed thigh, has quickened their blood. A novel's private parts are pronunciations only. We caress concepts like courtesans, as Gass would have it. Spent, we doze off, the splayed volume fallen away from our hands, from our latest virtual conquest composed, and in dreams make utterly lexical love.

"When my love swears that she is made of truth / I do believe her, though I know she lies." As Shakespeare's speaker knows, she is made of language. She swears by it. But vanity has ever been his significant other. And when the intercourse occurs between consenting adults, who is to say what's legitimate and what corrupt? "Therefore I lie with her, and she with me, / And in our faults by lies we flattered be." In fact, if there's any real treason, it's this: that we may transform the authentic into artifice in order to love it better. Line by line the writer limns his Galatea, until it's his own poetry he falls for. "'Gainst death and all-oblivious enmity / Shall you pace forth," he promises in another perdurable poem, but it's the poem's cadence, not her footfalls, whose beat we keep. Be reasonable, he might console her. No mere girl could undertake eternity outside the writer's devices. I do what I do out of love.

Just so, out of love, Doctor Frankenstein scavenged a motley protégé, compelling from the cemetery a man of parts. Out of love, Duane Hansen sculpted a prosthetic population so convincing that you feel a real shot of self-consciousness when you sense the rigged-up museum guard on your shoulder. Although Hansen's old woman, collapsed in a chair with her shopping bags dropped nearby, has a body built of the same stuff as the bags beside her and chair beneath, your compassion for her predicament registers much as it would for someone's real Aunt Rose. For eventually you will break down out of sight into a couple of bucks' worth of chemicals and ash in a sunken box, and out of love people will tend your plot. They'll come to pay their retrospect. They'll romance and remember you in flowers, words, and stones.

In hopes of making sense in retrospect, Lot's wife looked back upon an unsupportable past. Of all the characters in the Bible, of all the sage, sinning, reverent, and errant fleshes become words in that blessed book, she is Kurt Vonnegut's favorite. As he explains in *Slaughterhouse-Five,* he adores her for that one useless and most human reflex. And so he looks back on her looking back, and over what is in the end nothing more than a pillar of salt, he lets go a genuine sigh.

Excerpts from the Vertical File

Harold. Winston Towers (Canal Street), Lift #3.

When I retired from Roosevelt, where I had taught zo-
ology for twenty-seven years, I knew that I would continue working in some capacity. With requisite grace, I
accepted the conventional trappings of reprieve—the
recliner, the slippers, the rod and reel, the golf bag em-
bossed with the university crest, and all the cards, caps,
and t-shirts sporting jokes about my escape into indo-
lence and impotence—but I had years before begun
plotting to subvert expectations by staying useful. As a
graduate student I conducted my first meaningful research in a building called Noyes Lab, a venerable,
hulking barn of a place over a century old even then,
which in all that time never surrendered one of the
stains or stenches that constituted it. That lab remains
my model and motto. Students used to carry the carcasses they experimented on in sacks. The dissections
were performed on the top floor to keep the shrieks
from disturbing folks on the Quad or passing senti-
mentalists committed to softer disciplines. *Noise* Lab,
that was the joke. Although the equipment is now
largely obsolete—newer facilities on campus have gar-

nered all the upgrades—Noyes still functions for un-
dergraduate courses. There is a considerable distance
between diminished capacities and incapacity, you
know, inconvenient as that fact may be to the adminis-
tration. (Not to mention between diminished capacities and decapitation. Nevertheless, people tend to treat
retirees as though they'd gone suddenly and utterly
stupid. They speak slowly and loudly to you. People
who once wouldn't have dared whisper behind your
back now put their hands on your shoulders. It's humiliating.) And you can forget Florida. Have you *been*
to Fort Lauderdale? Have you *seen* it? One giant landfill for doddering, severance-packaged carcasses, not
much better off than those moldering bags of cat the
lab students used to lug about. Residents with awful
handicaps golf every day there, and it still takes them
seven whacks apiece to get to the green. Some life, Florida, being stared at every damn, changeless day by an
imbecile sun. Really, can you imagine me firing up a
Winnebago and abstracting myself to Boca or St. Pete?
I need seasons. I need weather that's *weather.* I need to
hear news and be in the mix. So, fine, I won't pretend
that operating an elevator is equally as stimulating as
extending the boundaries of scholarship. But I tell you
frankly that it's the position I'd fixed on years before I
left Roosevelt. In the margin, agreed, but not marginal.
Cruising a black tube in a viewless room may not seem
like much to you, but it's my golden parachute. I wanted something that was relatively free of stress, and that
made no physical demands upon me—I'm seventy-
one, after all, nothing below the neck is what it used to

be, and statistics suggest that an assault on the citadel will eventually be launched from somewhere deep in the interior, if you know what I mean. Most important, I wanted a job that freed me to think. I considered other post-retirement opportunities that covered these conditions, but none surpassed the satisfactions afforded by the metrical regularity of elevator operation. The predictable rhythm of throttle and glide. There's a meditative quality to it, no denying that, and world enough and time to apply myself to something more significant than simply counting floors. And what do I think about? Well, yesterday it was a couple of articles I had saved from my bulletin board in my old office, which a colleague in chemistry gave me, I think, to cushion my impending departure with perspective. One had to do with spin anomalies among subatomic particles—muons, they're called—which are opening cracks in the so-called Standard Model of how the four principal forces in the universe interrelate, or rather, how they fail to relate as predicted. The other reported on the most disastrous extinction event in history: a lava flow that covered an area half the size of Australia to a depth of more than a mile, which some 250 million years ago caused ninety percent of all species then in existence to die off. So there's perspective for you. Thus are we punished for presumption. Thus is the definite set off and, perhaps, validated by the dim. These are the sorts of things that keep you busy and humble, assuming that operating an elevator is insufficient to accomplish both. For every topic I consider, I calculate how many circuits from the lobby to sixty-six and back again it merited. For instance, the ethics of human cloning was worth a dozen; the dark matter science introduces to keep their equations intact, a dozen more; the regular presence of diabetes, clinical depression, and sexual misadventure in my family history and the chances of any one member evading all three maladies permanently, seven; the increasing number and variety of skeletal and pseudo-skeletal manifestations identified by oceanography, five; the likelihood that the Red Sox will cobble together a pitching staff adequate to take a real run at the Yankees this year, four; the fact that my baldness is advancing from the top of my head downward while my father's progressed from his temples back, whereas his father never balded at all, three; the pyramid scheme that has recently absorbed my youngest son having proved hardly preferable to his obsession with that divorcee with the two unmannered kids and the tulip tattoo curling over the small of her back and visible during the Lake Geneva vacation last year to which he brought them all unannounced and, if we're being honest about it, uninvited, three; the ubiquity and magic of cell phones, especially how the calls find their proper targets without colliding, and that glass is made of sand, two apiece; whatever happened to Lee Remick, one; just the tulip tattoo itself, how it must have hurt, and how far its roots might reach, one more; the mysterious way my downspouts keep clogging with leaves even though no trees hang over my roof, maybe six floors. And so on, on and on, up and down. Figuring conservatively, I have enough issues stockpiled to last me another six months, excluding the calculations required to determine their tenure, and that's not adding in anything that might arise on NPR or catch my eye in *National Geographic* in the interim. Anyway, as you might expect, my first month on the job was full of science. Once I'd sufficiently mastered the door's torsion, committed the oily give of the brass helm to muscle memory, and matched the floor-by-floor timing to my body clock, I indulged in some general formulations regarding acceleration, resistance, and so on, familiarizing myself with the physics governing the car and shaft, imagining the long-range impact of all those the hoists and drops on my organs. Just think: nothing but a thousand feet of physics and oblivion. We're at the event horizon, folks, so please stand away from the door. But I don't dwell on it, at least not any more, and not to the exclusion of other studies. I plan to branch out into art history soon, with a particular emphasis on the Italian Renaissance. And political science. Religious philosophy. Internet gambling. I mean to become the generalist emeritus I hadn't the chance to be in career tow. Why slump your way toward an end that's empty and contemptible if you don't have to? And I don't have to. Old age may seem to be only a syllable's difference from dotage, but at seventy-one, although I'm not gearing up for any marathons, I feel entitled to more than narcotics and the odd compliment for not drooling at the dinner table or keeping my sheets clean. Don't cluck your tongue at me, now. An elevator may seem a reprieve from your particular brand of chaos, I'll grant you that, and being boxed up in Winston Towers is arguably comparable to being secured in an ivory tower, but it's no diversion. Like any other office, this room is fraught with purpose and direction. A freight elevator, eh? Puns are worth enjoying for a floor or two. My point is, I'll just keep performing for as long as I can manage and they'll let me, thank you very much. An avatar of compliance, that's me. Just keep contributing, quietly, in the years my doctors allow me, still, in my own way, counting for something.

Lester. Broadmeer Building (La-Salle Street), Lift #2.

So get this. So Jeannie, that's my wife, says, she says, that that was exactly the sort of thing Ralph Kramden would do, knowing, right?, *knowing* that that would set me off again and even worse, not because the Ralph Kramden crack insults my weight or my intelligence or my job, though he could—she could, I mean, by mentioning him—but because it makes her Alice, long-suffering Alice, and smarter and worth more than him, who could have married better and why didn't she, which he realizes only when he's at his best at the end of each show, when she forgives him for being Ralph Kramden and accepts the bum deal she's gotten living with him, since she could have done better, but because he can't help it she stays anyway. That's the thing: the Ralph Kramden bit reminds me that she didn't have to settle for what she settled for with me. But I tell her that I'm not cut out for other jobs, that I'm not *interested* in the damn Civil Service exam, and screw her brother Marvin anyway because can you imagine me selling leather goods, especially for Marvin, with Marvin breathing down my neck. Okay, maybe, *maybe* I could do suits or sporting goods, and that's maybe, but ladies' handbags, and add to that answering to Marvin with the way he grabs your shoulder like we're old buddies and that mouth on that guy. Forget it. I've had it years ago with those jobs where sooner or later you have to have it out with some boss who has it in for you. Whenever—and here I'm not just talking about that time working for Ben Brillstein with his idiot son-in-law with the retainer and that condescending crap, and who wouldn't who didn't have as little as a dog's dignity quit—I left a job or decided not to go after one I knew I'd have to leave anyway so why not cut to the chase, and Jeannie, she says I'm just afraid of success or change or what it takes for success or change, I want to tell her, Just try it yourself for a month or ten minutes and see if I don't know what I'm talking about walking out or not walking in in the first place. At least here it's not Where is the Jensen file? or Did you restock Aisle Five? and biting back every single day the comments you wish you could make. It's honest work—it's *work,* no matter what they tell you, they don't just hand over a paycheck, no matter what Marvin says—and nothing to be ashamed of. I don't have to pretend to be something I'm not for anybody. And, okay, maybe the math on the licensing exam isn't up to SAT standards, but it's no milk run. And the safety manual is a real bug crusher. What to do when you're stuck between floors, when and how to override the automatic operations, how to work and repair the interlock, the limit switch, the governor, the buffers, the whole dispatch panel, especially when you've got whining kids aboard or angry commuters who have someplace other than up and down to go even though you don't, and don't think they don't let you know about it. And there's combustibles, inspection procedures, compensations for peak traffic hours, estimates like how many passengers per day on average you have to handle if the area of the building is, say, 100,000 square feet. Guess. See? And I'm not even getting into things like what's wrong with the hoistway cables because the car keeps skipping or you're picking up these sounds, you know? Or things like courtesy, or when—okay, here's one—say the only elevator in a building is being repaired and has been shut down by the mechanic during his lunch hour, and the county commissioner comes in and wants to get up to his office quickly. Or maybe just some guy spills coffee or freaks or passes out, what then? I'm not doing a Walter Mitty in here, idling at some curb, stroking my stick. You have to *know* these things. So I don't appreciate the jokes like how do you rest up from a whole day of sitting on your ass anyway or like the graffiti, you know, Elevator Men Do It Up and Down, like *that's* one nobody's ever heard before. Ralph Kramden, my ass. And anyway, I'm past fifty now, so there's nowhere else to go and nothing much else except like taking Marvin up on it the next time Jeannie has him and the kids over for dinner or we have to go over there and vomit all over the new dining room set or the pool table they've got in the basement because we're so impressed.

Which isn't, believe me and Jeannie knows this if she knows anything about me at all after twenty-two years, going to happen.

Sam. 1001 Grand (Grand Street), Lift #1.

Better than the other building, at least. Blessings count, so you count them. There it was like the whole place was clearing its throat, hocking up something awful every time you started up. The cables ached and complained all day long. A purgatory of betweenness, that shaft, a grieving, gasping factory you couldn't trust but had to. Labored climbs and stammering descents, the functions chafed and ragged, like something was gumming up the gloom you were in. You didn't dare move in the cube for fear of waking gravity like some monster that would gobble you down if it ever caught your scent. You had to pretend for the passengers' sake that all of you weren't marionettes played by massive, arbitrary hands. But the Grand, well, I won't ever say I'm not lucky to have gotten it. It's like a dream so precise you don't feel cramped or confined. You can stretch out, metaphorically, I mean. Clean, necessary, minimalist art in here, making me King of Sparta ten feet square, between oak molding—real oak, that—and polished mirrors. The doors barely make a sound, and the car slides through the shaft without a murmur, too, oily smooth as a new boot. At night you can imagine all the cars roosting like owls, alert but composed in the perfect pitch. Where you're standing now? Over a thousand pounds depends on lines slim as your wrist, each barely more than a furl of nerves. You have heard the ghost stories of shafts inhabited by dead residents, by revenants trapped forever by the routines that defined them in life. You cling to legends of anonymous heroes who risked everything to compose the armed claustrophobe and compelled him to surrender his gun or to engineer the rescue of a troop of visiting Girl Scouts stuck between floors. The lush, dense network of machinery above and beneath you inspires and nurtures stories of optimism. The Grand is . . . generous that way. One delicious rise and one plummy plummet after another through the indolent dark, a la Lewis Carroll's Alice adrift in the rabbit hole, riding a column of air. But for all that, there is no denying that you are on the way out. As a species, you are indexed with lighthouse keepers and whooping cranes. Future fossils, all of us, consigned to twilight, routinely striving toward that end. "The uniformed elevator men are gone," writes Carl Sandburg in "Skyscraper." Almost, at any rate. The rest of us are going bad in our cans. Automation will relegate all of us to museums in time. In time, we'll have to adjust to another brand of syncopation. The eternal cadence awaits us all. Who knows but that in other elevators, flustered by these thoughts, the operators have gotten sloppy about their execution, stingy with small talk. Maybe they aren't helping the Mrs. Garfields with their packages anymore. Maybe they aren't bothering with the bows the manual still mentions. You cannot help but wonder what the state of the art has become elsewhere, but because all elevation is parallel, there is no way to catch your brethren in the act, or rather, in the failure to act. Hard on the concentration, these considerations, and bad for morale. Who would blame you if you missed a greeting or a stop, if your hand grew slack on the tiller, if you slid off your stool. Massaging the spine of the Grand, like scratching a rash, or like lulling something. Up and Down constitute a kind of Manichean faith, don't they, and that's what holds us here. A false dichotomy, perhaps, but it's what we have, it's what we do and credibly inhabit, more or less. Here we grow heavy and light, we sink and aspire, from emptiness to emptiness, we fall and rise. Trust if you must in the coming floor, but our lives are spent in the transitions. That's where the action in this uniquely antipodal profession is. Up and down, over and over, like suturing a wound, sewing up the hole after you. You couldn't be blamed for losing track. Only natural. Eventually, you cannot help but give way.

Earl. The Sherman House (Randolph Avenue), Lift #5.

I *heard* that. Look, just because I'm stuck here like a post in concrete doesn't mean I'm deaf as one, too. All right. No one plans for it or wishes for that—what? *career* is close enough—when he's a kid. Kids think of firemen, doctors, and baseball players, that's about it. Who knew there were insurance adjusters or investment counselors or guys who restocked shelves for a living, not just to make a few bucks in the summer to put gas in the car? So, this, too, is something you don't aspire to. It's something you arrive at. It's the kind of thing, you look around, and there you are, and you've been doing it for years, and that's that. I mean, with my record, with the papers I have to show, what? What else do you really figure is out there? Astronaut? Talk show host? Exactly. Anyway, with my insomnia, it's just as well I'm here as anywhere. Me, a poor, bare, fucked animal in my sanctum sanitarium. Surprised you with that one, right? That'll teach you. What are you looking at, anyway? Eyes front, pal, just like in the latrine, the same goes here. Which is what I'm saying—we're not so different, you and I. We all sit to shit and lie down to die. Don't kid yourself. Or kid yourself if you want to, as long as you can get away with it. This is where you get off. Watch your step.

Jerry. The California (Armitage Avenue), Lift #1.

All in. All in? Eighteen, was it? Six? Right.
Nine? Oh, nineteen.

No problem, sir, it's right on my way. My
little joke. Ride with me

Again and you'll hear it again, you can bet
on that. Eye the numbers

As if there's a trick, you'll miss the entire
ride. That's the problem

With these new-fangled floor signals:
you've gotta watch them every

Second. Six. Yes, one more. Never at your
expense. No charge,

No tipping. Even that snot Donlen, who
handles the toilets on two

And mostly just brushes your coat for you
when you come out gets

Tips for that. Whereas I have lives in my
hands, whereas I'm with

You for the trip, the duration. Nine. Not
some coat I'm holding on

To. And not even the quarters you'd drop
on the sidewalk to keep

Away the cripples nesting by Wrigley Field
for my sake. Always

It's eyes up, eyes front. As for banter or
small talk, look, this ain't

Some taxi or barber shop. Maybe for the
regulars, and that's only

Maybe, and only when they know my name
first and use it because

What's so hard? What's it cost you, really?
Eighteen. Well, a bit

Of inventory as we go, take stock, take advantage, necessity's the

Mother, and so on, so, more bananas. Have
to let Jake out before

He pisses the kitchen again. And the pills,
first, in case the Bills

Vs. Colts knock me cold on the couch like
on Monday. Nineteen.

Going down? Eleven. And? Ground. Well,
let us put our faith in

Gravity, and we just might get there. My
little. Pay on the electric.

And the gas. Pay off Mike on the bastard
Rams. And rent already.

Why the first surprises me monthly I have
no idea, but there it is

Again. Plus him ragging on me for two
weeks, which who could

Blame him, Marty, but what's it, twelve
years I know the guy, so

You'd think, you might think. Eleven.
Maybe a beer left, unless

The last one this morning was the last, let's
see: three, two, better

To be safe than sorry, just to be sure, so I'd
better stop. All out.

The Orders of Magnitude

Because nothing is ever enough, not ever, nor is everything, nor everything and nothing taken together, like the world robed in mottled sky, enough, we look elsewhere for reconciliation, knowing that we will not be reconciled.

Each day, busloads of tourists arrive at the Precious Moments compound just outside of Carthage, Missouri, to bask, to sample, to marvel, and to buy. A promotional brochure for the main chapel attests to the "warm Renaissance tones" that prevail throughout the sanctuary. Although purists may quibble about this description, there is no mistaking the feeling that the jostling congregants—those milling about the chapel, as well as those depicted around and above the visitors—are being perpetually basted in satisfaction. In this friendly interior, the skies are rinsed in bliss and preside over a G-rated Genesis. It is a miracle of undifferentiated serenity. The main cast of the Old Testament adorn the walls and ceiling, but the tumult and travail, the rigorous dimension and bloody expense seen in the depictions of the Sistine Chapel have been bleached clean. At Precious Moments, religion is chipper and pristine, as ecumenical as any local currency exchange or neighborhood mall. Like pop singers who automatically reference the stars and blithely adduce the moon, the good folks at Precious Moments are very much at home with immensity.

The Biblical figures share three obvious attributes: they are mute, having had their mouths reduced to prim blips; they have massive eyes, like satellite dishes designed to obtain the highest-fidelity signal; and they are children. Each saint has been trumped by sentimentality and merchandising—a transubstantiation in softest pastels, with replicas on sale as you depart the complex. Each prophet is swaddled in his raiment like a toddler playing in the living room drapes or pretending eminence in his father's bathrobe. Moses looks readier to coo than to contest Pharaoh. Noah looks unlikely to be trusted to feed the cat, much less guarantee the future of every species. Even Methuselah bears no mark from his many centuries but hovers in unassailable contentment with the blessed rest.

This is devotion's nursery, impregnable to conflict or complication. The message of Precious Moments, the message that keeps the house full and maintains the gross, is that you are right. You are all of you all right.

༈

Because nothing is too much with us, and everything is, too with us and too much, we would rise sublime together, riding the thermals of public desire, at once collected and unencumbered, for once at one.

꩜

At the Rothko Chapel in Houston, surrounded by the artist's luminous, misty planes, we recognize Mark Rothko's intention to establish a visual counterpart for spiritual contemplation. In his poetic tribute to the artist, Baron Wormser sums up Rothko's vision as "ecstatic mass." And yet, as everything seems to succumb to color, all the pulsing, enveloping "blacks, tarnished plum reds, and Stygian violets" appear to cancel rather than to consecrate. For art critic Robert Hughes, the effect is one of "pessimistic inwardness": "[The chapel paintings] represent an astonishing degree of self-banishment. All the world has drained out of them, leaving only a void. Whether it is The Void, as glimpsed by mystics, or simply an impressively theatrical emptiness, is not easily determined, and one's guess depends on one's expectations." The artist has sacrificed calibration for vanquishment. Rothko either may be urging prostration before the Utmost, the better to be ravished by holiness, or he may be giving up on achieved form as a false or impossible version of serenity. Viewing these paintings, one thinks instead of the imposition of Wallace Stevens's "tinted distances" in *The Auroras of Autumn,* with the paradox of "form gulping after formlessness / Skin flashing to wished-for disappearances." Or as the poet puts it in *The Comedian as the Letter C,* "Crispin was washed away by magnitude." The artist—and by extension, the worshiper—becomes the conduit for, not the conductor of, "Ubiquitous concussion, slap and sigh, / Polyphony beyond his baton's thrust." Faith is equated with entreaty, then erasure; magnitude does not amplify its beholders but swallows them whole.

ॐ

Because we would extrapolate beyond mortal dispensations and mortal attachments, as dying animals fastened to our dying features and animal cravings, frail as nothing else and everything else in Creation, irremediably subjunctive, a dependent clause.

ॐ

R. M. Fischer has provided a plaque on the wall adjacent to his *Fountain,* an exhibit on display at the Nelson-Atkins Museum in Kansas City. Even as he defends the work's theological basis, Fischer confesses a tentativeness befitting its hybrid form: "*Fountain* is almost some kind of quasi-sacred or religious object taken from the church of commerce and industry." Composed of salvaged chemical drums lashed by black cable, the main structure noisily marinates in dirty water and yellow light. It gives off a complicated aura, something akin to that emanating from a Mercury space capsule lifted dripping from the sea. The artist anticipates and invites responses to *Fountain* that are as contradictory as its origins: "One may take comfort from its illuminated waters or be intimidated by its steely electrical charge."

Fischer's refusal to be prescriptive about the argument or the impact of his artwork is very much in keeping with the contested space it occupies. One important question that *Fountain* occasions, for instance, has to do with the confusion and mutual provocation of realms—the ramshackle and the venerable, the technological and the sublime. As evidenced by his reliance upon ungainly expressions ("almost some kind of quasi-religious object"), it is clear that his creation remains "anxious" for the artist himself.

Experiencing Fischer's sculpture is like trying to process such reversible figures as the Necker cube or the duck-rabbit illusion. How a given viewer adapts to, then judges, *Fountain* largely depends upon how comfortable he or she is with the coexistence of seemingly incompatible components. Are those portions of the sculpture stolen from manufacturing, which seem oblivious, if not inimical, to its religious implications, modified or mollified by this appropriation? Perhaps the transfer of our awe to our technology does not diminish its intensity; or perhaps piety is debased by the introduction of profane elements, a situation anticipated by E. E. Cummings in his sardonic review of our "world of made," in which "unwish returns on its unself."

ॐ

"Things are awash in ideality," writes A. R. Ammons in *Garbage,* a book-length poem that implies on every page that things are impossible to discredit and perilous to discard. We must waste not even waste.

In *A Natural History of the Senses,* Diane Ackerman explains that an apple isn't really red. In the sense that red is what the apple reflects—it is the color that the apple does not absorb—when it comes to red, an apple is anything but. Thus one is known by what one rejects. It is possible that our essence lies in our excrescence, that what we bleed out retains us.

Suddenly something close to you is gone. Suddenly something gone to you is close. Hold tight.

۲

Aesthetic responses to magnitude in some way occasion the deregulation of the sacred "to stroke faith the right way." Recent intimidations of the self—what Robert Frost called the "larger excruciations"—compel renovations of conventional sites of worship. For John Updike, "The welter of religious phenomena is not necessarily comforting to the professor of a specific faith; the very multiplicity and variety suggest that none of it is true, other than manifesting an undoubted human tendency." What appear to have been lost in the renovation processes are the endowments of belief. Precious Moments suggests foster care, not fortification; the Rothko Chapel engulfs instead of enlarges; Fischer's *Fountain* fosters an industrial trance. The self is pulverized to a minus; more to the point, the self seems to welcome the effect. As a beleaguered character in Don DeLillo's *Underworld* muses, "There are times when you want to stop working at faith and just be washed away in a blowing wind that tells you everything." The language precisely echoes Stevens's account of the predicament of Crispin. The irony here is that faith seems to be just another kind of foundering. Awe does not ignite a launching out or an incipient collaboration with the sublime; instead, awe becomes its own (and only) authentication, destination, and reward.

Rumor has it that the numinous was once easier to access, simpler to afford. If we can believe the Transcendentalists, deific qualities migrated past specifically religious locales to include other immensities: oceans, mountains, constellations. And the artistic imagination was the engine of moral understanding. Grand latencies and greater human dimension could be articulated out of local forms and forces. Obviously, this reasoning featured the artist in a favored, even a prophetic, role. From God's Beyond to Nature's splendors to Man's imagination, the infinite percolated down to us, thanks largely to the pioneering raptures of painters and poets.

And yet, one of the principal characteristics of the sublime has always been its elusiveness: what we call "sublime" is that which cannot be adequately transmitted through language or image. However impressive the creations of the artist, they are cursed with surrogacy; they inevitably testify to the shortcomings of their expression—of *any* expression. Or perhaps, to put the case another way, they are solely an expression of desire, not of desire's object. The most vivid depictions are entreaties at best, from which the ultimacies we seek remain detached.

So our handling of magnitude is no more likely to exalt our apprehension than to emphasize our diminishment and our incapacity to deliver the occasion. Every formulation, whether stanza or shrine, confesses itself provisional and insufficient. Awe condenses into our representations of it, which simultaneously stage and renounce their object; like desire, awe certifies and defers. And all the while, the absolute looms—enveloping, rapacious, charismatic, entire—teasing and deflecting in countless guises, with inexplicit grace often indistinguishable from gruesome doom.

Better to restrict ourselves to buttons on a coat, an infant's rhythmic sleep, a shaft of light on a sill than struggle to apprehend an expanding cosmos on its own incommensurable terms.

Disclaimer demonstrates the artist's integrity. As Mary Oliver writes, "Isn't everything, in the dark, too wonderful to be exact, and circumscribed?"

Because there is nothing more natural than to rebel against our biology, to bring our petitions to the door of the Divine, to collect in petition like all of the wind-blown leaves in the neighborhood swept and shivering against the chain-link fence, we rebel and petition, we collect and shiver.

Annie Dillard is ambivalent about size. She adores what dwarfs her. In *Pilgrim at Tinker Creek,* Dillard consistently displays what Theodore Roethke called a "thingy spirit." Especially in the section entitled "Fecundity," Dillard praises Nature's quality of fermentation without ebb or concession. Her God runs a mad laboratory of roiling, boisterous, ravenous forms; if He is mean, He is never miserly. Dillard immerses her imagination in the extravagant spawn of everything from grunions to lacewings to protozoa to rock barnacles to horsehair worms, reveling in existences countless and improbable. But the spectacles are so expensive! While Nature rolls about in its plenitude like a lottery winner lolling in dollars, Dillard wonders how value can inhere in each of the anonymous, squandered particulars of life: "I don't know what it is about fecundity that so appalls. I suppose it is the teeming evidence that birth and growth, which we value, are ubiquitous and blind, that life itself is so astonishingly cheap, that nature is as careless as it is bountiful, and that with extravagance goes a crushing waste that will one day include our own cheap lives. . . . Every glistening egg is a memento mori."

Dillard thinks of milky tides of fertilized eggs, of explosions of locusts and lemmings, of the conjectural aphid breeding "unmolested" for a single year and producing "so many living aphids that, although they are only a tenth of an inch long, together they would extend into space twenty-five hundred *light-years*," and of numbers uncovered by the microscope "that swell and would split my skull like a shell." "What if God has the same affectionate disregard for us that we have for barnacles?" she thinks. The essence of these marvels, writes Dillard, is "holocaust, parody, glut."

In *For the Time Being,* Dillard specifically turns her attention to human history, where this verdict becomes even more sobering in the context of mass graves and the terrifying fission of statistics: "How can an individual count? Do individuals count only to us other suckers, who love and grieve like elephants, bless their hearts? Of Allah, the Qur'an says, 'not so much as the weight of an ant in heaven and earth escapes from him.' That is touching, that Allah, God, and their ilk care when one ant dismembers another, or note when a sparrow falls, but I strain to see the use of it." In other words, how can anyone pick purpose or dignity out of the vanished and vanishing generations, out of the numbing jungle of us?

ॐ

Because we live in the midst of abundance at a loss, we would contract with the intangible. Because the firmament blurs like a blow to the eye, because the sun comes out of a commotion of clouds to stun us, the first rule of prayer is to stay low.

ॐ

When Mark Doty observes a painting of the penitent Magdalen raveled in a voluptuous gown and finds that "every saint / in the gallery / flaunts an improbable / tumble of drapery," he does not denigrate the vulgar show but celebrates the lavishness of disguise; for adorning the emissaries of the spirit, be it with clothing or with poetry, does not sully their epic renunciations but rather furnishes our longing. Indeed, he comes to wonder, "Maybe the costume's / the whole show, / all of revelation // we'll be offered." The irony is that divestiture may deny the spirit instead of liberate it. (Love may be love of encumbrance after all.) In the language of Richard Wilbur, we must contest the "sensible emptiness" of "pure mirage": "auras, lustres, / And all shinings need to be shaped and borne," lest we be immolated by their glare. For brief, bright intervals, stubborn matter comes stubbornly to matter.

Yet even if through such compromises the horizon does not prove fatal, it may be nevertheless foreclosed, as it is by the impacted atmosphere Stevens describes in *Sunday Morning* as "this dividing and indifferent blue." God is equally indeterminate whether ghost or galaxy. Divine dispositions are scrambled, so we batten down as best we can against the onslaught of abstraction.

"Poetry is a species of thought with which nothing else can be done," wrote Howard Nemerov, who had to live with poetry's embarrassing relations. Well, consider the source.

᳒

Because by nature and necessity we linger before the sunrise and the sunset, exposing ourselves to too much light and too little, we rely on these devices to protect and provide.

From Walt Whitman's sturdy verses strung like cables across our manifest destiny to the most ordinary objects abiding in pockets, gutters, and drawers, we commandeer what we can to anchor us against the dark.

Or as Ruth Krauss puts it in her children's book, *A Hole Is to Dig,* "The world is so you have something to stand on." In case your children wonder, too.

᳒

In Donald Barthelme's short story "Lightning," a reporter for a glossy weekly magazine is assigned to track down and interview people who have been struck by lightning, the hope being that some unifying (and hot-selling) profundity may emerge. But the results are inconsistent. One man became a Jehovah's Witness, but another joined the American Nazi Party; one woman decided to marry her boyfriend, but another took it as a sign to dump her husband. No ready uplift, no divine message, no terrible beauty is born, and the afflatus goes flat: "In his piece Connors described the experience as 'ineffable,' using a word he had loathed and despised his whole life long, spoke of lightning-as-grace and went so far as to mention the descent of the Dove. Penfield, without a moment's hesitation, cut the whole paragraph, saying (correctly) that the Folks reader didn't like 'funny stuff' and pointing out that the story was running long anyway."

Magnitude submits to satire in Barthelme's story. But even if art cannot land the infinite with formulas or phrases, art does not simply suggest that we swoon in unison before it. The dilemma is how to respect the complexity and the intensity of "the infinity out there" and still posit an intellectual, emotional, and aesthetic presence.

In Richard Powers's novel *Galatea 2.2*, a computer competes with a human subject on a comprehensive examination in English literature. The test comes down to a single task, which is to interpret the following passage from *The Tempest:* "Be not afeard: the isle is full of noises, / Sounds and sweet air, that give delight and hurt not."

Alluring and inscrutable, these "noises" are the means by which Caliban is enslaved by his master Prospero. The human contestant—a one-woman control group for the human species—delivers a reading that is brilliant, allusive, and imbued with her fluency in cutting-edge critical theory. "She rendered *The Tempest* as a take on colonial wars, constructed Otherness, the violent reduction society works on itself. She dismissed, definitively, any promise of transcendence." Meanwhile, Helen, the computer, still getting her linguistic bearings, channels for Caliban himself: "You are the ones who can hear airs. Who can be frightened or encouraged. You can hold things and break them and fix them. I never felt at home here. This is an awful place to be dropped down halfway."

Whatever their differences, the two readings do coincide when it comes to the matter of transcendence. In the first instance, transcendence is a historically based treachery, which it is the perceptive reader's responsibility to dispel; in the second instance, it is a linguistic amputation from an authenticity we may presume but never penetrate. Yet dismissal strands us, leaves us (despite Thoreau's warning in *Walden*) "shipwrecked on a vain reality" while yearning leaves us homeless, estranged and starving after hypotheticals. Yes, this *is* an awful place to be dropped down halfway!

Absent an assured object of transcendence, the incentive toward the transcendental does not abate. Irony does not deter our appetite for elevation. That appetite survives in manmade simulations and ordinary disguise. It is variously constituted as panoramic landscape and patriotic zeal, in flights of rhetoric and rocket launches, in gilded monuments and toxic waste sites, as the Mall of America and the mushroom cloud. It is as likely to examine state-of-the-art technology as the mysterious titrations of the soul. In a pinch, any promontory may potentially serve as an exclamation point; any noun's noumena will do.

🍂

"When the Old God leaves the world, what happens to all the unexpended faith?" asks a character in DeLillo's *Mao II.* "It's not that people will start believing in anything; they will start believing in everything." Perhaps it is as ecumenical as that. "When the Old God goes, they pray to flies and bottletops." Perhaps it is as indiscriminate as that.

🍂

In contemporary literature, God tends to persist as a proposition. When art advances that proposition, it is inevitably speculative. For He will not be coerced like a prize buck into the clearing. We may remember John Updike's *Roger's Version,* a novel in which a computer-smart divinity student, who contends that God can be flushed out by a program, discovers that the reach of deity exceeds digital grasp.

The question is whether an ever-broadening context for the sublime represents its vitiation. Truly, these days it is not necessarily belief that brings us to our knees. The sky intimidates us. Newscasts warn that it may not be rain that next rains down.

Our writers labor under the awareness that language often must serve not just as the announcement but as the very repository of the holy; that transfiguration is commonly treated as being solely the province of clever figures; that the work of art—earthbound, artificial,

223

engraved—is all the higher valence that beckons us and all that we can finally esteem. Nor can we deny that today's visionary is no more likely to be the one who instructs us in euphoria than the one who ducks first.

Do you own a television or read the paper? Then do you really expect each day's annunciation to come in a voice so sweet it leaves dew in your ear? "No use to linger over beauty or simple effect," writes A. R. Ammons of the garbage in *Garbage*. "This is just a poem with a job to do."

In "So Sure of Nowhere Buying Times to Come," Jorie Graham is transfixed by an uncannily acrobatic plastic bag. It seems to win for once over the stuff we heedlessly entrust to the dump:

- a small brown plastic grocery-
- bag, empty, handle-straps pointing earthward, apricot-beige, soapsud
- beige, like a voice in the next room one can't quite make out, rises, up
- into the throat, the congestion, up high, in the grip of heat-fumes and the
- nervous embroiderer's pause—hand mid-air, needle mid-flight—dream
- tired but knowing still to rise.

There is something animate about its operations, as if it were an unidentifiable organ caught in a purgatory of pointlessly enduring function: a lung sprung from its rib cage, dutifully soaking up gases, or a tumbling stomach still gorging on the void, or a woolgathering brain. It appears to manifest some destiny or some ambiguous gesture of resolve, simultaneously swallowing and pouring forth great gouts of oxygen, giving out and onward as it does. Graham witnesses a passion forever spending but never completely expended. Her subject seems almost wistful over everything, over nothing, culling and lulling, like a gondola indolent and opulent in its drifting, in its dips and eddies complying with the indefinite, undefeatable air.

What else to make of it, this air bag inflated against invisible collisions? What aim or analogy, what silent seismic activity does it accommodate? The poet would fill it with spiritual significance, and she takes it shopping on the bargain floor of the Sublime. The bag has been magically provided to bear off reciprocities between the Infinite and the material world. Balking at parameters, accepting a dimension in the world but not of it, it takes the very shape of vision.

In another poem, Graham advises us that this is part of "The Way Things Work": "the objects of desire / opening upon themselves / without us; objects of faith."

But these conjectures are as unstable as the bag itself, and as frail. It is an image that is *almost* until it alters semblance and position again, in a constant fit of innuendo. The bag translates itself continuously: it is a doffed bonnet or dropped cowl; a gown the worse for wear; a cave haunted by drafts; Shelley's painted veil concealing annihilation or Stevens's extended wings become a parachute to break the Fall; a hole opening or the spirit's sloughed skin, and so an emblem of abandonment, still engaged in its idiotic dance; an image of ullage; a gas chamber; an everlasting last gasp. The way the wind goads the bag into greater ambition, the poet would push it to graduate into a soul, and indeed, for the space of the poem it does not betray her: the wind has lifted it from the sullen pavement, and eloquent attentions keep it aloft.

Graham's bag may serve as a precursor to the one that rivets and invigorates the darkly eccentric Ricky Fitts in the film *American Beauty*. It is the prize feature of his secret videotape archive, by which he claims to be rooting out and preserving the Beautiful, a commitment that presumably defines and justifies him. (This is no small feat, given the boy's voyeuristic compulsions, not to mention the fact that he finances his fetishes with money earned from dealing drugs.) Ricky maintains that his gaze consecrates what it objectifies, whether it be an wayward garbage bag or Jane Burnham, the neighbor girl for whom he debuts the "piece" and who proves, by virtue of her sympathetic response, to share his aesthetic sensibilities. (Young love has been based and brokered on flimsier evidence, to be sure.) Better than any drug, more magnificent than the sexual encounter it precipitates, the tape of this skittish, elliptical bit of debris insinuates for Ricky and Jane a rich metaphysics on the order of what William Carlos Williams called the "radiant gist" of the mundane.

Should it bother us when Ricky tells Jane that he once saw God looking back at him through the eyes of a homeless woman who had frozen to death? In the economy of Ricky Fitts, in his fixed stare, a plastic bag and a human being are promoted to the same status. The question is, as Ammons asks, "will this abstract, hollow junk seem beautiful / and necessary as just another offering to the // higher assimilations. . . ."

In his acceptance speech for winning the Academy Award for Best Original Screenplay for *American Beauty*, Alan Ball thanked "that plastic bag in front of the World Trade Center so many years ago for being whatever it is that inspires us to do what we do." That original bag is gone now, of course; so, as it happens, is the World Trade Center. It is up to the artist to redeem the world so as to be redeemed by it in turn.

"The way things work," writes Graham, "is that we finally believe / they are there, / common and able / to illustrate themselves."

Because, as Ricky Fitts insists, there is an "entire life behind things" to reckon with. "I need to remember. Sometimes there's so much beauty in the world, I feel like I can't take it, and my heart is just going to cave in." This is something he tells Jane Burnham, who lifts his heart, who makes it dance like a blown bag, who empties and fills it like a cave.

At the Cranbrook Academy of Art, Kun-Ah Yoon placed fifteen hundred goldfish (symbolizing Jesus) in clear cups of water and covered them with a Plexiglass platform, which people could walk upon. As each fish suffocated, its water clouded over, blotting out the word "sin" that had been inscribed on the bottom of every cup. The artist's expressed intention had been to illustrate how Jesus died to eliminate our sins. However, the protests of animal-rights groups convinced Yoon to take down the exhibit a week earlier than planned. The eighty-five surviving fish were collected by the Michigan Humane Society and were adopted by sympathetic area residents. Although Ron Kagan, the director of the Detroit Zoological Institute, condemned the sacrifices, he confided, "It's unfortunate, because the piece of art was quite intriguing." In art and religion alike, transubstantiation is a tangled business. There is no innocent altar.

⌇

USA Today reports that baby boomers are getting religion, but they tend not to adopt conventional affiliations. They want a more fluid, interactive brand of worship. David Kinnaman, vice president of Barna Research Group, a California market research firm that specializes in faith and culture, says, "They're not loyal to specific churches like their parents were, and they don't want to just sit there as passive participants." They like to study the Bible online. They like to dabble in "virtual religions." They like to pick and choose among teachings and practices from several denominations. They like to shop around.

Research also reveals that the top five reasons why boomers are turning to religion are, in ranked order of incentive, spiritual well-being, a sense of community, the prospect of offering service, concern about mortality, and guilt.

According to the article, the results of the survey are somewhat surprising and, clearly, good news.

ॐ

Aiming at grace, our temples and our texts verify the exile they would defy. In spite of this condition, we remain tenacious in inventing strategies of supplication and building structures of praise. Because adoration, even from a distance, is not an empty discipline. In time, we even come to adore the things we fill the distance with, and, possibly, the distance, too.

Meanwhile, we blunder upwards as best we can.

Inadmissible Evidence

When elections roll around, I keep my distance from the scrum of pundits. Most strictly held political positions remind me of complex sexual positions: plausible in the abstract but, ultimately, difficult to hold for very long. Because I find it a strain to maintain commitment on political issues, I tend to stand clear of debate and watch the fray fray. My stance is more of a crouch, a la Groucho Marx, who is reputed to have issued from that infamous position the following bulletin: "These are my principles. If you do not like them, I have others." Generally speaking, his bent is my bent, too. I have Groucho's quotation taped to the window of my office door, which makes it harder for prying eyes to determine if I'm in or not.

Politically diffident by nature, I am at best a swing voter. Like the man hired to make the balloon animals, I am available for parties, but I don't stay for cake. You may catch me peering in from the edges of rallies from time to time, but you won't find me planting signs in my lawn or proclaiming any cause, concern, or candidate on my back fender. I am perpetually avid and just as perpetually unsure. What reaches me exceeds what grasps me. So that's my public record: many arrests, no convictions.

To be honest, I am more than a little intimidated by those who navigate without qualm the ambiguities that wreck hesitant, tentative ships, who day by day brazen out the doubts that I avoid like stray dogs. Resolutely irresolute, I cannot help but be taken aback from time to time by the unabashed. I don't know what to make of those people who are about as bothered by alternatives as a band saw. And so, even as I hang fire and hang back, quibbling in limbo, I wonder about those unswerving sultans of single-mindedness, those dashing captains of denial who damn the torpedoes and drive full-speed ahead, those entrepreneurs inspired by the philosophy of "Ready, Shoot, Aim."

Call it forthrightness that incites them. Or call it executive action. Asked during his grand jury testimony about the status of his illicit relationship with Monica Lewinsky, Bill Clinton garrisoned himself behind the following words: "It depends on what the meaning of the word 'is' is. If the—if he—if 'is' means is and never has been, that is not—that is one thing. If it means there is none, that was a completely true statement. . . . Now, if someone had asked me on that day, are you having any sexual relations with Ms. Lewinsky, that is, asked me a question in the present tense, I would have said no. And it would have been completely true." Clinton sat back in his chair, confident that no prosecutor could undo this Gordian grammar.

Conjecturing at graveside among a row of fusty skulls, Hamlet conjectured that one of them "might be the pate of a politician, which this ass now o'erreaches, one that would circumvent God, might it not?" For nothing ruffles the aplomb of the dauntless and the dead. Regret never pangs after their impulses. Whatever the crisis, politicians breathe forever evenly, and their unencumbered judgments run smoothly as atomic clocks.

᳙

Paragons of circumvention certainly ran the annual commission meeting of the Big Ten in 1990, during which Penn State University was officially admitted. At the time, the collegiate sports scene was alive with speculation. Innovation-minded alumni applauded the move, sensing that the addition of so prestigious, so successful, and so lucrative a program could only enhance the reputation of the conference. On the other hand, many purists complained that such bald accommodationism could only lead to ruin—had we so soon forgotten the harsh lessons of Neville Chamberlain's catering to the Axis appetite? Over the course of three years, which was the time allotted for the integration of Penn State's major athletic teams into the Big Ten, campus newspapers and talk-radio hosts from Erie to Waterloo debated the issue with the disproportionate passion that only sports ever seem to compel.

For me, however, the real interest was onomastic. What would they call the transformed conference? For decades the member schools had spent millions of dollars in advertising on the name "The Big Ten." "The Big Ten" blazed up on sweatshirts, sports equipment, coffee cups, and stationary throughout the Midwest. "The Big Ten" had the same sort of concise impact and

estimable heft as "The Supreme Court," and to devo-
tees (some of whom had named children after prominent gridiron stars), its stature was at least as certain.
By comparison, the Trans-America Conference had
little tenure and less gravity. What could it boast? A
Tradition of Excellence Since 1989? No, "The Big Ten"
conjured images of leather-helmeted Hectors unleash-
ing picturesque fury on legendary turf gashed gold ver-
milion, of Crazy Legs Hirsch and the Galloping Ghost,
of century-old stadiums whose walls were bronzed with
renown. An eleventh team, even one so substantial as
Penn State, threatened all of that. For what rough coin-
age could "The Big Ten" be exchanged? The League
of Eleven? The Flatland Conference? The *Bigger* Ten?
Better to drop Northwestern from that august company, some said, than jeopardize their good name.

Finally, the decision came down. By 1993, Penn
State University would be a fully participating eleventh
member school. And the conference would then be
called . . . The Big Ten.

The panel took questions, but these focused on the
mundanities of scheduling and profit sharing. Did
even one reporter note that the Big Ten emperors had
no clothes to ensure that all eleven teams could suitably
suit up? Did even one square-hatted rationalist suggest
that there was now too much baloney to fit in the same
old bag? If so, it didn't make the Six O'Clock News,
which showed the panel handling every question—
there is no better word for it—qualmlessly. And to this
day, the conference retains its title and its cachet, while
so far as I know, no opposing coach ever fires up his

players by mentioning the affront to common sense of their having to play against one of the Big Ten's eleven teams.

ॐ

As I say, there is something remarkable about the way some people paint themselves into a corner, then go striding imperiously across the paint. Far be it from them to go Gradgrinding through life, fending off facts like fussy kids. Dither over details, they complain, and you'll end up flossing all Friday night while your waiting lover dozes off. Instead of spending your time wondering if you are doing what you've intended, you need to start intending what you've done. Have you seen the way a farmer, driving his rear disker through his field, cultivates a plot after the protagonist has passed through? Have you seen the way county maintenance workers lay down lane dividers from the back of the moving truck? They learn by going where they have to go. Even their errors endure as design. (Listen, God never ran quality control checks on his mountain ranges, either.) The moral is obvious: don't plan your progress—paint your wake.

Balking at actualities is one of the essential reflexes of literature, too. Think of Dylan Thomas's high-falutin' refusal to mourn the death of a child in a London fire. His diction rising with his dander, Thomas is so incensed that he spends his first nine lines in high dudgeon before bothering to announce the main clause of his complaint. Then he throws his rattle to the floor again and crabs for another stanza or so before he can be quieted enough to get the sense of his anti-elegy out. Or think of Robert Frost, ordinarily conceived of as being a genial sort, dismissing the proof that the birch trees he sees were likely bowed by ice. He submits instead a patent fancy: "I should prefer to think some boy's been swinging them." Your brittle facts snap as soon as you lean on them, he says. Give me a meaning that will hold my weight.

For her part, Emily Dickinson tries to run a bluff all the way to heaven, but she betrays her daintiness by disclaiming her thesis. "I know that He exists," she begins one poem, opening blind, and ending the line with a rare full stop. The steady iambs of the constant heart persist for just three beats, until "Somewhere" pops the clutch. So the poet invents excuses, playing press secretary for Him: God is in the vicinity, but hiding "Somewhere—in silence," and she cannot speculate on where or what he's up to. Maybe, ever the prankish parent, He's just playing hide-and-seek with humanity; maybe we can ambush bliss and catch a peek of Him just past the curtain of mortality.

"But—should the play / Prove piercing earnest—/ Should the glee—glaze—/ In Death's—stiff—stare," a voice follows up from the floor. What then? She'll have to get back to us. When she does, in "This World is not Conclusion," another poem whose annunciation sounds as if it came off a church billboard, she is still stammering on behalf of her Master. After rattling off the positive party line, she confesses a slip of faith and scrambles for reassurance, lest anyone catch her in the breach. It takes little more than twenty lines for

Dickinson's belief to dwindle from the opening salvo to "Narcotics cannot still the Tooth / That nibbles at the soul." There's the rub. If God is consciousness—specifically, consciousness of God—when consciousness falters (notoriously leaving the poet, in another stalled meditation, "Wrecked—solitary—here"), God departs the premises. That troubling sound you hear is metaphor seizing up, overheating.

Still, regardless of the anxiety that overtakes her poems, Dickinson's iffiness is kin to the conjuring of Thomas and Frost, in that all three writers practice stylish avoidance. In a manner of speaking, all imagery is denial, and the greatness of poetry may chiefly be a matter of the size of the escape. Surely, all of that fustian Dylan Thomas sets off is like the tear gas they lob into the warehouse to cover the cops as they try to get the hostages out. Meanwhile, Robert Frost's hankering for a childhood idyll allows him to give adult "considerations" and Truth's matter-of-fact the slip. (No wonder most of us wistfully misremember "Birches" to be a poem about how those trees have been for generations subdued by agile, imaginative boys.) In one way or another, each poet rides a horse that refuses the hurdle.

Thus did Hamlet dilate and metrically repress. So, too, does the modern stage provide rich veins of disavowal. Ask anyone at Hickey's bar in *The Iceman Cometh* if you don't believe me. Catch Edward Albee's Honey upon her return from vomiting in the bathroom when too much undiluted reality went down. She emerges from her purge and announces, "I've decided I don't remember anything." Then she greets the redeemed company with the jerry-rigged brightness of a nurse in a managed care facility. "I don't remember anything, and you don't remember anything," she explains to her husband, who is still groggy from a drunken adulterous bout with their hostess. "Hello, Dear," she chirps.

Or take a seat in the steamy gallery of *Inherit the Wind* and witness the exchange between Henry Drummond and Matthew Harrison Brady. Drummond's client, you'll recall, is on trial for having had the temerity to teach about evolution in a Tennessee high school. Drummond puts his fundamentalist adversary on the stand and confronts him with the rapid-fire "begattings" of the holy men and women of the Old Testament, seemingly in persistent transgression against Original Sin. He presents him with a fossil of a pre-historic marine creature that scientists have estimated to be millions of years old as hard evidence against the argument that Biblical calculation puts the age of the earth at about six thousand years. He submits the logical tangle of the description in Genesis of the first day of Creation, the problem being that no sun had been fashioned until the *fourth* day to measure it. "What do you think?" he asks. Brady flounders a little, then replies, "I do not think about things that . . . I do not think about!" This is the impunity of eminence, the eminence of impunity. "Do you ever think about things that you *do* think about?" Drummond volleys.

Possibly you can't afford the legitimate theatre. But you may remember what they did on TV's *Dallas*. In response to Patrick Duffy's impending departure from the show, the writers killed off his character, Bobby

Ewing. Perhaps the actor discovered that he'd overestimated his prospects outside of South Fork, or perhaps the producers realized that they'd underestimated his impact on the ratings. Whatever the case, Bobby was resuscitated, and he rejoined the cast. The explanation? It had all been a dream. A protracted hallucination of his wife's, one apparently contagious enough to have overcome every other character on the show. Wouldn't you love to have been at that meeting? Imagine the trance of rationalization as it overtook the writing staff. "Well, we could just pretend that it never happened." "What about the viewers?" "They could just, you know, play along." "Great! That's lunch, everybody!"

You'd think they couldn't possibly have pulled it off—that is, if you were one of those people who think about things they think about. You'd predict that the public would never have bought so transparent a finesse. But the ratings *did* improve after Bobby's return from the dead, sustaining the show for another season or so. Go figure. Henry Drummond lost his case in Hillsboro, too, because they'd had the goods on his client from the start. For all his eloquence, the attorney could never shake the statute.

⌖

"The Truth must dazzle gradually," Dickinson concludes, "or every man be blind." But for the majority, the truth is more brunt than dazzle. (We better understand the dangers of taking so much sun these days than Dickinson did. This is thanks to a proliferation of media she couldn't possibly have foreseen, which assails us daily like acid rain.) The bigger fish eats the smaller fish, and the biggest eats the bigger, raw. There's truth for you—a concussion. A punch to duck from. A thousand natural shocks that flesh is heir to. You have to prepare to take the day on, much the way a mover must steady himself beneath the sofa he means to lift.

We now know more than anyone ever knew before, and the more we know, the more we want to shun. That is why we see an epidemic of deflection nowadays. Somewhere a guy at a party is wincing at the voltage going through his chest when his ex-girlfriend appears on the arm of a rival; he tells his buddies, "It's nothing. Hey, can somebody crank up the music?" Somewhere a fellow at a given gym is complaining to the kid at the desk that the scale in the locker room is registering too heavy. Somewhere a woman is being wheeled through ER and insisting over her swell that she is not really pregnant. Somewhere someone is rejecting the findings, ignoring the seatbelt, inhaling another cigarette, feeding the readout through the shredder. What can you say to people determined to disregard the data you wave in their faces? There's no denying denial. As the Yiddish proverb says, Sleep faster, we need the pillows.

Of course, I am not above pulling up the covers when I can. For example, if I take the ads on the radio seriously, as the ads on the radio say I should, I can keep my vessel of self intact. I can hold on to my hair, retain my waistline, and stockpile an inexhaustible arsenal of erections. I can stop every mutinous atom in me and, coiled tight, stave off time entirely.

While I scramble to keep myself together, my psychologist calls me immature and tells me I need to keep my poise in face of my corrugating face and reconcile myself to my inevitable decline. Without changes to map the impact of the years upon us, he argues, we would be deprived of crucial information about ourselves. And knowledge is power, he says, knowingly. Our bodies are developing nations, naturally extending in time and space. If I feel an unprecedented pain in my shoulder after exercise, awaken to a new squatters' settlement of arthritis in my wrist, or detect any other wrench in my infrastructure, I should drop my peevish opposition and, instead, marvel at the ways evolution has remembered me.

My psychologist is nothing if not an angel of equanimity. Shall I presume that he has never had an unguarded moment in the bathroom when he flinched before his reflection in the mirror, that behind the foggy glass of the shower door he never palpates or probes himself at all?

ॐ

Ultimately, all incentives for denial come down to one sort of survival or another. It is with a mixture of outrage and amazement that I recently discovered a worldwide growth industry in Holocaust denial. There is a Committee for Open Debate on the Holocaust (CODOH), which is dedicated to contradicting some of the most infamous events on record. Significantly, the principal spokesmen for Holocaust denial refer to themselves as "revisionist historians," thereby putting a more wholesome, scholarly finish on their contentions. They hold conferences, publish papers, sponsor web sites. They maintain that there was no single "Master Plan" for Jewish annihilation, nor was there a net loss of Jewish lives between 1941 and 1945. There were no gas chambers used for mass murder at Auschwitz and other camps, nor does any objective documentation exist to prove any premeditated program of Nazi genocide. The Nuremberg trials were a "farce of justice" staged for the benefit of the Jews and the furthering of their own ongoing conspiracy. The perpetration of Holocaust "mythology" (or "Holohoaxes") in the media, in educational curricula, and in rituals of public remembrance, is designed to instill a disabling sense of guilt in the white, Western Christian world, so as to advance the international Jewish agenda. Merciless and imperturbable.

The *International Holocaust Revisionism Newsletter* provides a ready lexicon of rebarbative terminology. Readers learn, for instance, that the "Zionist racket" has engaged in "systematic allegation" and "blood libel." It is misprision of the highest order—deliberate, hard-won, and rigorously honed to a single, incontrovertible point. As one editorialist writes, "Don't for a minute think that indoctrinating wide-eyed school children with the lies and slanders against Germans, Slavs, Catholics, Christians, Europeans, and whites in general isn't a primary purpose of the Holocaust-mongers. . . . The Holocaust is a religion. Its underpinnings in the realm of historical fact are non-existent—no Hitler order, no plan, no budget, no gas chambers, no autopsies of gassed victims, no bones, no ashes, no skulls, no nothing. . . . Secondly, it's a religion for losers. . . . Suffice it to say that the rise of religions such as this generally coincides with the decline and fall of nations which tolerate them." So no one climbed through piled corpses to tell anything other than tall tales. The numbers that blush upon the forearms of all who withstood the camps are not the residue of some demonic accounting but the stigmata of hallucination. All Holocaust testimony furthers a pyramid scheme of the highest order—the most profitable scam in the world today. Suffice it to say.

Your instinct is to think that those who can believe these things are anomalous, or alien, or insane, just as you are convinced those who carried out the crimes themselves must have been. Nevertheless, we have studied about citizens whose ignorance was so accomplished that they could decline to realize the extent of the evil. By all accounts, millions of victims nurtured disbelief during the census that disqualified them, nursed it in spite of dictates and disappearances, barricaded themselves behind it to withstand rumors of atrocity, kept it warm beneath their rags in the crowded railway cars.

Would that science could fathom the pith and marrow of their attributes. Would that psychology could pierce their dispositions or melt that solid flesh.

In my mind I have assembled a squad of doctors. They line the deniers up against the wall for delving. They fire a barrage of X-rays, invading their infrastructure, taking their blinding ideology down. Imagine that mural of negatives, in relentless black and white. (Poetry lets us pretend for a time what the real world, lined with lead and lawyered up, would never submit to.) If only we could break into each adamantine trunk and rummage for clues. If only we could loosen the valves of their willful inattention, slip their seals and fire back their bolts, by indirections find directions out. If only we could dare to look deeply in, we might just glimpse something dense, elemental—just to the left of every wretched heart, I suspect. We might find that knot or nodule, lodged like a bullet, which does not divide or fade. There it is, the very nucleus of denial, and it lies in all of us, and it does not budge.

Waiting for Takeoff

BERNARD: But sometimes, Willy, it's better for a man just to walk away.
WILLY: Walk away?
BERNARD: That's right.
WILLY: But if you can't walk away?
BERNARD [after a slight pause]: I guess that's when it's tough.
—Arthur Miller, *Death of a Salesman*

Be sure to prepare an escape route in case of emergency. Go over it with your family so you will be able to get out quickly when the time comes.
—*Fire Safety at Home*, free brochure obtained at the Northpark Mall Home Show

More and more often as the years go by, a woman finds herself drawn to the attic to see if her old ballerina slippers might fit. They are stiff and discolored, by now beyond remedy, and useless to hand down even if her daughter were to suddenly demonstrate an interest in dance. But the ribbon laces are still supple, and while the last of the breakfast dishes soak, she sifts them through hands grown graceless and, unaccountably, without her realizing it except when she sees her slippers in them, old.

During his drive home, her husband, who has never seemed able to make his tie lie plumb for an entire day's work, adjusts his rearview mirror to repair it and briefly sees the ghost of his former self. Unlike him, the ghost stuck out the minor league contract he was offered at nineteen, rejecting solid judgment the way one can at nineteen, just to see where it would lead.

A siren forces him to the side of the road. He watches the fire truck hurtle past, and he does not edge back into traffic before assuring himself that it has passed the turn to his house. There was a time when he didn't give fire trucks a second thought. No tragedy could touch him. What did he have to lose? In graduate school he rented a room in what had once been a sorority house. His kitchen privileges included being able to store his two plastic plates and plastic bowl, a saucepan he'd inherited from an old girlfriend, and a fistful of unmatched silverware on a shelf above the stove. The furniture—ambiguously soiled and never dear to anyone—had come with the room. What else? A few pairs of blue jeans, some T-shirts, socks and underwear. Three plates, a frying pan, a pot. Tapered for the quick getaway. He'd lived in several rooms like that. When the place became unbearably dirty or bleak, he filled a couple of boxes (courtesy of the local liquor store) and in no more than three trips to the trunk of his buddy's borrowed car he'd sprung himself. When it came to escaping from material trappings he was the equal of any ascetic; he abstained with a thoroughness even Thoreau would have envied.

Now that he has station and property, of course, it is a different story. Actually, the property is principally the bank's, at least for another twenty-two years, but that only tightens the squeeze. There is no denying it: he is as dug in as a soldier in a pillbox or, for that matter, a cemetery.

For a good five minutes after he gets home, he cannot find his wife. He gives up on her, opens a beer, sweeps a little clearing at the kitchen table, sits. He recalls the satisfying, almost sinful, anonymity of eating dinner in a strange city, the pleasure of being unimportant to anyone there. When was that? Well, Cincinnati, for instance, where he'd spent two days on business. Not knowing for sure when he would be able to get away for dinner, he had made two dinner reservations at the same Indian restaurant under different names—his own and his ghost's, perhaps—and he still recalls the sinful rush it gave him to two-time himself like that. Yes, now he recalls it precisely: it was the hypothetical self that dined that night. Flirted with the waitress, too.

His wife knows he's down there—she heard him shake his keys free at the front door—but she does not call down. Tonight she will imagine that the bed is a black raft on blue water and ride the night out alone. Upon awakening, her eyes still streaked with dream, she will not recognize her room, the sound of the shower, her children's voices. That sound is the sound of the shower, she will realize. Those voices are the voices I know. The word for shower is "shower." Alone for the moment in her bedroom, she will says words aloud, remembering. Shower. Voices. Theirs and mine.

It must have begun with the chest of drawers, he tells himself. That first significant purchase and durable good. The initial buy-in and domestic ante. Now the house is laden with furniture, expensive and heavy and positioned with care, like statements of principle. He meditates on the newly painted walls—they'd needed it—and he remembers reading somewhere about how it was lethal to paint turtles. If you do, their shells cease to grow with them, so they eventually strangle inside. Yet even though we know better, you still see them sold that way.

After a difficult day with them and a worse night getting them down, she sees her children as bats, dark and unremitting in their unstable cave of sleep. The television is purring about pharmaceutical breakthroughs. The names are utopian, intoxicating, stalwart, rich with ambition. "If it's a boy, we're calling him Rogaine, after his grandfather," she thinks. "If it's a girl, well, we're torn between Drixoral and Viagra." In only a few hours the children will emerge again, opening like fists.

"You'll miss being the baby," she had told him one evening. He'd been resting his head in her lap, what there was left of it late in her first pregnancy, and she was tracing the contours of his ear, pretending her finger was swirling down a drain. "You get to be the baby only until the baby comes." She unplugged his ear, letting the words circle. A suburban pieta—one of the last opportunities they'd have like this, what with the baby about to arrive.

She would probably have to return to temping as a word processor to make ends meet. Back to typefaces. "And these are the twins, Garamond and Helvetica," she thought. Now *there* were names that made an impression. She did not move. With his face nestled against her, he wondered at the faint aroma there. Homely and decadent. He did not move.

"How dreary—to be—Somebody! / How public— like a Frog," croaks Emily Dickinson from her Amherst keep. Who hasn't wondered what it would be like to tiptoe off on the ellipsis of his likely fate to be lost, without even a single footnote to find him by? To be a fugitive from the injustice you believe all you've built your life on has levied upon you? To leave behind all your evidence as if life were the scene of a crime, to withdraw from your smudges, scents, and identity— the pictures that frame you, the hairs stuck deep in the brush—and, having secretly mastered a false dialect and a different signature, resume at some undeducible remove, elsewhere and otherwise? I am talking about asserting your alienable rights here. This is more than simply wondering about dumping a love grown dreary or quitting a dull job, although if you've ever done either you may have an inkling of the exhilaration I mean. No, I am talking about wholesale abandonment, the self's ritual undressing, as if you could slip out of yourself by undoing a few central screws. As if you could outflank who you are: start down the street toward the bus stop and, suddenly, split off from what you've become, letting your slough go through with the usual while your decommissioned ego departs, leaving no forwarding address. As if you could calculate the drag coefficients of your routines and muster just enough thrust to break free. As if you could walk away.

Nathaniel Hawthorne tells the tale of a man who left his wife and home to take up residence directly across the street—an almost involuntary experiment that grew into a self-banishment lasting twenty years. There was nothing particularly furtive or original about this Wakefield, so far as the rest of the community was concerned, which by all reports was not very much at all. His own wife, we are assured, would have described him as displaying nothing more extraordinary than "a quiet selfishness," which had anyway "rusted into his inactive mind"; his secrets, if he had any, were certainly petty and "hardly worth revealing." Whatever strangeness he might have been suspected of was "indefinable, and perhaps non-existent." Indeed, whatever specific purpose may have lain behind this singular, unprecedented project was never especially clear to Wakefield either, and even that vague inspiration steadily dissolved over time.

That Wakefield was able to recover his life in the end is by the author's reckoning a matter of wondrous good luck, for through this bizarre maneuver he had nearly forfeited his membership in the human community altogether, so tenuous is the privilege of being included in the fold. "Amid the seeming confusion of our mysterious world, individuals are so nicely adjusted to a system, and systems to one another and to a whole,"

Hawthorne insists, "that, by stepping aside for a moment, a man exposes himself to a fearful risk of losing his place forever." But the story may just as well suggest an alternative lesson: once established, one's life is ruthlessly possessive. Destiny sets in like arthritis. Essence is tenured, and we writhe in the custody of custom. Wakefield may be AWOL, but he is never out of range. Because he cannot seem to achieve sufficient escape velocity, he merely becomes a satellite of the world he once inhabited, and his departure demonstrates his constancy. Faithful even in his defection, he is like the house pet that, rambling about the yard as far as his chain allows, pantomimes wildness in an illusion of open country. Spying on his absence for twenty years from across the street, Wakefield practices a firmly centered sort of eccentricity. It is said that you can't go home again, and Hawthorne sternly reminds us that Wakefield barely made it back; however, the point may be that you can't really leave in the first place.

Eudora Welty's Mr. Marblehall is just about as questionable a flight risk as Wakefield. Out for his evening constitutional, the old man who "never did anything, never got married until he was sixty" keeps to a gait that is measured and slightly bent over, making him look either conspiratorial or merely frail. He leaves behind his rather nebulous wife, whose "untidy head trembles in the domestic dark," and whom Welty barnacles with pitiless, ossifying adjectives: "She is only looking around—servile, undelighted, sleepy, expensive, tortured Mrs. Marblehall, pinning her mind with a pin to her husband's diet. She wants to tempt him, she tells him. What would he like best, that he can have?"

As it happens, Mr. Marblehall, "still exactly in the same degree alive and old," is on his way to his second house, wife, and son, to whom he is Mr. Bird. The fact is, however, that the most remarkable thing about his double life is how unremarkable (and unremarked upon) it is. His other home is as stagnant, his other wife as pinched and grotesque, his other son as irremediably vile, as their counterparts on the other side of town. And while the old man entices himself with imaginary scenes of shocking revelation, nobody cares. His delinquency is really a duplication. Welty concludes that "he has even multiplied his life by deception," lying like a cadaver in alternating beds to last out "the clocking nights." Shuttling from circumstance to identical circumstance, Mr. Marblehall is a weak charge oscillating between fixed, equivalent poles. "Otherwise he dreams that he is a great blazing butterfly stitching up a net; which doesn't make sense."

While American literature is loaded with anxious characters looking for the exit, it ends up to be a compendium of foiled escapes. "Whenever I find myself growing grim about the mouth; whenever it is a damp, drizzly November in my soul; whenever I find myself involuntarily pausing before coffin warehouses, and bringing up the rear of every funeral I meet; and especially whenever my hypos get such an upper hand of me, that it requires a strong moral principle to prevent me from deliberately stepping into the street, and methodically knocking people's hats off—then, I account it high time to get to sea as soon as I can." So Melville's Ishmael begins his saga by confessing that evacuation is his "substitute for pistol and ball." After one hundred and thirty-five buffeting chapters, though, he is gathered up from the sea and restored to shore, indentured to dry dock and the writing desk. In Melville's economy, his travels notwithstanding, he proves a "Fast-Fish" after all.

Similarly, Huck Finn pinballs downriver for hundreds of miles before civilization reels him in. "But I reckon I got to light out for the Territory ahead of the rest," he decides at the end of his story, not realizing that as far as his readers are concerned the Territory has been relegated to adventure books. His belief in the frontier is the only thing that remains unbridled about his future.

And with respect to *On the Road,* for all its author's celebrated trespasses, it is not a breach but an expansion. Try the trip yourself, and you'll find that every highway is hemmed by the same contingencies and K-Marts. Anyway, it turns out that Kerouac's desire to give convention the bum's rush is conventional, too. The impulse to bolt is about as bourgeois as a Sunday barbecue.

And would it have been any different for Wakefield had he opted out of his office hours, let the mail mass unanswered, exorcised himself from his old haunts, battened down his ordinary hatches and burgled out of town? Would it have mattered if Mr. Marblehall had forsaken his compounded families for the first train out of Natchez Trace?

Ask Yetta, a woman now in her seventies, who has never liked her name. Her birth certificate shows where she once penciled in "Anne"—she used to dream of something untainted by Eastern Europe, something out of *American Bandstand*—only to erase it. She worked for years in the state licensing bureau, and she regularly refused the job's sole perk: free vanity plates. "Why didn't you ever change your name? Why not just change it now?" I asked her. "I can't," she said quietly. "That's who I am." A rose by any other name would hold its odor nonetheless. Her children know not to personalize her birthday cake or to commemorate the occasion with jewelry bearing her name. Phone calls, application forms, pages searching out the hospital waiting room—it is impossible for Yetta to avoid having to answer for herself. Meanwhile, there are so many Susans who never shun a survey, Heathers who eagerly raise their hands in class, Rebeccas unruffled by public broadcasts, and Annes who never wince.

Or ask Tom, who took me golfing one sun-flushed afternoon to fill out a foursome with a couple of his business associates. When we all reached the fourteenth green, I started to set up my putt and noticed that my three playing partners had all broken out their cell phones. Seeing my expression, Tom explained, "This is really a terrific gadget. Thanks to this, wherever I am, people can always get in touch with me." "And that's a *plus* to you?" I said. It was a dazzling afternoon, zephyr-teased and lacquered with French Impressionist light. And all about, the sweet green reaches were being strafed and buzzed.

As for that, you might have asked me on the day I was interviewed by our college newspaper for my mandatory new faculty profile. It was my maiden semester of teaching at the only school that offered me a position—the only place in a down decade for the humanities that would have me, and, more than twenty years later, has me still. The student reporter caught me in my office, had me pose for a picture ("Pretend that you're reading or writing something, you know? Just do what you do"), and ran me through a gauntlet of prescribed questions about my experience, hobbies, and philosophy. I could have said anything so far from home, a couple of states at least away from any acquaintance who might have corrected me or objected. I could have reconstituted myself with perfect impunity. I could have invented a painful affair with a soap opera star. ("You've probably seen her on *Days of Our Lives*. She goes by another name now. Stephanie or Monica Something. Really, I don't like to talk about it.") I could have trumped up a previous career as a prizefighter, a drug habit, a nickname, a police record, a war wound. I coulda been a contender for anything instead of admitting to the lockstep march toward the doctorate I'd actually made. Which, I'm afraid, is what I ended up doing.

When the paper came out, my colleagues congratulated me because there were relatively few errors or embarrassments in the profile. (Many of them had once suffered clumsy translations of their comments at the hands of freshman journalism majors.) I was lucky. And the photograph could have been worse, we agreed. Everyone said it looked just like me.

Shelf Life

Mortie

The night is a solid bruise, blue-black and unremitting, spread absolutely and everywhere. A private rain angles wickedly in.

Perhaps she seems a pluckier version of Joe Bfstplk, with his thundercloud always nagging him. She should be pouring the salt before her, to steady her over her slick supposed passage—it's only common sense. Instead, as if automatically deferring to superstition, she douses her wake with dissolving crumbs of light. The darkness laps them up. Another winsome Gretel, you think, vainly marking her way back. But no, she has no interest in what's behind her. Like the weather harassing her from behind, the past never touches her, and she has no plan to return. Abstracted as she is, recrimination is as foreign to her as appointed rounds or a worrisome mole. Neither, for that matter, does she look forward but sights along the shaft of her umbrella to where her foot is poised. Poised is it exactly. She does not falter at all. She maintains a calculated grace.

The night is a contour sheet tugged flush against the bend of horizon.

She holds her umbrella, its protective lavender billow big as a pup tent, with the studied daintiness of a Daisy Miller. Almost prissy, the way she curls her hand over the stem, although not out of character for her. Her stride, too, is contrived, with her white tights gleaming against surprisingly meaty limbs (modesty should forbid so flimsy a dress!) illuminated by no apparent light. Joints locked, she is intent upon the turn of her foot, as if she were obeying an absent dance instructor. (Second position, please.) The wind has swept her hair into a blond cowl, but her expression is placid. Consider the self-absorption, the self-satisfaction. A Mona Lisa in imperturbable motion. Rare to find such insouciance in one so young. You can't help but admire her, and decency does not deter you from watching how the light clings to her, climbs her legs. And you see by the distribution of her weight that she intends no progress at all. She hovers, posing to verify an accomplished end, which is self-possession. The purgatorial career of Keats's painted maiden occurs to you, along with the arid aesthetic the poet comes to denounce, but in her charmed circuit this girl enjoys perpetual consummation (just look at her face!), in spite of the rotten weather.

She shows not a single crack or access. She is all aplomb, insulated from assault. Demeanor is the one domain she can govern absolutely. She is perfect, in her way, in the perfect gloom of an implacable night.

Does she realize that it is all snowing inexorably away? If you alerted her to the loss, she still wouldn't flinch. Although she is up against it—a monolithic

darkness, as well as the law of diminishing returns—
she is content. If that is contentment. Perhaps she believes that no calamity can disturb the success of her
measured step. Perhaps it is enough for her just to get
one lovely thing right. She is inscrutable in that way,
taking care of an errand impenetrable as the night itself. Her bearing is the only achievement she needs. It
braces her against the rain and contains her entirely.
All of her attention is compressed into posture.

What tells her not to dread a night like this? A night
of secret violences and hostage takings. A night made
to cover muggings.

Will she waste away in the cave of herself until
neighbors notice the odor? She does not know enough
to care about what she is losing or may lose further on.
She does not know enough to come in out of the rain.

A final night has descended like a spell. A night fit
for significant fables and Freudian snares. A night to
dim any depth or destination, which you'd assume any
innocence must succumb to. One more step, surely,
and she will fall down a mineshaft of night it would
take a team to lift her out of, if at all.

From no discernible direction comes the light that
somehow spots her and makes a halo of her umbrella.
The other ravages don't matter. She is in her element.

The Lady of the Lakes

What boy didn't know that if you forced her smooth,
bare knees against her chest, they became overripe
breasts about to burst? The other abundance she of-

257

fered—the bright, mutinous bounty to come, the rich organic spill that could not spoil—no boy ever bothered with, having but one proof of her plenty on his mind. That may be the reason that her current estate has been stripped of all of that juicy congestion: only a grassy knoll before flat blue water is left from that previous Eden.

Yet she put up with that mischief, that perverted regard, beatifically. To be sure, that same steadfastness, that supplicant's patience and repose, remain intact. Although she may yet occasionally be handled like a freshman girl who's strayed into a frat party and been loosened up by too much booze, she nevertheless radiates an almost maternal aura. That dissonance—it's someone's *mother* whose buxom promise you're slavering over, a woman whose melons swelled for babies—snaps you back into the wholesomeness of Minnesota. For it is ultimately the landscape she offers, this strangely rosy Native American mother and model Indian giver, so serene in her commitment that, although she shows unmistakably Caucasian features, she transcends racial implication altogether.

For it is her willingness that wins us over. If she is motherly, she is motherly without a mother's judgment or admonition. Go ahead and have another helping—a healthy appetite flatters her. She is no stickler, after all; she is not one to fret over a starved father's cholesterol count or to chide the kids for using their fingers. She balances a box like a chalice between delicate hands. It is the very box you've bought, featuring the same image of the fetching squaw, box in hand, and so on, regressing ad infinitum deeper into the pastoral interior, drawing you on to pleasures, drawing you in.

Jem

Looking at her, it is hard to say whether plastic surgery or protracted illness accounts for her transformation. Whichever the case, the effect is startling. Gone is the dark meringue of flesh that once billowed beneath her scarf. Her wattle has been lopped off and her ample cheeks carved down to the jaw. So much for her membership in that sustaining, high-fat sorority of cloying maiden aunts and plump grandmothers bearing breakfast provisions dense as love. Today's revised kitchen counter intelligence demands severity. She has recreated herself to suit the times.

For years she suffered a chain of associations that political correctness no longer abides. In this way, art has been the instrument of not only beauty but also emancipation. Jem shows an almost ferociously made-up face now; her pride in the upgrade occasioned by defter cosmetics and quality dentistry is undeniable. She is forthright, imposing, in a way the rest of that culinary coalition have never been and do not aspire to be. While they are satisfied to take their nourishment vicariously, sublimely beaming as you gobble their sweet provender down, Jem (too fashionably recreated to be identified as anyone's aunt) almost glares her good will at you. For a second, your breakfast glut seems vulgar; the drenched batter clogs your throat. She watches you in a way that the deferential serving line of Stepin Fetchits, Butterfly McQueens, and rascally Sambos never did. Self-consciously, you lift the newspaper slightly higher, chew in secret and more slowly.

And yet, despite her contemporary aspect, Jem's past shadows her. Just as the crash dieter's face and figure subtly betray her former weight—recently emerged bones seem freshly dug, somehow, and evacuated folds of skin drape, cumbersome as the clothing she needs to replace—Jem is haunted by her former self. In a way, its absence continues to define her. Although it has been reduced, that once-sumptuous flesh is not forgotten; the formerly incarcerated cannot completely forget the conditions she came from, although conventional wisdom insists she is free.

Mr. Clean

It was probably Kleinschmidt or Klinhoffer once, back in the old country. (The exact location is uncertain, but going by looks alone, somewhere in the upper latitudes of Europe is a reasonable guess.) Then some overworked immigration officer probably got hold of it and performed the sort of nominal surgery that was commonplace on Ellis Island, so that after a generation or two any memory of the original name had been sponged utterly away.

Kleinstein. Another possibility.

Or maybe he made the change himself because he was on the make or on the lam. He may have been looking for a streamlined, media-friendly moniker with the one-punch virility of "Wayne," "Peck," or "Grant"; on the other hand, he may have been ducking under that sleek, clean cover to escape a criminal history. Definitely, he has the look of a man who'd been forced out of the merchant marine for taking a swing at a superior and who never found his footing on land, or a guy you'd find working in a high school boiler room. He lives alone in a rented room that's spotless and somber as a scene taken out of Edward Hopper. He eats his dinner over the sink, and he lies in bed (a can of beer held on his belly) reviewing his gripe against the manager who twenty years ago reneged on his promise to put him on the undercard for the heavyweight title fight. It's all conjecture, however, since he doesn't talk about his past. But you see something in the knob of his chin or the frankly vicious knit of his brow—a brow like a bulkhead, not to mention those roughly bunched arms—that implies a demanding physical history of some kind or other. Whatever it was, he has clearly come through it, and, forever flexing, he dares you to comment on the earring. He dares you to dare him.

I know a Klinkowitz. That could have been it, too.

It's tough to keep his luster in the company of housewives, where masculinity is a matter of muscling grime. Worse for him, macho is out. Check the manuals: real men these days do the dishes, even escort their daughters to dance class. But his current circumstances floor him. He is galled by his employment; the petty crises and petty raptures of the women he caters to equally insult him. What has happened to the once-robust

American culture? Ours is a heritage of men before whom Nature bowed. These were men who cleared forests, drove steel, routed obstacles. They blasted past; they rammed through. Now it's all domestic fluster and feminized delight. Does even one of the women who surrenders the premises to him, their feckless, suppositious husbands out of sight and consequence, ever suspect him of motives less pristine? As they eagerly admire his biceps and accomplishments, do they consider him capable of more? For it is there for them to see reflected in the gleam he leaves: his smirk, his glowering, and the intimidation inherent in industrial strength.

Kingsford

It isn't that he doesn't love his wife. When she brings the platter of steaks to him like a blood sacrifice, although there is precious little godliness about him, she is not taking him for granted. Although there has never been anything of the astronaut or congressman in him, she is still able to detect in him the man she pledged herself to. (He has kept himself in shape all these years, which she takes as an indication of his commitment and self-respect. She also treats it as a compliment to her.) She lets him in on her pleasure in small ways: the care she takes with her hair even when she has nowhere to go; the smile she lets him see, the one that harks back and forward to intimacies that they both continue to burn for; and, yes, the plush, tender way she has arranged this evening's slaughter for his delight. On his best days, his best Sundays, days of designated solidarity and mutual appreciation, he is a backyard Zeus ritually anointed, complete with aromatic nimbus. She keeps this image to herself—the allusion never makes it through the fumes. Of course, it's all in good fun.

Sufficiently liberated to handle the bills on occasion while he beds down the kids, she has never vied to do the grilling, not once, not ever. She respects his domain, that he needs one. This is why she puts out chips and beer for him on Sunday afternoons during football season and doesn't begrudge him the conventional trappings of masculine distance from her. He is a good man—she knows of none better—and while some husbands are purportedly lusting in other directions in other yards, he is home putting down steaks. If he is constrained in his aspirations and accomplishments, neither has he shown symptoms of mid-life crisis. She counts her blessings, calling them "ours."

She isn't in anything she means to dream her way out of.

It isn't that his children aren't dear to him, rising and subsiding in volume, scrabbling (mercifully) out of sight while with a menacing fork he steers the main course through the fire. To say that they believe in their father would be an overstatement, but it is fair to say that they depend on him, which provides more compensation than sociologists credit. When they bray like a couple of cub reporters through the screen door—- "*When?*"—it is more than dinner they need.

The rest of the family lies outside the scope, undepicted yet impending. The package implies them. Figure it out: he wouldn't go through this trouble for his own sake alone. If dinner were only up to him, he'd have been just as happy to order in or pick something up instead of giving his Sunday up to undertake another project.

Honey?

Don't be fooled by the mawkish apron he wears as a joke for the whole family to share in. He is good at what he does. Grilling is his gift and, therefore, his incontestable portion. The assumption of his sole tenancy of the pit honors and subdues him at the same time.

An icon of regular guy-ness, he is easy to underestimate. Don't be distracted by the cheerful rictus in his face or the jaunty Superman coif. Don't let neighborhood pleasantries (these we must infer as well) take you in. This is serious business he's up to, the bright Sunday afternoon notwithstanding. Toxic fumes may accumulate and cause death. We are talking about essential threats: fire and hunger.

The gasps of relief when he bears the finished food safely back inside gratify him, certainly, but they fall short.

Dad?

Everyone else has been cropped out.

Housed (presumably) in the background, his wife has spent the last hour looking at photographs. Absently, she blots out the boy with her index finger, smothers her daughter with her thumb. Some of the grease from cutting fat did not wash away, so her prints will be over the pictures. The implication is not lost on her. With her ring finger she rubs out her husband. The irony is not lost on her. She surveys all her decapitated darlings, all her obliterated dears. Nor does she spare her own head. Thus with a simple, measured gesture—not even the full span of her hand—she subtracts her world from the world.

Only connect. That was E. M. Forster's advice. Does the family ever remember that there is an English major still among them? Her education was not completely lost on her. Now that "only" sounds like meagerness instead of ease. Now it sounds like the instructions on a box of Tinker Toys.

Meanwhile, the children have been occupying themselves in secrecy, too. At this age, their parents cannot endure their racket, and they do not trust their silence. To be honest, it was ever thus, nor do they envision it ever being any different. This is what it is to be middle-class parents sensitive to the frail state of the family unit these days: the children get too much attention or too little; they are forsaken or spoiled; they are ruining their appetites by exercising them. How much time does it take to huff kitchen cleanser or to download porn? Their mother calls for them to wash up because Dad will have dinner on the table in a minute, and her voice breaks a bit when she does.

And this model, dimpled Dad never looks down at the fire. He has done it so often—two hundred and fifty Sundays is a reasonable estimate—that muscle memory is enough to guide his hand. The rate of searing is predictable. Without once consulting his watch, he turns the meat.

I wake to face the day each day, he thinks. It is only a matter of turning the meat once more.

It isn't that he wishes some genie would build and beckon from the smoke. There is nothing specific he watches for in the suburban middle distance, and indeed, no discernible figure dawns out of the foggy ground. But even if he doesn't look up Nina's sundress or down it when the opportunity presents itself, even if he doesn't long for Mitch's time-share or Jerry's Porsche, the way his gaze is fixed makes you wonder whether some other fantasy or squandered fate, some past transgression or future plot consumes him, so close to the lick and snap of the flames.

Without adequate ventilation, he'd be done for.

Although the cooking takes place on a wooden porch, only a few feet from the house itself and everything it contains, there is no need to tend to the embers. Experience dictates that the coals will die out without anyone having to douse them, completely on their own.

Trash Talking

> Can't we learn from this materialism instead of
> taking the trouble to trouble it? Can't we remain
> content with the "real, very dirty window"—a
> "thing"—as the answer to what ails us without
> turning it into an ailment of its own?
> —Bill Brown, "Thing Theory"

For the second time in the past three months, my garbage can has been stolen. Rather, a second can has been stolen. Like the first, it was full of garbage when it was taken. What's more puzzling, it contained the same sort of unremarkable garbage the first one did, as every can I put out always does, the same mundane run-off I've always produced.

Now, I don't think I've grown delirious and begun dragging bounty to the curb each week to tempt the neighbors. I'm sure that I've been leaving the same useless, putrid, maggoty, unidentifiable take-out as ever. I can the same ambiguously spattered and soiled stuff, the usual oily clutch of vegetable skins, coffee grounds, and slick debris I've always abandoned to freeze, congeal, or steam, depending on the season, each Friday morning for the fifteen-odd years I've lived in this house. Once I've extracted anything the city's deemed recycla-

ble—liberal guilt makes recyclers of us all—what's left
in to be left out contains no scandal to incite the *National Enquirer,* no telling excrescence to cause the FBI
to alert the lab. It's only junk mail they'd be restoring,
church flyers they'd be uncrumpling. Why bother to
reclaim my tattered Reeboks, buff up my broken toast-
er, or debride the peels, pencil shavings, plastic wrap, or
party favors fallen into disfavor? They might as well in-
terrogate the plumber who unplugged my pipes for all
that it would profit them. There is nothing better than
wretched in my refuse, nor anything beguiling there,
not by any reasonable estimation. There is nothing to
disgrace, incriminate, or betray me. At most, the occasional line of saliva, the odd corpuscular smear. Otherwise, unprepossessing, homely trash—scruff only a
mother could love. (Surely only Mom would want to
preserve Baby John's first curls as a charm or wear his
inaugural snot in a locket around her neck.)

So have the intelligence community stand down.
Let the psychologists eager for deviance ease back into
their overstuffed chairs. It's garbage, okay? I'm happy
to have another rat pack it. He who steals my trash
steals trash.

Yet someone is managing to salvage what for me
does not merit saving. To someone my issue issues a
challenge. Something for someone transcends the regular shambles I've made of things. So one of us is mistaken. At least one of us is mistaken, at least, about the
state of these spoils.

Once I whip out my Ockham's razor to cut the crap,
what's likeliest? Common sense dismisses that crack

squad of mutant raccoons, outstandingly diligent and endowed, as well as a single intrepid skunk descended from Robert Lowell's line: "She jabs her wedge-head in a cup / of sour cream, drops her ostrich tail, / and will not scare." If it's only one burglar who is squandering his stealth on effects I am more than willing to surrender to the landfill, if it's just one fellow who is casing my waste and who's made off with both my cans, he's deranged. A filth fetishist, a crackpot after cracked pots, and more disturbed than disturbing. A lunatic clawing at my fringe, crazily excavating by the light of the moon. Or no one quite so exotic: just a kid with insufficient supervision or homework to keep him at bay, the sort of student who before leaving the farm for college used to topple dozing livestock for fun. Possibly it's a fan too cowed to confront me personally but prizing items that retain my taint, much as disciples rabid for anything touched by Elvis once clamored for towels he'd used during concerts to mop his brow. I can even conceive of the ghost of Joseph Cornell, doomed to forage to fill posthumous boxes for all eternity . . .

But given how cumbersome an operation this must have been—like our own bodies, garbage seems mysteriously to take on weight as it settles over time—I am moved to consider a larger conspiracy. Such as a demented ringleader with besotted accomplices, comparable to those comic book gangs Batman had to break up in every other issue. Or guerilla survivalists who will stop at no edict or odor to obtain provisions. Or possibly a bunch of eccentric antiquarians or relic hunters. Perhaps an ecological cult of some sort. Rogue chemists on the prowl for novel polymers. A roving over-sight committee. Or a sullied underground network comparable to Thomas Pynchon's Preterite, denied but enduring, like a collection of irregular, unregulated verbs, ambiguously active, populating and plotting in the sewers, making their persistent exceptions to the System.

Whatever the means or motive, though, I can't get annoyed, indignant, or vengeful about someone wanting what I no longer wanted as badly as that. (Hey, if I'd intended it to be an art installation, I'd have cordoned off the can with velvet ropes.) Shakespeare went so far as to place a warning against rummaging his grave, but I have no bone to pick with anyone who'd bother to pick my bones.

Is it peace,
Is it a philosopher's honeymoon one finds
On the dump?

At times, desperation is as impenetrable as it is acute, I guess. Desire for what's down and out composts down and out of sight. Indeed, no matter how deeply I delve, I remain confounded that anyone—more than one, mind you!—would take the trouble.

I will show you fetishism in a handful of dust.

I wonder if it's really the cans themselves they're after, but only briefly. For if there's any logic at all in their dismal enterprise, the perpetrators would simply have waited for the haulers to empty them and not contended with the added mass. Or say they did not have the patience to let the professionals lighten their load. If stealing cans is what the ransackers had in mind, wouldn't the street be strewn with trash on the days they struck? On neither occasion has that been the case. No, the only plausible explanation is that it's the garbage itself they crave, those foul rag and bone shoplifters. It's the discharge I deem unredeemable each week which they deem desirable, my forsaken et cetera and incontinent ordnance, the disgusting ding an sich.

Ho-ho . . . The dump is full

Of images.

Which provokes a question: is their stealing my trash or my dispatching it to the curb in the first place the greater violation? In other words, how impulsively, how fatally do I weekly deceive myself by winnowing down this way? Does something still obtain in my mulch? Does a pregnancy yet reside in the residue? Have I abridged too far? I feel silly appraising my improvident slops, scrutinizing my swill, and it is difficult to bring myself to inspect that obscene distillery of mine, not to mention credit all that's stale, squalid, disqualified, or defunct, the rusted nuts and unwholesome bolts of being me. Bagging up trash, I basically abide by an out-with-the-old attitude on the order of Emerson's in "Circles": "We grizzle every day. I see no need of it."

Nevertheless, I may have unwittingly let a piece of my ego go down with the shit. Who hasn't at one time or another been seized by an indiscriminate fit of renunciation? Family, clothes, job, and company are bound to chafe eventually, and convinced that nothing is better than good riddance, we may not even grab after the baby as the bath water drains away.

A diary of my detritus might enlighten me. Maybe trash can look back at you, insistently if you give it time, the way books do. With that in mind, allow me to present one man's Rorschach, corrupt and curdling even as I speak.

January 21: cotton swabs bent into L's, their tips hard and showing a bit of sheen from scouring the bowl of each ear; newspaper and nail clippings, creased and yellowing together; old ballpoints, whose dried-out cartridges look like collapsed veins, as well as a pencil worn so close to the hilt that it could not accommodate another sharpening; a broken snow globe whose immoderately humid weather leaked out a crack in the firmament; a few disposable razor blades, still glinting menace and looking like robot vertebrae; wrappers, napkins, tissues, and other papers betraying recent meals, kitchen accidents, cosmetic efforts, rent fleshes, spat aftertastes, and assorted effluvia. What I've lived with lately and through, now consigned to the pit, the full, indifferent docket of a hundred hours or so. My very own LaBrea, if you will, which I continually replenish. Everything that's been siphoned, exhausted, ripped, reamed, wrung out, used up, left for dead— taken together, not enough to constitute one modest still life or stay a vagrant for two seconds, much less inspire a crime.

Why go on? Why itemize further the variegated rejects, the fusty crumbs and anonymous clumps? All of it shunnable, unsensational, barely worthy of comment, let alone police protection or a listing in the Fodor's guide. These, my seamier manifestations, are more embarrassing for their ordinariness than for any mystery about me they might expose. I have been offered low-rate credit cards. So what? I have strangled toothpaste tubes. I have eaten Italian—note the mangled spaghetti, the telltale stains. I have fingered *Victoria's Secret* and fought a cold. Turn me in.

And yet, apparently, one or more people have found my grunge agreeable. It has stamina I had not foreseen—not only its reek exceeds my grasp. Some nuance muscles through. The question my swiped trash begs is whether I might be unwittingly slicing away decent meat with the gristle. Am I missing something here, or will I eventually? Am I guilty of reckless abandonment? Am I unfairly predisposed?

I must focus. Before casting it out, I peel back the glistening innards of an onion that I'd left to rot behind the bread. I strip a wizened orange to reveal the overpopulated colonies each swollen segment comprises. I carve the knotted heart out of an artichoke I'll never eat, whose vile mush holds to the stone like vernix after a difficult birth. Nauseating, all that viscid interiority. Saturated and vaguely genital—not vaguely enough, in fact. And yet.

One feels the purifying change. One rejects
The trash.

A theory: There is an epidemic of reclamation around here, of which my garbage is but one target. But I've consulted with my neighbors, and it appears as though I've been singled out. Conceivably, no one else has noticed a similar loss, or no one else who has suffered a similar loss sees it as loss or suffering to be so deprived. However, these are people who chase loitering kids off their lawns and shoo any unleashed dog that begins to lift a leg against their property. For instance, the officious Mrs. Pearlman, who with arctic resolve watches over the block from her living room window, is the emblem of the neighborhood attention to whatever is going on. Oh, she's constant as a gator on a lagoon, that one, and as implacable. If these strikes stretched even half a block beyond just my driveway, she'd notice. They all would. And no one has.

Another theory: I am being laid out in effigy. In some fenced yard or unseen garage, I am being re-formed via synecdoche: my mouth implied by something I've mouthed, my nose by something I've sniffed and found noxious, my hands by something I've handled, and so on. The better to worship, insult, hex, or invade me.

And another: scholars are scavenging my middens for manuscript. Strange, though, that prose that no publisher yearns for might compel such yearning. At the office I've convinced our on-site computer wizards to demolish all encrypted checkpoints and password barriers to my documents because they were primarily stymieing me. Why protect my work, whose privacy is the very problem with it? It would be like asking to patent the way one picks at his pimples or to copyright a shopping list.

Conjecturing again: I am unwittingly serving as my own antagonist. In a somnambulistic daze I am responsible for putting out the garbage and then taking it back. What deep-seated neurosis such recycling might manifest is unclear, and quite possibly unprecedented, but I wouldn't be surprised that it speaks to my having had to comply with the conventional practice among suburban mothers of the 1950s who stoppered with bottles the babies that boomed on them and kept their breasts to themselves.

To drill in another direction: My refuse uniquely offends, keeping me from returning incognito from the curb and alarming the Neighborhood Watch Program, as if how I monotonously bottom out constitutes a kind of exhibitionism, a kind more blatant than other area evacuations might be. I presume that if I were spilling piles of thumb-smudged or even more intimately abused pornographic magazines into the street or planting crops of sodden diapers to ripen further in the sun, I might be held accountable. Yet I cannot reason my way into my garbage or out of it.

No, it is hard to imagine my meager output putting anyone out.

To think that there are those who might perceive my leavings as advent instead of culmination. Whoever they are who are finding value there, they must have a more sophisticated waste facility than I do.

More than once, having left the closed can to bake for a day or so in summer, I have lifted the lid for my latest deposit, only to discover a roiling casserole of tiny white worms winding about the walls and floor; in the lid itself, which I held away from me like a giant platter, worms were pearling, too. Writhing like tiny glands under duress. A colony of commas and ampersands cooking away, twisting blindly in the uneditable mess I'd left.

To think that even here my premises are not secure. I had assumed—as who would not?—that in this regard at least I was immune. Trash manifests our fall into the quotidian, I'd figured, which then falls into further disrepute, but not out of the ordinary by any means. Certainly I could cast my swinishness before Mrs. Pearlman and get no reaction. I had believed that I could relegate this much matter to the perimeter with impunity, without fear of incursion upon that disintegrating edge, my surface layer, as it were, the self's topsoil and odd impasto of my recent past. But no. Evidently not.

I might benefit from consulting current literature on litter to help me understand what my garbage is up against. I spoke of Pynchon before, who consistently glosses garbage—most infamously in the shadowy W.A.S.T.E. conspiracy that underwrites *The Crying of Lot 49,* but also, in a more general sense, in the agglomerative quality of his novels. *Gravity's Rainbow* in particular is besieged by materials, not only their dissemination but their entropy, as things inexorably capitulate to "ions and earth."

Put simply, Pynchon dotes on *stuff.* The poet John Ashbery once wrote that there are two basic ways of proceeding as a writer: to try to put everything in or to try to leave everything out. Pynchon is a peerless putter-inner, as his initial visit to Slothrop's crammed, "godawful" desk demonstrates:

It hasn't been cleaned down to the original wood surface since 1942. Things have fallen roughly into layers, over a base of bureaucratic smegma that sifts steadily to the bottom, made up of millions of tiny red and brown curls of rubber eraser, pencil shavings, dried tea or coffee stains, traces of sugar and Household Milk, much cigarette ash, very fine black debris picked and flung from typewriter ribbons, decomposing library paste, broken aspirins ground to powder. Then comes a scatter of paperclips, Zippo flints, rubber bands, staples, cigarette butts and crumpled packs, stray matches, pins, nubs of pens, stubs of pencils of all colors including the hard-to-get heliotrope and raw umber, wooden coffee spoons, Thayer's Slippery Elm Throat Lozenges sent by Slothrop's mother, Nalline, all the way from Massachusetts, bits of tape, string, chalk . . . above that a layer of forgotten memoranda, empty buff ration books, phone numbers, unanswered letters, tattered sheets of carbon paper, the scribbled ukulele chords to a dozen songs . . . an empty Kreml hair tonic bottle, lost pieces to different jigsaw puzzles showing parts of the amber left eye of a Weimaraner, the green velvet folds of a gown, slate-blue veining in a distant cloud, the orange nimbus of an explosion (perhaps a sunset),

rivets in the skin of a Flying Fortress, the
pink inner thigh of a pouting pin-up girl .
. . a few old Weekly Intelligence Summa-
ries from G-2, a busted corkscrewing ukulele string, boxes of gummed paper stars in
many colors, pieces of a flashlight, top to a
Nugget shoe polish can in which Slothrop
now and then studies his blurry brass reflection, any number of reference books
out of the ACHTUNG library back down
the hall—a dictionary of technical German, an F.O. *Special Handbook* or *Town
Plan*—and usually, unless it's been pinched
or thrown away, a *News of the World* somewhere too—Slothrop's faithful reader.

There may be important documents or sentimental
possessions among the clutter—a crucial command, a
viable memory, even a key to winning the war—but
in this blasted context, which recalls in miniature the
bombed-out surround of *Gravity's Rainbow,* everything
give way to inconsequence.

Nor is any one of us—each a body containing the
"coiled whispers of decay"—exempt. Mocked and
marked by dispossession, each of us is a man on the
dump.

Meanwhile, in *Underworld,* Don DeLillo grants
cameo appearances to a garbage scow that no city will
harbor, and which perpetually circles the narrative like
a nightmare patrol. Like Pynchon, DeLillo fixes on
the repercussions of what we refuse; with how the slag
of history, big business, war, government, technology,

and language returns to haunt us, much the way that buried nuclear waste threatens to leach out of sealed drums; with "the sand-grain manyness of things" and the fearsome revelations of the "dug-up self"; with how our dereliction defines us and how our rubble hums. Our cities rise on garbage, claims DeLillo's Detweiler, a "garbage hustler" and former "waste specialist"; garbage has its own momentum—it pushes back. Elsewhere in *Underworld*, Nick Shay concludes while contemplating a landfill on Staten Island that "Waste is a religious thing," so consistent and sizable is its claim upon us. Even humble, domestic waste—one unexceptional man's unexceptional trash—looms large, as we learn in *White Noise:*

> An oozing cube of semi-mangled cans, clothes hangers, animal bones and other refuse. The bottles were broken, the cartons flat. Product colors were undiminished in brightness and intensity. Fats, juices and heavy sludges seeped through layers of pressed vegetable matter. I felt like an archaeologist about to sift through a finding of tool fragments and assorted cave trash . . . I unfolded the bag cuffs, released the latch and lifted out the bag. The full stench hit me with shocking force. Was this ours? Did it belong to us? Had we created it? I took the bag out to the garage and emptied it. The compressed bulk sat there like an ironic modern sculpture, massive square, squat, mocking . . . I picked through it iterm by

> item . . . why did I feel like a household spy? Is garbage so private? Does it glow at the core with personal heat, with signs of one's deepest nature, clues to secret yearnings, humiliating flaws? What habits, fetishes, addictions, inclinations? What solitary acts, behavioral ruts? I found crayon drawings of a figure with full breasts and male genitals . . . I found a banana skin with a tampon inside. Was this the dark underside of consumer consciousness?

These metamorphic confines cannot ultimately contain us. Our covert lives threaten to burst through, contaminate, and level indictments. "It is necessary to respect what we discard," writes DeLillo, but respect will not spare us from the verdict.

Then there is Donald Barthelme, who positively revels in *dreck*. In *Snow White,* his seven dwarfs are as enchanted by the current "trash phenomenon" as by the fabulous potential of the title character; they stock up on junk, extol the manufacture of buffalo humps—sublimely useless!—and prefer "books that have a lot of *dreck* in them, matter which presents itself as not wholly relevant (or indeed, at all relevant) but which, carefully attended to, can supply a kind of 'sense' of what is going on." And what is mostly going on is garbage. Barthelme's stories rake shamelessly the vulgar, glamorous shatter—the brand names, swatches, jokes, memos, and slogans of the American idiom. There is Stanley Elkin, who in dizzying sentences sweeps the kitsch of postmodern culture. No one is so eager to "franchise" the fabrics and textures of ordinary life; no one is so enchanted by our country's "mansard roofs and golden arches and false belfries, all its ubiquitous, familiar neon signatures and logos, all its *things,* all its *crap,* the true American graffiti, the perfect queer calligraphy of American signature, what gave it meaning and made it fun." There is William Gass, who sets himself the task in *The Tunnel* of "giving grandeur to a shit." No mean feat, when your featured speaker is filled with spew, to keep a visionary gleam burning in a burrow, to light your way through the murk by metaphor alone.

But for truly dedicated attention to trash, none can match A. R. Ammons, whose devotion of some twenty-five hundred lines to it earns him the mantle of American literature's High Priest of Debris. His *Garbage* protests that it is not a waste of consecration to consecrate waste. In this protracted Sermon on the Heap, Ammons steeps us in the "staid gross" so as to ground our penchants and fancies—our poetry—in its priority:

> what else deflects us from the
> errors of our illusionary ways, not a temptation
> to trashlessness, that is too far off, and,
> anyway, unimaginable, unrealistic.

For the grime we scour out and the scum we flush finds its way back to us. The record of our jettison clings to us like the stench itself, our fluid ruin bending back upon us like conscience, following us back into the house; it lingers on the skin, dogs us like a criminal record, infiltrates our food, water, and atmosphere, infects our beds.

"O, let me kiss that hand!" cried the sightless Gloucester upon recognizing his decrepit king. "Let me wipe it first," replied Lear, "it smells of mortality." Another "ruined piece of nature" most would just as soon be rid of, yet who returns from exile like an awful judgment upon them all, like history and destiny together.

For our garbage augurs our own plutonic fate; garbage is the avant garde of our succumbing to time. Garbage is no digression, but the secret thesis of our ramshackle days and waning nights. Call it the endless undercurrent of our dying, the viper coiled in the ticking, the core life rots to. Would that we could forestall time as routinely as we have the city haul its evidence off. But Death always catches us with our hands in the till. It is as undeniably nested in the cells we make as in the cells we slough. Although one plunges each fistful deep down the pail, the fact does not stay down: thus we are undone.

Who hasn't uttered the phrase "I'm just killing time" when obviously it is the other way around?

Suspicious, the way our erstwhile contents silt down into unexpected densities, the way we still occupy our parsings and paraphrases, sunderings and cinders, ferment and flux. Impossible to believe completely that we and this great world shall so wear out to nought. Amazing, the way it all deteriorates together.

Like a book, a garbage can can be an echo chamber.

So Beckett's Hamm potted his legless parents, Nagg and Nell, in ash cans, and they ragged at him without mercy or meaning much at all. They took up what slight residence they could muster in the same interiors that later in the play became their tombs. Whose destiny is very different? One need only turn the soil so often.

That corpse you planted last year in your garden,
Has it begun to sprout? Will it bloom this year?
Or has the sudden frost disturbed its bed?
Oh keep the Dog far hence, that's friend to men,
Or with his nails he'll dig it up again!

So Eliot confronted the Waste Land with other clutter of his own devising: "These fragments I have shored against my ruins." More brutish than his Prufrock, I have measured out my life in garbage cans. And in so doing sought to shore against my ruins as well.

While I am on to other matters, they balk and reposition, shift and congeal, simmer and devolve. Whenever I thunk the can beside the curb, I seem to feel the contents shrug, as all that's given out that week gives up. All my squander, my would-be ballast, my canny subtractions. An orgy of organic material going on under cover of darkness and decay. A shudder in the litter engenders there the broken wall clock, the burned roux and towel, and double-A batteries dead.

"What are the roots that clutch, what branches grow / Out of this stony rubbish?" One cannot stay the fractious atoms in the alley, the chaos in the can. This one can't, at any rate.

ॐ

And so, in lieu of conclusion, a coda, a detachable tag. In sit-com lingo, they call it a "throwaway," the summing up that succeeds the last commercial, which in reruns they tend to omit altogether.

"You have reached USA Waste. If you are calling to start garbage pickup service, press 1. If you are calling because your garbage was not picked up according to schedule, press 2. If you are calling to suspend garbage pickup temporarily, press 3. If you are calling to terminate garbage pickup at your business or residence, press 4. If you are calling to activate automatic withdrawal from your checking or savings account to pay for garbage pickup, press 5. If you are calling to arrange an alternative payment method for garbage pickup, press 6. If you are calling to ask about our optional curbside recycling service, press 7. If you are calling to obtain copies of billing transactions or additional printed materials related to USA Waste operations, press 8. If you are calling to register a question or complaint about how your garbage has been handled, press 9. If you would like to have these options repeated, press 0. If you do not have a touch-tone phone or would like to speak to a representative of USA Waste, please hold the line, and your call will be answered in the order in which it was received. If you are calling after regular business hours, please wait for the tone and leave a brief message about your garbage service. Otherwise, you are invited to call back during regular business hours, 7:30 to 5:00 P.M. Monday through Friday, except for garbage holidays, which are national holidays. Thank you for calling USA Waste."

"Yes, I want to report stolen garbage cans. My garbage cans have been stolen."

"Stolen, sir?"

"Well, I presume they've been stolen. I mean, they're gone. They couldn't have blown away because they were full of garbage both times. Two cans. I mean, one can on two different occasions. No, what I mean is one can on one occasion, one on another occasion a couple of weeks later. Yesterday, actually. The second can."

"Are you sure they were stolen?"

"I'm sure they're gone. What other explanation could there be?"

"I'm sure I don't know. Could it be that your haulers thought that you were throwing away the cans, too?"

"How would they know that? Why would they think that?"

"I'm sure I don't know."

"Are you saying that my garbage cans were so ratty that they decided to take them, too? Do your people ordinarily make those decisions on their own?"

"No, sir. We just remove the garbage our customers leave out. From time to time a can is damaged or there is some spillage during dumping, but we can't be responsible for that sort of thing, as I'm sure you understand."

"I do understand. I'm just wondering how in the world, you know . . ."

"You're upset. You want them back. That's understandable, of course. You are welcome to come down during regular business hours and look for your garbage, if you'd like."

"It's not the garbage, just the cans. Just the garbage *cans.*"

"Can you describe them, sir?"

"Can I describe my garbage cans? No. Who remembers what his garbage cans look like? They're . . . what? They're *dark*. Okay? Dark and with handles. You know, just regular *garbage* cans."

"And what reason do you have to believe that USA Waste has taken your garbage cans?"

"No reason at all. That's my point. Why would you take my garbage cans? Why would *anyone* take my garbage cans?"

"I'm sure I don't know, sir. As I say, you are welcome to come down during regular business hours and see for yourself. But you should prepare yourself: most garbage cans look pretty much alike, especially after they've been emptied. In all likelihood, they are either not here or gone. If you want my advice, better to let it go."

"Let it go? As in 'move on'? I'm not talking about a lost love here."

"Precisely. All the more reason."

Whether it is a sign of obstinacy or immaturity on our part, it is characteristic of literary types, as well as of the texts they treasure, to cling and linger. They get hold of something as obsolete as a failed relationship or a fallen leaf, and they won't relinquish it. It's easier to strip rings from a corpse or to separate a cow from its cud than to convince some writers to release an obsession. "You're surrounded, pal. There's no way out. Be smart. Just lay the anthology down gently and step away, and no one will get hurt." The tragedy is, more often than not, you end up reading the next day how maintenance had to come to scrape the sidewalk of his remains.

Environmentalists will tell you that it is not advisable to put out every fire. In certain instances, the forest benefits from a purging burn. What looks like a calamity may really be healthy and integral to the natural order of things.

Which is to say that I have deferred to the experts after all. I let it go.

Getting Known

Richard Burton used to tell interviewers that the key to his success as an actor was neither his classical training nor his Welsh accent, with its intimations of elevation, ennui, and ale, but rather his bad complexion. As a boy, Burton had contended with the ravages of acne, leaving his adult face ripped and divoted as turf following a football match. But he counted that an advantage in his chosen profession. Because he was not conventionally handsome—not a "pretty boy," he would claim, prolonging his disgust with the concept by letting the vile phrase out much the way he pronounced "murder" in *Becket*—he could be taken seriously as an actor. (Now *there's* a sneer that in two seconds would have withered the pretensions of any unblemished Elvis.) Instead of being relegated to the usual roles for promising young actors—the dull run of proteges, fiancés, and fops, all wide-eyed, sprightly, and dim—he could sink his unaligned teeth into meatier challenges.

Even in his twenties, Burton already looked as though life had plundered him somehow, as though he had worn the world awhile, taken some knocks, tasted his own blood in his mouth. In a word—in a cliché—his face had character. Directors could assume by such a face that the man had something to show for himself simply because a substantial self showed in his face. Talent and hard work take you the rest of the way, of course, but first you've got to get through the door. The hard-bitten among us, like Burton, burst through, and when they do, they burst through face first.

If your goal is to get the whole room nodding, one reliable strategy is to denounce contemporary culture for its shallow fascination with youth and beauty. Blast fashion magazines and cosmetic ads for the vapid, vaporous ideals they teach. Make a show of your ignorance over the quantum difference between a model and a supermodel; speculate aloud if perhaps the latter can fly. Spit on the polish of primetime television stars, gleaming indistinguishably out of predictable nonsense. Complain that the film icons of Generation X all share the same calibrated, predictable dimples and indistinguishable Euclidean chins.

If you are accused of general misanthropy, explain that glitter won't do for you. You prefer to hold out for smolder, thank you, because you appreciate the acids that create the heat underneath. Forget those baby-smooth faces that have never had to face up to anything. You want a countenance that's been held accountable. I mean the deeper, contemplative fires of a Tommy Lee Jones, whose name may sound as though it could adorn a pair of designer jeans but whose hardscrabble looks suggest that (his actual Harvard education aside) he's had to carry the weight of what he's learned out of the pit on his own back. The same brand of beleaguered genius governs Robert Duvall, presiding over the looming cliff of his brow, the unfinished masonry of his jaw's rough jut. Surely you see it in Robert Mitchum as well, the movie embodiment of November, darkly lumbering and embering out. These are men who have weathered hard luck and hard liquor, who are as willing and as likely to take a pounding as to dish one out, who, however rumpled, bloodied, or dispossessed, remain unbowed. Memorize their faces and the faces of the wrecked and rugged dead who were plugged into a hundred films, anonymous and enduring icons of anonymous endurance, whom you deem (lifting your drink with a snort to seal the argument) *real* actors.

Oh, one may counter that the inflexibly sour expressions of the actors you champion betray a lifetime of digesting sour grapes, girls regularly having wrapped themselves about more glamorous men. On the contrary, tell them, these men have known the arms already, known them all, and resisted, having long ago realized that women would drain their rigor from them like syrup from a tree. "I won't play the sap for you," Sam Spade declares to his duplicitous lover, Brigid O'Shaughnessy, in *The Maltese Falcon,* sucking it up, sucking it in.

☙

Before you cry "foul"—Mary Astor may have been ripe for comeuppance, but what would it have cost Bogart to cushion with couth the fall she was taking?—keep in mind how difficult it must have been for him to hail a taxi or finish a meal without interruption. Bad manners can be as useful a bulwark against assault as blisters or bad breath.

When Don DeLillo writes in *Great Jones Street* that "fame requires every kind of excess," he is referring not only to the limos, the luxuries, and the lurid surpluses of the adored but also to the overflow of doting they occasion. It follows that obscurity requires every kind of abnegation, which, paradoxically, is a kind of excess, too. It takes almost heroic determination in our super-mediated environment for the recluse to assert his inversion successfully. To resist signing up and signing on in every instance, to dodge the junk mail and telemarketing entirely, to evacuate the vicinity like a bowel would these days seem to require vigilance as extensive as that of the communications industry that seeks him out. No wonder those pioneers of retraction, the withdrawn and the ingrown, those resolved to evade the obsessively cultivated field of vision, who pull up the ladders after them and leave no forwarding address have inspired cults of their own—stealth bombers, if you will—aggressive as any fan club. No wonder that two of our most renowned American authors, J. D. Salinger and Thomas Pynchon, have invented seclusions more notorious than their novels. Thus a rumored Salinger sighting incites a riot on the Internet; a handwriting expert matches a handwritten editorial's with his scribble and conjectures that the man who brought us Holden Caulfield is still delivering incognito. A Pynchon blurb surfaces on another writer's dust jacket like a sudden evanescent shape rising out of Loch Ness, and relic collectors crowd the coast. Duck and cover is clearly an art all its own. Arguably the greatest performance Garbo ever gave was her starring role in her own recoil, just as the most exorbitant thing Howard Hughes ever bought was invisibility.

Maybe we do not respect the repudiator's perimeter because solitary confinement represents a negative judgment upon the rest of us. They want nothing to do with the due we would give them? After we've come so far to worship they won't unlock the church? We'll show *them* not to show themselves!

ᚹ

It is bad enough that the stars in *my* private firmament do not care who recognizes their glow; it galls me more that so much celebrity is squandered these days on the undeserving. For nothing is more ecumenical than fame. I've read that there are now actually more personal web pages on the Internet than there are people on-line, so eager are we to guarantee our niches, virtual or otherwise. It has gotten so that the famous are not primarily those who daunt us or dare us to fathom them, only those who happen to sit up in the shallows.

In fact, it now appears that Andy Warhol underestimated the half-life of fame when he predicted fifteen minutes apiece for each of us. Think of the television celebrity who engineers a career out of conspicuousness. Exploiting sentimental vestiges of a sit-com she starred in a generation ago, she will haunt game show panels, hawk hair care products, or otherwise trade on her ubiquity, and persevere, a stubborn mote forever lodged in the public eye. ("Off-camera lives are unverifiable," someone says in Don DeLillo. At the baseball game, fans clamber over one another to be caught by the camera's seventh-inning sweep of the stands, then hurry home in the hope of glimpsing themselves on the late news. No one wants to settle for being parenthetical if they don't have to.) Closer to home, there is the gridiron hero who applies the legacy he developed as a teenager to a viable career in insurance—a more modest example, true, but the principle is the same. You can be a local weatherman or reformed heroin addict and be featured at mid-afternoon assemblies (holding forth on barometric and cardiac pressures, respectively) at junior high schools throughout the area. If nature bestows unusual favors or misfortunes upon you, you can be a prodigy of the body: whether your age, weight, height, strength, flexibility, or I.Q. is off the charts, whether you are especially decrepit or wondrously endowed, you might secure a seat on a prominent float in the holiday parade. Hit the lottery or survive a hostage situation, be the millionth lucky customer or suffer some spectacular bereavement, smack the record-breaking homer or snag the ball from the scrum in the stands, charm a senator into your hotel room or cherish the biggest ball of aluminum foil in all of Oklahoma, and gird yourself for worship either way.

"Let X stand for the unknown," my math teacher would say, never considering how increasingly rare it has become for any X to stand for it.

Figure that out of about 275 million Americans, maybe as many as a million fit fame's billing in one way or another, and you begin to realize just how unnotable being notable is these days. When it comes to recognition, *Who's Who* shows us what's what: a numberless slur of worthies strain the bindings and burst the appendices of volume after annual volume, any one of which is massive enough to anchor a schooner. So many Who's end up moving into Whoville—the Reference Section's San Diego—that it overwhelms the census. It is becoming a mark of distinction not to make the cut.

This may be why the magazine we pass the time with in the checkout line is called *Us* when you'd assume that if its inhabitants were uniquely deserving we'd be reading *Them*.

Meanwhile, *People* magazine each year comes out with its list of "Twenty-Five Most Intriguing People," who are anything but intriguing. Yes, they are enviable enough, the slick felons and film stars, the huge-breasted and the highborn, the outstandingly handsome and the lusciously corrupt among us. But once we've peered into their diet regimens and underwear drawers, intrigued is the last thing we are. If royalty is a product of dazzle and distance, access doth make commoners of us all.

A question for the astronomers: if there are so many stars in the firmament, why isn't the night sky ablaze? How does the outer dark swallow so much luminescence anyway?

☙

After I alerted her to the copy of my latest book tucked snugly among the 800's on the library's Recent Acquisitions shelves, my fourth-grade daughter narrowed her eyes at me and asked, "Daddy, are you famous?" This with what I imagined to be the same intonation a daughter would ask if you had gotten into her cache of Halloween candy. More than a little taken aback by the question, I hesitated before answering: "Yes, sweetheart, in a way, I guess. I guess you could say I am famous." "Does anybody *know* it?" she asked. The remark might have cut deeper if it hadn't been for the fact that I was the one who'd requested that the library purchase my book in the first place, making me (in a way, I suppose) the center and circumference of demand for me. There is an incisive and sobering line to that effect in Beckett's *Krapp's Last Tape* when the grotesque ascetic learns that sales of his *magnum opus* have crept to seventeen. "Getting known," he cackles. It's a big club.

My mother recalls how the world made way for her when she was a child growing up in a Chicago orphanage. "Reminisces" would be the wrong word here: the Marks Nathan Home was respectable and hospitable enough, as far as institutions were concerned, but that was never so far as *Annie* or facilities in Victorian fiction stripped of the sinister for Christmas nostalgia suggest. Those are not wistful tears she sheds in remembrance; it was "a hard-knock life," indeed, but without the winsome choral support of the Broadway musical. Yet she did enjoy—"enjoy" is not right either, I know—a sort of neighborhood ascendancy. Call it the royalty of dispossession. Because she was an orphan, my mother got permanent dibs.

For instance, every week the choice seats at the movies were cordoned off for her and her kind. Once everyone else had settled, the orphans were led in procession, single-file, like prisoners or the somber cast of a fire drill at religious school. They sidled their way to the center of the seventh row and domino'd down. The last one dropped into position, and only then did the theater go black and the show begin. In this fashion were the orphans compensated by public deference mixed with something like survivor guilt. Adults smoothed their hair as they passed and rubbed their shoulders the way trainers prepped boxers between rounds, but the infamously bereft never had to endure actual parental supervision and full-blooded love. ("Endured" is probably mistaken, too, in this context.) There was no one for their transgressions to echo out to, no one to gainsay their adventures or admonish them for failing to brush; there was no one to interrupt their play to wipe smutch from their faces. (This was something on the order of what the rest of the gang saw as Huck Finn's lucky lack of sponsorship: while their parents made them put on and put up with starchy clothes every Sunday for church, he was blessed to wallow about in fashion-free comfort.) In this way, orphans were automatically compelling. They awakened already exotic in their institutional beds.

So, apart from true family, the orphans were consecrated in every significant way imaginable. If, by definition and by virtue of a variety of family catastrophes, they could not have everything, the orphans could have everything else. Like dealers siphoning off the house's take from the final pot or ministers skimming tithes the way shearwaters did the brimming seas, they laid unspoken but undeniable claim. The neighborhood regularly laid the lagniappes on. From the virgin plunge into the fresh, sweaty cylinders at the ice cream parlor on Kedzie Avenue to the last licks at the batting cages off Kimball before the night proprietor whoomed the halogens off, their special status was assured.

And yet, if you consulted the bureaucrats of mercy who ran the orphanage, they would have told you that the dream of every child they cared for was to desert them and dissolve into the undifferentiated crowd of ordinary, parented kids. Like the State that Marx theorized would from obsolescence wither away, the Marks Nathan Home looked forward to a utopian future that did not include it.

ॐ

The truth is that, in the manner of E. A. Robinson's Miniver Cheevy, who "scorned the gold he sought, / But sore annoyed was he without it," my admiration of the prodigious contempt of the Bogarts and Burtons who like bruised and fallen angels slum among us does not prevent my wishing for the "ripe renown" of those whose public way is paved. For instance, I have craved the shared election and country clubbiness of guests on late-night talk shows. Booked to promote a new movie, a series debut, or other show-biz foray, each guest saunters on stage, busses or backslaps the host (as gender dictates), and negotiates the caresses and glad-handing of precedent guests. Then, having accepted touches from all assembled as if she were a Torah scroll passed among the orthodox, she beams at the band that played her on stage, takes the seat nearest the desk, and, with an oversized sigh, settles in for a four-minute segment. And at some point during the conversation, she refers to "the business." As in "We in the business," or "As everyone in this business knows," or "My son is interested in the business."

It isn't the excessive public tenderness I'm after. (Actually it was this sort of display that made the '60s most uncomfortable for me—all of that unwarranted hugging among strangers, all of those ambushes of affection among people whose sole affiliation was a basic solidarity regarding our role in Vietnam or the use of mild hallucinogenics.) No, what I want is the embrace of elite shorthand terminology. In the heyday of Las Vegas, major players were billed by their given names alone: FRANK, DEAN, SAMMY, BARBRA—the starting Elysian infield—towered over the Strip. And they all worked in what was and unmistakably remains "the business." With the possible exception of Congress or the Cosa Nostra, no other business enjoys this privilege. And while I might openly deplore the outbreak of inflation among the members, privately, like Miniver Cheevy, I confess that I "would have sinned incessantly / Could [I] have been one."

As it happens, just as whatever accomplishments I can claim on the resume have earned me limited eminence, whatever sins I've committed have not been newsworthy enough to stop passersby from passing by me on the street. I confess to consorting with ordinary mortals on a daily basis without raising the rate of a single pulse. I've never been asked to appear at any store opening as a come-on to consumers; I've never made the front page for committing a felony or kicking a winning field goal; I've never been publicly cheered or stoned, never rode the shoulders of an exuberant multitude nor been ridden out of any town; I've never been featured on a bus's flank, mountainside, or marquee. "I do not think that they will sing for me," sighs Prufrock—yes, that selfsame disdainer of women's arms I alluded to before—who accidentally bumps into me as he slinks off and pays me no mind.

No, the venues where I'm most visible lie well beneath the radar. I do not mean the classrooms I teach in or the bathroom walls where frank and florid opinions about my personality and personal life are broadcast. I am not referring to the shelves of omnivorous libraries where my writings, nestled in with the other literary S's, resist disintegration on acid-free paper. I mean the vestiges of me that survive through the subtle ways I subsisted in graduate school.

One of the most enduring lessons of graduate school was that you could make a serviceable dinner out of Minute Rice and Italian dressing. Paychecks for teaching assistants were never as elastic as months were long, so when it came to the basics, I prided myself on my resourcefulness. I found out which campus bars on what days provided free food with drinks. Nursing the one beer I purchased like some rich, fickle invalid who held my prospects for inheritance in his hands, I made a meal out of the bland sandwiches and incidental edibles, all the while pocketing enough to ride out the next day's appetite. I scanned the campus paper daily for notices of public largesse because I knew that open banquets followed opulent regard. At dedications of every shape and kind, there were none so dedicated as I. I raised a plastic glass of champagne to the new wing, slapped backs at commemorative unveilings, honored alumni risen to chair impressive boards, and laid hands on retiring deans, for all university functions functioned on food. In humanities departments they may have prosecuted over stolen paper clips and kept the Xerox machine behind velvet ropes, but the true essence of higher education was crustacean, and by probing carefully for the plush parts, I learned where bits of sweet meat were reachable and tweezed out my fill. Yes, the wise graduate student conducted his hunger with aplomb, keeping his social insinuations deft and his one decent sport coat clean.

Ask anyone who pushed through the grad school snake and you'll hear the same story. There were valuable classes at college, certainly, but then there was what you needed to know to get by. While my mentors plotted for prime parking spaces or fended for tenure, while senior researchers emerged from endowed chairs to sabbatical in snowless climes, I bent to the necessary gleaning, picking through their garbage for subsistence. I was like one of the low browsers paleontologists talk about—more economically constituted than the towering brontosauruses that would sweep only the tall trees and, ultimately, able to outlast them. A request to edit conference papers for an agricultural journal, a bite-sized commission for a thousand words on a currently obscure poet for a soon-to-be obscure reference work, a pittance for a paragraph—they had not yet invented the enterprise that was beneath me. Clinging to the frayed hem of the profession, I scrounged for dignity and the odd dollar.

I also checked the classifieds for short-term tasks to supplement what my department called (without irony) my income. I developed a real genius for ferreting out the extra hour's employment. I cosseted funded profs to let me type findings or swab cages. Let no ongoing research go on without me, was my motto. Let no quota close quotes nor gathering of data shut down for the day before adding me to the tally. For two cents I urged upon dozens of researchers my two cents' worth. For a guinea I'd pig for you. Over the course of my graduate career ("career" in this instance being another of those questionable expressions best handled with tongs), I must have volunteered for a couple of dozen psychological surveys to swell the statistical piles of hopeful Ph.D.'s. I considered it a personal mission to guarantee that no psychology dissertation left the dock without some semblance of my objectives, dreads, preferences, recriminations, longings, tastes, and lusts among its cargo.

Nor like some mouse from the calculated jolt did I shy from the behaviorists. How long can you hold your arm in a bucket of ice? Take this pill and try it again. Now how long? Negotiate this maze while Mozart plays. Now try it under heavy metal duress. Placebo or poison? I swallowed unlabeled brews while they watched and docketed me. I wore glasses that scrambled my sight to test my recovery time. I held a minor fire sale on the premises of my body, letting them scrape cells, clip hairs, fill pipettes with bubbles of blood.

Love me, love my scurf.

So I was one of the legions of cheerful, petty mercenaries on whom research institutions secretly depend. For the price of dinner I'd auction off my fluids and aptitudes, submit to measure, broadcast my vitals, or sell my idiosyncracies out. I spread the secrets of my aggressive tendencies, blood counts, sexual preferences, inhibitions and frequencies, political opinions, spiritual assumptions, drug tolerances, and fear of house pets. Whatever the experiment, I signed up, I signed on.

I also posed nude for drawing classes. Graduate school had prepared me to be inert and hidden, and these were traits admirably suited to sitting still. The work required no greater talent than opaqueness; I did not have to be a model model, just a slump of shapes to take the light. So long as I did not shiver or flinch, I served the purpose. In this sense, the rhythms of my skin proved no less useful to the aesthetic end of campus than they did to the internal organ grinders. And so, as a site of intersection between arts and sciences, I was a living refutation of C. P. Snow's theory of two cultures, and I regularly inspired delvings from opposing disciplines. For every psychological study that divined me, there was a charcoal sketch detailing my clefts and crevices, my gradients and shades. Then it was grab your pants and your cash and get your body to the next inventory. And so, in my own small ways sustaining the attentions of fellow students, I was sustained.

And this is where I probably most reliably persist: on slides to enchant the annual batch of freshman chemistry and biology students, among the classified molecules of their required classes; as smudged, scumbled charcoal on yellowing paper; as unsung yet essential statistical evidence serving to ground projects in the hard sciences and the soft. "Sweetheart, it is a strange sort of fame, at best," I say to my daughter, who is too young to wonder if any nod to Bogart lies behind that endearment. Off she goes, casually carrying my genetic code around like allowance in her jeans pocket. Today she is generally known as my daughter; one day I may be better recognized as her dad. For the time being, however, and in blithe defiance of concerns voiced by ophthalmologists and publicity agents, we risk the outdoors without the protection of dark glasses.

Mistake and Identity

Lewis Thomas, that sunny pundit of the microscopic, writes, "If we were not provided with the knack of being wrong, we could never get anything useful done." In this instance, Thomas is musing on the fallibility of human thought, thanks to whose ineradicable talent for error we sometimes find ourselves moving fortuitously toward insights and discoveries that bland exactitude could never have disclosed. "The capacity to leap across mountains of information to land lightly on the wrong side represents the highest of human endowments," he claims. But if to err is human (as Lewis claims in the title to this particular essay), it is not only human; in fact, the potential for error is embedded in the very DNA from which all organic life—the whole blooming, buzzing, blundering confusion—has evolved. "Without this special attribute," Thomas tells us in "The Wonderful Mistake," we would still be anaerobic bacteria and there would be no music. . . . The molecule of DNA was ordained from the beginning to make small mistakes."

Certainly it is consoling to think that when we miss an appointment or mismatch our socks, modern science supports us at the molecular level. We are compounded of ramshackle cells, and all creation comes from Nature's mutinous moments and mutant moods. From fleeting paramecia on up to tenured full professors, our personalities and purposes, biologically speaking, are patchwork; every species has its origins in glitch. Basically, we have all bungled our way to the present day. What but the unexpected might you reasonably expect of us?

This may be a hard precept for precisionists to swallow, who believe that perfection is the ideal and destiny of science. We are the future beneficiaries of meticulous, wholesale cellular manipulation, they presume, and we will ultimately dwell in a utopia purged of disability, disease, and all the mitigating deviations from standards human beings now suffer from. And no doubt there is much to admire about the prospect, especially when one considers how currently incurable afflictions like cancer, dementia, and the decrepitude of aging—may this list eventually strike its readers as being as curious and obsolete as typhoid and manual typewriters do today!—will likely as not descend upon our loved ones. Nevertheless, I find myself worrying that a doctrinaire version of DNA will somehow, in some essential way, diminish us.

Cloning, of course, is the trendy exemplar of this fear. True, bruiseless apples, Euclidean peppers better suited to stacking, and other effects of barnyard eugenics have troubled no one all that much. But once such chromosomal breaking and entering takes place on the premises of higher mammals, the argument that we're talking about a difference in degree, not kind, is a tougher sell. Dolly out dozens of genetically identical sheep, utterly comparable cows from whose preconceived beef countless Platonic patties might derive, and chickens whose zygotes Xerox would envy, and it is hard not to extrapolate from them a human congeries of *op. cits.* to match. It's still science fiction for the time being, but the notion is enough to put you off your feed, even when the meal features streamlined meats or unblemished, beveled eggs.

In terms of human repercussions, the closest to cloning I ever came was observing the Gott twins, Jerry and Gary, in elementary school. The Gott parents dressed their identical twins identically, gave them the same haircuts, and named them as much alike as common sense allowed. Jerry and Gary were always that, a couple, indistinguishable when together and unimaginable outside of one another's company. It was a condition and connection that, even then, they must have realized that choosing separate colleges or disparate careers would not change. And as for that, whom God has brought so completely together let no marriage tear asunder. Meet the Gott boys, a set with the honed sameness of steak knives, looking less born than engineered long before we learned about letting the laboratory into our intimacies.

There were childish pleasures to be had, perhaps, in being half an entity: sleight-of-self pranks to be played on teachers, fellow students, and even (when a hard day shook their focus) their own parents. With their masks by nature forever in place, masquerades were easy to pull off. Jerry (or was it Gary?) would answer roll call on his brother's behalf, allowing Gary (unless it was Jerry) to dawdle in the hall, a favor Jerry or Gary would repay the next day, or vice versa. They reacted to everything at the same time and in the same way, braiding their celebrations, blurring their surprises, blending their whines. Yes, even their voices overlapped exactly, so that the Gott twins sounded off like tines on a tuning fork, simultaneously struck.

Actually, I found them pretty spooky myself. I had an irrational fear of running into them alone in the hall because I worried that they might reach out their freakishly interchangeable hands and command me, in robotic monotone, "Join us." The memory haunts me still. So if you mention cloning to me nowadays, I envision squads of like-minded, like-bodied, efficiently begotten Gotts on the prowl, relentlessly spreading solidarity, and shudder.

For even when Nature perpetrates it without our prompting, there remains something unnatural about absolute congruence. Apart from the products of office machines, we don't tend to look at copies and think something has gone *right*. God may not be an artist, but he is definitely no stock clerk, either. We are talking about the same Deity who cannot craft a tide or corrugate the coastline it will dash against for more than ten meters without transgressing against the tolerances. He may be the Alpha and the Omega, but a Lord who cannot get as many as two mountains anywhere in the range alike wouldn't have lasted half an hour on the assembly line for Henry Ford.

In truth, if to err is human, it is apparently just as much divine. Take a good look at Creation and tell me honestly if you believe it's ever been proofread. There is no contesting the evidence: although His animating breath may lie behind the universe, we inhabit an unedited draft. Is it possible that no pastoral poet or landscape artist ever recognized that land and sky were incommensurate not only because of their respective magnitudes but because blue and green simply do not go together? Granted, throughout the cosmos God plays it safe, cloaking the whole of it in formalwear. To last out the unrelieved evening of outer space, He recommends basic black. It is the color that covers a multitude of indulgences, covers up the embarrassing bulges. But in the end there is no hiding that God plays havoc with the tabs and slots, quality control be damned.

If in the beginning the Word became Flesh, at least occasionally that word must have been "whatever."

Plainly, disorder is in the order of things. We live in the midst of mishaps, of which *Homo sapiens* itself constitutes billions of matchless examples. What dread hand designed what's warped and distorted and gave shape to the ragged, the bedraggled and the ruined? Did He smile His work to see? Did He Who made the acne'd, the swaybacked, the macrocephalic, and the mauled make me?

It takes a most forgiving faith indeed to overlook corruption and see only constancy. Science may evade the spiritual stalemate by reminding us that it is Nature's aptitude for error to which evolution—our own included—is due. Accordingly, the undeviating Gotts, conformist down to the last discernible freckle, are anomalous. Exceptions to the rule, rule. Otherwise, after billions of years of simmering, nothing would have splashed its way out of the primordial soup but occasional drops of broth, engendering nothing more advanced than stains, whose content, pattern, and value would be about as unpredictable and prepossessing as a roll of dimes.

As one of the molecular biologists in Richard Powers's novel *The Gold Bug Variations* maintains, the fundamental role of science is "not efficiency or mastery, but the revival of appropriate surprise." And wonder is best cultivated in mess. (Rest assured, they haven't found a galaxy yet that looks more like a gridiron that a pot of gorp.) Woe to the scientist who cannot see the aberrant forest for the solid symmetries. Thus let us invest in the deckled and the flecked, revel in the variegated, brood upon the accidentally arrived at and the rudely made. Maybe Nature's mistakes, not its maintenance plan, suggest a more fruitful avenue for exploration after all.

Now when it comes to scientific principles, I confess that I rather quickly come to the end of my tether. However, I do find a similar urge to embrace novelty in the literature I know well. In this realm, the counterpart for the clone is the cliché; the equivalent of dressing identical siblings in duplicate outfits is dressing one's sentiments in metaphors so exhausted from their long run that you can see them coming stanzas in advance of their arrival and collapse. The way Jerry's plaid shirt, blue jeans, brown belt, and loafers anticipated Gary's ensemble down to the penny—Mother Gott alliterated them daily, remember, in every way she could—so too in tuckered poems does "love" drop like an overdone waffle from "above" and each "hand" reach out inevitably for "understand." (Lovers should resonate as long as their limbs and their longing will let them, but must they rhyme dull-tonguing like that in public?) "The creator is no puritan," writes Annie Dillard, admiring his cornucopial energies. Let's assume the He is no poetaster, either.

And what is a Hallmark card if not the cloned sheep of all the heard, the TV dinner of desire, imagination's Model T? Shall we consign our poets to the coop to produce batches of unvarying verse to service all the birthdays, graduations, and anniversaries an occasion-driven nation requires? "The freshness of night has been fresh a long time," writes Wallace Stevens in "The Man on the Dump." Perched upon the compost of decaying images and outworn expressions, he wonders

how many men have copied dew

For buttons, how many women have covered themselves

With dew, dew dresses, stones and chains of dew, heads

Of the floweriest flowers dewed with the dewiest dew.

Clichés sustain vain resemblances with numbing redundancy. I am talking about sweatshop language here. Just imagine sculptors shackled to replicated gestures like slaves in a galley or painters all linked to pantographs, and you'll get the sorry picture. Having weavers repeat their same seaming forever, and so on, like having poets repeat their same seeming forever, and so on, leaves us uninspired. Such art advances after a fashion only. Hence, every cliché is destined only to redo itself, like the aggravating school kid whose punishment is to copy out his most recent offense a hundred times during after-school detention. Then the proctor will take up his papers and add them to the other garbage.

I submit that readers who decry poetry at its most peculiar and venturesome have opted for impasse. Peering through a cataract of orthodoxy, no wonder they claim there is nothing unusual on view. Those who hope to scrape adjectives off like burnt parts of the toast, who would sober up besotted nouns and train verbs to become the clean-running engines of clear intention—those who would blank verse, if you will—are losing out on what Stanley Elkin so notoriously celebrated as "the range of the strange." Purging the page of metaphors like suspicious mutagens is as irresponsible, and potentially as fatal to our potential, as clear-cutting a rain forest to build more condos. Who knows what serums and what extensions of common sense we might miss?

Poets in particular realize "Such savor's in this wrenching things awry." So Richard Wilbur puts it in one poem, and puts it comparably but otherwise (for that is what metaphor *and* evolution do) in another when he concludes, "A graceful error may correct the cave." In that latter poem, entitled "Mind," by which he not only means to anatomize intelligence but also to summon us to attention, Wilbur likens the movement of the human imagination to the finesses of a bat in a cavern. But while the bat aptly manages to avoid every bump and obstruction, the poetic impulse is to allow for deflection; moreover, it mandates it. Do not exterminate error, in other words; exploit it gracefully.

A poet may make a virtue out of flying blind. So might a species exceed the confines of its cells.

What I mean is that metaphor is the error that charms us, the misdirection with good PR. When the Romantics celebrated children as natural poets, what they meant was that they make interesting mistakes. A kid can't sleep because the trees in his back yard are demons reaching gnarled fingers out from the underworld: even as his parents coax him back to bed, they extrapolate from his nightmare an artistic career. When college students make diction errors too elusive for their Spell Check programs to catch, we chasten them for their haste. However, when their baby brothers and sisters concoct malapropisms, we find those goofs as dear as the misshapen ashtrays they made for us in camp, and we are as eager to show them off. Let her little boy mangle a fact or a phrase, let him suggest that asteroids must be the fragments of the shells planets break out of when they're born or contend that something can be "taken for granite," and it won't be five minutes before Mom is on the phone alerting the relatives about what Johnny, her genius son, just said. "Somebody called you, Art," my mother told me one afternoon when I came home from first grade. "Everybody calls me Art," I replied. By the end of the day, the whole mah jongg team was in on it. On the other hand, were I to respond that way today, she would say "Don't be smart" and not mention my remark to a soul. Go figure.

No discipline should be so severe that it repudiates mistakes altogether. It is that sort of logic that led some to insist in the middle of the nineteenth century that there was no reason to keep experimenting because there was nothing left for science to discover. It is that sort of logic that now leads some to pronounce the novel dead as the 8-track players gathering dust in their attics. To skeptical representatives of both cultures, I'd say that a little adventitiousness is in order.

As Lewis Thomas advises, the phrase "trial and error" appears to discredit as arbitrary and doomed what is really a successful method. Were it not, researchers would have lost heart several centuries and inventions ago. Happily, their hearts keep beating like bats in a strange cave, still craving, still believing in the breakthrough. It is in this commitment to the usefulness and the beauty of error that scientists and poets, each uniquely crucial, conspire. They take in all who read and rely on them as well, reaching out hands, surpassing understanding.

Join us.

My Animal Instincts

It was a palpable relief even to the most stolid
to see this savage animal thrashing about in the
cage that had been bleakly lifeless for so long. He
lacked nothing . . . even freedom he did not appear to miss; that noble body, endowed almost to
bursting-point with all it required, seemed to carry
its very freedom around with it—somewhere in
the teeth, apparently, and sheer delight at being
alive made such a torch of the beast's breath that
the spectators had difficulty in holding their
ground against it. With a conscious effort, however, they crowded round the cage and, once there,
would not budge.

—-"A Hunger Artist," by Franz Kafka

Let's talk credentials. To paraphrase Stanley Elkin, another incurable urbanite, I am not by Nature by nature.
I was raised like something engineered in a research
lab, a one-kid control group sealed off from interfering
elements. In summer my mother would slather me in
emollients that kept me safe from the treacheries of the
sun and amphibian-slick; in winter she layered me in
enough insulation to make a member of the Peary expedition sweat. My entire childhood was conditioned

314

by central heating and air to refute the extremes of the seasons; if the vicissitudes of temperature triggered the system during the night and awakened me, I counted on the view of the radiant towers of the WEAW radio station to comfort me. Not until I entered my thirties did I live out of eyeshot of neon altogether. In fact, the first apartment complex I lived in after leaving home was no more than two hundred yards from the cloverleaf, and it was indistinguishable from the motels that barnacled the ramps to and from the interstate. The insistent murmur of a refrigeration truck put me to sleep like a mother brontosaurus lulling her young.

What else? I have never ridden a horse, never eaten anything taken directly from a tree, never hunted or fished, never slept outside—you'll find me camping closer to Woody Allen than to Walden Pond and contending that any deity determined to inflict mosquitoes and ticks on Creation is dubious at best—and never owned a pet. As for the goldfish I won at a carnival by landing a ping pong ball in a cup, which they presented to me in the kind of carton typically used for leftover Chinese food and which, like leftover Chinese food, almost didn't last the trip home, the goldfish which had barely taken up residence on top of my dresser before expiring and therefore never had a chance to grow dear, I don't count it.

Like the rest of my Disney-infected, Lassie-besotted friends, I often petitioned my parents for a pet, prefacing my request with my willingness to compromise over its size and species. If not something conventionally huggable because it would whine to be walked or soil

315

the rug, I'd settle for a salamander, I said. I'd whittle my desire down to the size of a live-in lizard or fish if necessary. I'd room with a guinea pig and be content. I'd confine myself to a box turtle. Give me fish, flesh, or fowl, and I'd commend all summer long. What son worth any salt at all didn't deserve a gerbil? But it never came to pass. "The whole point of having a home is to keep animals *out*," my father would argue. "We pay the exterminator to get rid of termites, ants, and silverfish, and you want to bring a *dog* in here? What are you thinking? Bad enough we share walls with the neighbors. Bad enough that somehow that Bobby Greene kid gets in here, and you're talking about a *pet* now?" I admit that it did seem pretty arbitrary of me when he put it that way. Dad was big-city born and bred. (He came from Chicago and stayed there, and while he accepted New York as a legitimate place to live, he dismissed places like Denver and Phoenix as "towns.") Dad craved his urban fix every day: he trafficked in traffic and needed a regular dose of kosher deli the way some men needed dialysis treatments. His philosophy was that, along with fresh coffee and the Sunday paper, being separate from the beasts was what separates us from the beasts. So no dog.

In short, for better or worse, my childhood acquaintances were pretty much exclusively human. We covered the country in elementary school—when our reading primers had us "See Dick and Jane feed the horse," I saw them, their husbandry rudimentary and writ large—but I never came any closer than that. You can forget farms. Yes, Illinois was full of them, but that was another country far from Chicago. Years later, at the Illinois State Fair, my brother-in-law slipped one of the contending farmers twenty bucks to let me milk one of his cows. The episode proved no less intimate, unnerving, and ultimately humiliating than if he had bought me a prostitute for the evening. In any event, I have not had any occasion to repeat it.

So when it comes to contact with animals, allergies, landlords, and an exaggerated fear of rabies have in my experience conspired to keep them at a safe and mostly hypothetical distance. Oh, I, too, was weaned on nature programs that combed and curried the wilderness in such a way that its photogenic denizens seemed personable and cute. I happily fastened on the mice that gave Cinderella daily consolation and provided their shrill compassion and earnest tailoring skills until her fairy godmother took over the fable. I watched as rapturously as any kid could the way woodland emissaries wafted Snow White toward domestic employment with the dwarfs, even going so far as to help her complete her chores. Long before I was confronted by the spiritual advertising of Romantic poetry, I was a sucker for the purported sympathy between man and the rest of the animal kingdom. Then I grew up, of course.

☙

Even the local newspaper called her "Cat Woman," unable to resist joining in the joke. Her modus operandi was to check out the classified section of the paper for notices about stray cats and lay claim to every single one of them. "I'm calling about the calico you found? Yes, that's my Mr. Duffy. I've been so worried about him. Can I come by to pick him up?" And a dead ringer for Dickens's Miss Haversham would arrive at the unwary Samaritan's door, looking kindly, harmless and erratic. (Her criminal history had been scored into her hands and cheeks by recalcitrant cats, but only in retrospect did anyone read the signs.) I cannot recall what finally alerted the police to her scheme, but when they broke in on her they found dozens of cats in various states of malnutrition and disrepair. Dehydrated and dying cats, injured and ratty cats, rheumatic, infested, and frothing cats, cats with torn paws, open sores, and broken teeth. A photograph showed a soiled, paper-strewn chamber on the order of Dr. Caligari's cabinet, where for nearly five years she had visited ambiguous endearments or dastardliness upon them. It took a team of police to confiscate the remains of the living and the dead. As one officer confided, "The place was like a sewer. Freaky. All that lace and shit."

Evidently there's an epidemic of this sort of thing, sufficient to warrant investigations of pathologies and syndromes. "Perhaps the most prominent feature of these individuals is that pets (and other possessions) become central to the hoarder's core identity," explains veterinarian Gary Patronek, writing on behalf of the Hoarding of Animals Research Consortium (HARC). "The hoarder develops a strong need for control, and just the thought of losing an animal can produce an intense grief-like reaction. Preliminary HARC interviews also reveal that hoarders grew up in chaotic households, with inconsistent parenting, in which animals may have been the only stable feature." And so they determine to rescue as many creatures as possible from a negligent, unwholesome society and bestow upon them the benefits of witless innocence and incontinent love. Some are trying to recapture and consecrate a vision of childhood or to reify in their basements a private version of Edward Hicks's *Peaceable Kingdom,* where sublime lions cuddle up to beatified lambs, where predators and prey sit placidly for the class portrait. Some are just lonely and find people too complicated and severe a challenge.

Our Cat Woman made her kitties clothing out of paper and tinfoil and read to them from the Bible.

What surprised me was not that this particular dysfunction had manifested in my neighborhood but that so many folks felt threatened by it. There are more people than you might think who subscribe to a kind of unified field theory, whereby everything animate belongs to the same paradisiacal country club. For several days after the woman's arrest, the editorial pages were littered with references to "feline felonies" and "cat burglars." People vowed never to take their pets for granted and urged readers to do the same. There but for the grace of God go Bootsie and Tipper, they maintained, and they clutched their cats a bit closer than before, which clawed and complained because all they knew of human devotion was how much it chafed.

Quite frankly, this shouldn't have struck me as news. Even Sylvia Plath succumbed to the odd moment of sentimentality. "Your clear eye is the one absolutely beautiful thing," she wrote of a child, and by referring to animals she managed to sustain the romance for two more lines, anyway: "I want to fill it with color and ducks, / The zoo of the new." A desperate, distracted mother, Plath, but a mother nonetheless: in between her rants about being assailed by bastards and her suicidal bouts, she undoubtedly shopped for toddler clothes. Sylvia knew as well as any other suburban mom that when it came to acceptable fashion, she would admit no vengeful phoenix to the wardrobe—only chicks, bear cubs, smiling dinos and ducks and such would do. Thus were all of us swaddled with waddlers in buttery colors: yellow like Wordsworth's symbol-rich daffodils or blue like a dream of sky.

Ultimately, though, I was drawn to forests where darker fascinations awaited. Ovid's animals especially captivated me, maybe because the fell propensities that manifested in *Metamorphoses* coincided with the un-leashed animals I shied away from in the alley. Zeus alone provided plenty of evidence that it would be wisest to give unfamiliar animals a wide berth. To go wolfing among mortal women, he violated lower spe-cies first. Look what happened to Europa one myth-driven afternoon when she fell for his bull; see what became of Leda when he ambushed her while sporting swan's down and godly prerogative. Conceivably I had been primed for prejudice by all of those comic book characters who had been bitten, embodied, or other-wise infiltrated by animals and thereby hybridized into Batman, Hawkman, Antman, Spiderman, and so on. (The cities of Marvel and Dell were rife with such spec-tacular conjunctions, the fantastic and awful results of miscarriages of nature. Ordinary men and women cowered and took what refuge they could.) And so I learned to withdraw from incurring squirrels, refraining from staking a claim to my own property. I learned to avoid any dog and did not wait for it to consult the library of odors stored in its snout like a judge considering precedents before passing sentence (for I knew that every dog, even if I happened to know it by name, was strange). I continue to keep my hands back from inquisitive pets although their owners assure me they've only come to lap, to recoil from hummers before they strafe, and, indeed, to look away from any animal that looks at me, just as any sane person would avert his eyes from a thug on the subway. (Some pet peeves are literal and as tenacious as the critters they target.) And when I chance upon a doorway adorned with a deer's head or a den festooned with assorted slabs of animals, I overlook aesthetic issues and choose to assume that they were struck down in self-defense.

ℸ

As far as I can determine, the animals are none the worse for my evasions. Indifferent and uninsultable, they persevere. Bugs are busier than probationary faculty trying to enrich their resumes. A colloquium of crows is loudly brokering deals. Their eyes never meet our eyes; they look at us no other way but askance, if at all. When I witness a badger's principled indignation toward a cameraman, the hair-trigger nastiness of the goose that wanders from the pond to crap on an adjacent lawn, the otherwise dumpy possum's opulent disdain for my approaching Honda—I'd wager that even a Buick Regal wouldn't budge it from its course—I cannot help but admire how each finds everything about us, including our admiration, irrelevant. Like rock stars they bunch their furs and turn tail; with a flash of feathers they duck into the wings. Like bluestockings they turn up their moist and mucky snouts.

J. D. Salinger's Teddy, that prodigy of equanimity, said that he was impatient with poets because they took Nature so personally. But it's harmless arrogance on our part, I suppose, to suspect that a vendetta lies behind the snowstorm that grounds our flight to Florida or to watch the moon bobbing up out of a slosh of clouds and deem it a positive review of our sexual prospects. It is good fun to wonder if the latest lightning flash can be read as Nature's EKG. However, when we predicate stock purchases and surgical procedures on which way a gust of wind takes a given bird, we have taken the game too far, and what Robert Frost calls "sunset raving" gets us into trouble. "You've capitalized your Self enough," warns Howard Nemerov, when you assume that a flock of swallows are inscribing the sky with messages in invisible ink. How ridiculous to cry "Why me?" at Nature as if we more than half-expected a response on the order of "Oh, was that *you?* Sorry about that."

Unlike Teddy, however, I am very fond of poetry and, therefore, rather more forgiving of its tendency to rifle through every tide pool, nest, and burrow for directions as if the world were one everlasting scavenger hunt. Take up any anthology and you'll find it overrun with animals. Because they are slightly more sentient than the rest of their surroundings, we may ask animals to translate all that's mute and numb in Nature. For centuries, poets have been paying calls upon and interrogating animals, carrying their uncertainties and sorrows to their lairs, consulting them in their secluded offices, molesting them in their beds. Teddy is right: it's more than a little embarrassing, really.

That is why I prefer poetry that grants animals their distance, treating it as proof of their dignity. Give me creatures that do not give themselves up to me, that refuse to communicate but hold their sundry tongues until a prospective meal makes an appearance. Anyone who's ever seen a cheetah tackle its dinner on the dead run knows that concern for our congratulations never affects its stride. I have come upon a flattened rabbit at the curb, its blood rusted nearly solid, its viscera caked and brittle with the late November cold, and saw how its remnants of belly were worming with organisms wild for protein. I was enraptured by the dedicated vermin and the rabbit's ruins, but I did not mistake the scene as something performed for my benefit. I have been impressed by the industry of flies and grubs at work within some slowly imploding carcass, reminding me of nothing so much as stagehands striking a set. But the most impressive thing about it was how they brooked no interruption, much less bothered to break down the procedure for me.

One might as well trouble termites for their autographs or interview a virus. These creatures, caught up in Nature's daisy chain of appetite, give up nothing.

As I look through the poetry in my students' rental texts, I notice that Walt Whitman takes hiatus from his *Song of Myself* to envy the otherness of animals: "I think I could turn and live with animals, they are so placid and self-contain'd, / I stand and look at them long and long." I discover Elizabeth Bishop's "battered and venerable / and homely" fish, which does not return the speaker's insistent gaze; Richard Wilbur's accidentally mowed-down toad, whose eyes are likewise averted and unavailable to human interest; Philip Levine's defiant pig, scorning whoever is about to slaughter it, begging nothing from him but promising to assault him with its stench; Katha Pollitt's seals, which, "historyless, at peace," visit the dock for trash but never speak to, wonder about, or come for us; and Mary Oliver's seemingly infinite flocks, which ride the air immune to care or rhyme. So many recent poets seem to share my bias on behalf of the insouciance of animals. That very terminology, for instance, I borrow from Denise Levertov, who encourages us to "Come into Animal Presence" not because animals are eager to receive us but because they do not even answer the door. "What is this joy? That no animal / falters, but knows what it must do?" Take a lesson, Levertov suggests. Animals do not abide by poetic figures any more than today's birds deliberately adopt the postures Audobon arranged their ancestors' corpses in or insects emulate the geometries origami implies. Inherently and forever on the contrary, animals beg to differ, or they would were they beggars and were their supplications ever aimed at *us*.

Then there is Robinson Jeffers, who, when it comes to animals—it almost always does for Jeffers—best loves love unrequited and attentions unreturned. "[I]t is bitter earnestness / That makes beauty," he asserts in "Boats in a Fog," and animals accomplish this motto more effectively than humans do. "[A]ll the arts lose virtue / Against the essential reality / Of creatures going about their business among the equally / Earnest elements of nature." Put aside the corruptive legend of St. Francis, who presumably moved about in his raiment of robins and wrens. The integrity of animals rests in how consistently they do not give a good shit about us. So much for the poet's celebrated fancies. Jeffers' hawks, imbued with wilderness, have no time for temperance, forbearance, or meditation. (Ted Hughes concurs: "There is no sophistry in my body," maintains one imperious representative of the breed. "My manners are tearing off heads.") People are too cerebral, too "communal," to earn a bird's notice, much less its endorsement. For Jeffers, the closest one can come to such excellence is surrender. "To be eaten by that beak and become part of him," he imagines in "Vulture," "to share those wings and those eyes—/What a sublime end of one's body, what an enskyment; what a life after death." Our appreciation carries no weight with carnivores; maybe our carrion can.

In its preoccupation each beast is a living prime number, impenetrable by anything other than itself. From ciliates to sperm whales, the poet ponders, I have heard the animals singing, each to each. I do not think that they will sing to me.

Perhaps no poet appears hungrier for resemblance between man and animal than Galway Kinnell, who prowls after a porcupine for over a hundred lines, inciting no answer from it but boredom. No poet campaigns so grandly to know a creature and so grandly falls short, as is probably most memorably depicted in "The Bear." After picking up the bear's scent, Kinnell's speaker spikes some blubber with a whittled rib, then stalks the bear that swallowed it for days over the frozen landscape, gnashing down a bloody turd for sustenance along the way. When he finally encounters the dying animal, he hacks into it, eats and drinks his fill, then proceeds to "tear him down his whole length / and open him and climb in / and close him up after me, against the wind, / and sleep." He dreams the bear's final dream and torment. But like the very flesh and blood of the bear, the images prove indigestible. The poem closes with the futility of knowing anything beyond the speaker's own obsession, which endures: "the rest of my days I spend / wandering: wondering / what, anyway, / was that sticky infusion, that rank flavor of blood, that poetry, by which I lived?"

I have read that many Native Americans believe in spirit animals. Generally speaking, an animal can inhabit you the way a mouse might enter your house through a crack in the foundation to escape the weather. One thinks of the warrior fortified by a private eagle or wolf, but it could just as well be a less prepossessing animal—a sparrow, say—that finds its way in. In a different sense, the poets I've referred to are possessed by animals as well. (This is the more profound meaning of "animal magnetism.") They may mutilate them or try to coax them out with metaphor ("The better to see you with, my dear"), but it is their failure to achieve intimacy that becomes the subject of their poems. Animals slip the words writers lay out for them like the clumsy, obvious snares they are. What W. S. Merwin says of trees is true of everything else in the forest: "their names have never touched them."

ॐ

In college I met a girl named Penny who routinely pleasured her golden retriever, Gordon, with the side of her leather boot. She would do this in front of company. During a party, while eating her dinner, or as she dragged her joint down to the nub, you might see Penny let Gordon ride her instep into doggy delirium. "Hey, it doesn't cost me anything, and Gordon enjoys it so much," she said. It was the 1960s. The war was on, and no one had any idea what the future held for any of us. You took and offered satisfaction where you could.

Penny was also the first full-fledged vegetarian I'd ever met, and she made no bones about decrying the bones her less sensitive friends stripped and sucked in front of her. Now I customarily argue that only an overdeveloped sensibility could define my chicken salad sandwich as a crime scene. I'd never call a minion service together to mourn a McDonald's Happy Meal or say Kaddish over the patties at Burger King. Why not hold the pickle? Why not eulogize the lettuce? No, being at the top of the food chain has its advantages.

I survey the collateral damage of my appetite with my composure intact. Call me heartless—Penny always did—but neither the vile realities of the slaughterhouse the cows come home to nor the scandalous conditions in the coop, where the sleep-deprived are wedged tighter than in any tenement, have ever trumped my stomach. Hey, do you mind? I'm trying to eat here! Let the black ops that do my dinners in stay dark.

And yet, neither of our attitudes handles all of the facts. On the one hand, a dozen or so species are secretly expiring each year; they flicker and go out like bulbs gone bad in the basement. On the other hand, there are pests now feeding eagerly on toxins that laid waste to preceding generations and super-resistant bacteria mounting unseen insurrections in body cavities all over the earth. If we cannot nurse enough silver back gorillas back to prosperity or pander to pandas to make them reproduce, neither can we manage to alter the environment by mistake or design so that it proves unconducive to the cockroach. The situation is just too complex for dogmatism to cover.

In any event, as I write, the woman in my life is a vegetarian. We compromise: she doesn't recruit or proselytize, and when I must eat meat, I do it discreetly and leave nothing from the butcher in her fridge. Also, as it happens, she is an avid bird watcher. Although I am barely conversant when it comes to their names and distinguishing features, I occasionally join her, binoculars at the ready. It takes practice, seeing even after several minutes' surveillance what she is immediately able to see. Actually, I enjoy her enjoyment more than I do the activity for its own sake, but that doesn't dampen the pleasure for either of us. When you're in love, that's only natural.

At night, her cat, drawn by the sounds of our love's diminuendo or just by a fundamental desire to snuggle, will launch itself onto the bed to be with us. She winds herself like a spring in a clock and begins to settle in, her tiny motor idling. I have my own agenda, obviously, but here, too, compromise is key: instead of forcing her into solitary confinement, I gently tent the blanket so that she slides toward the foot of the bed, but no further. It is a cozy little humane society we've established. "Stay," I tell her, and, amazing me, she does.

Something Like a Particle,
Something Like a Wave

We need a word for it. Something long, ungainly, and difficult to pronounce, befitting a newly christened phobia. Some fresh term is definitely called for, intricate and delicate as the bones within the ear it is intended for. Something negotiated, something German, I think, in the schizophrenic style of *schadenfreude.* (Leave it to the Germans to link incompatibilities like boys and girls forced to dance together at a wedding.) Something at once user-friendly and abstruse, more kindly than science yet retaining the distinction of the task force it came from, the stature of the lab.

I am talking about the paradoxical fear that one's children will not resemble him and that they will. I mean the fear that he'll find no gesture or inflection that echoes him, no coloring, cleft, or curve to complement his coloring, clefts, and curves, coupled with the fear that his own worst propensities will come to the fore when he least expects them, like piranhas shattering the water's surface or maddened bees bursting from the hive. The fear, I mean, that his children will never take his meaning, and that he will involuntarily demean them in everything they ever undertake.

For instance, the day my eight-year-old daughter asked me whether we were rich or poor, I did not think to redirect the question against her teacher's insistence on antonyms. At least, I did not think to do so immediately. Earlier that year, as we reviewed her performance on a language arts quiz, I had suggested that a more accurate antonym for "fat" than "thin" was "fit," in that both fat and thin, as indications of poor physical condition, belonged on the same side of the health ledger, and both were opposed by "fit." "And for that matter, Lizzie, what's the opposite of blue? Since it is one of three primary colors, red and yellow are both adjacent to it, but neither is really opposite."

It is a game we play in my family, answering a question with a better question, stirring in another spice instead of straining the offending ingredient from the stew. Even "ambivalence" doesn't exactly describe the situation because the word suggests that we have come down to the final two. As I prod my daughter, so my parents prodded my brother and me. (I have a terrible memory: I remember everything. In this, I am like my parents, and theirs.) Saltzmans seem to take such perverse pleasure in protracting the issue, in watching their brood brood, that nothing can account for it but love.

What a fidgety reflex to inflict on a little kid. But simple division—true and false, right and wrong, fat and thin, parent and child—doesn't hold up over the long haul.

I had been similarly flummoxed by fill-in-the-blank fussbudgets when I was in grade school. "Which of these things does not belong with the other three?" posed Miss Ogren, showing us "fiddle," "trumpet," "table," and "clarinet." In retrospect, she was obviously after "table," its eligibility scotched because it was not an instrument, not properly. But I was too young for retrospect and couldn't know that not even age would ever bring obviousness into my direct line of sight. Even as early as third grade I needed an essay to explain why "fiddle," "trumpet," and "table" could team up while "clarinet," the sole three-syllable word in the group, got benched. Then again, a trumpet was the only item not made of wood, so that the fiddle, clarinet, and table could reminisce about the respective trees they'd been recruited from, but the trumpet would naturally have to keep to the officers' club and consort with the rest of the brass. Taking another tack, how could "fiddle" smuggle its way past the customs that "trumpet," "table," and "clarinet" moved smoothly through when authentic passports had to carry a "t"? Ultimately, I could not intuit the essential trio from the greater audition nor isolate the inherent solo act from the noise.

Yes, I was dealing with the same Miss Ogren who daily pulled down the map of the United States to direct us in directions: "North is toward the ceiling, south is toward the floor, west is out the window, east is out the door." And so Canadians resided in the continent's attic—America's insulation, as it were—while Mexicans busied themselves beneath our feet. Which was fine, unless we left the classroom. And how am I supposed to find my way around outside your perimeter, Miss Ogren? Where are directions then?

Actually, getting back to the orchestra, the conventional answer to which items would play had occurred to me, but I'd dismissed "table" in favor of "trumpet," my contention being that a beaten table was somewhat more like a percussion instrument than any trumpet I'd encountered was like wood. And I probably did contend, seeing as I was already the sort of person who never dispatched a response without its portfolio. I may even have gone so far as to drum my desk for emphasis. Yes, I recall being rascal enough for that. My grade card said as much: "Art is an alert, capable student, and in general he is a pleasure to have in class. However, he does not take criticism well."

In telling my daughter about this incident, I had meant to ally myself with her, to demonstrate that in her aloneness she was not alone. From her perspective, however, I was indicating just how deeply rooted was her exclusion from the norm. No kid wants to stand out that way. My congratulating her on her philosophical rigor wouldn't get her befriended on the playground. It is said that while his classmates sat apart from him in the lunchroom, Socrates drank his fateful draught alone.

Small comfort for her to be told that her manner paralleled mine in so many particulars that she might have been a metaphor for me. (Each of us is a restless tenor tied to a moving vehicle, daisy-chained all the way back to the core of our origins. Each of us is a figure of species, a foregone conclusion.) Small comfort to realize that the ego can improvise only so far and to hear that she was part and particle of her father. Yet my impulse was and remains to reach back a hand for her, the way (love descending to crush depth) Orpheus groped for his bedeviled darling or, more simply, the way any dad naturally asks his child to latch on as they launch into traffic. It is a gesture so natural, in fact, that he'll continue to do so long after she's too old to take it. It is the fidelity of futures going down together.

Forget the premise upon which every guide to parenting is built. For better or worse, we are always too late to stir the batter of personality before it hardens, for better or worse.

⌘

There is always something on the boil in my little girl's mind. Today it's money.

For the longest time, time was for her the only currency needed to obtain what she desired. A special doll or device might be hers if she could wait until her birthday came or my paycheck cleared. Gifts eventuated; the method of their translation from the store's shelf to her hands was utterly obscure and held no interest anyway. But as adolescence loomed closer, she began to appreciate the rudiments of transaction. Things *cost*, in other words. Her clothes, her food, her toys, and even she herself were, in every sense of the word and in ways she was just starting to realize, dear.

Plenty of parents complain of the avariciousness of their kids, of course, whose addiction to getting and spending precedes, and in most cases outstrips, the threat of any other drug. Blaming television, consumer culture, or the permissiveness of other parents in the neighborhood, they clamp down as best they can. But the opposite condition afflicts my daughter, or nearly the opposite, or a possible opposite, given the slipperiness of opposition. If anything, she has an overdeveloped sense of our expenses. At age six she was already a prodigy of thrift, who realized that one couldn't reliably infer that one's money wouldn't give out before the supply of checks did and that credit cards were a ruse, too. And even younger than that, didn't she refuse to remove the tags from the ears of her Beanie Babies as if she'd intuited that unrestricted intimacy might depreciate its object?

Other parents are amazed when I describe her checking the price tags, mulling ruefully over a limited budget she has only limited understanding of. Call it guilt that keeps eating away at the cravings her friends exercise freely. "Can we afford it, Daddy?" she asks in the garish center of Toys R Us, and the way court society marveled at tiny Mozart playing pieces he must have composed in the crib, brisk employees and hyperventilating moms stop to marvel at my girl.

But I was hardly different, like Lizzie a savant when it came to the family savings account. I remember how when I asked my mother about money—I might have been four—you'd have thought, by the way she winced and prickled, that the question had caught in her collar. I had interrupted her while she was kneading raw eggs into a bowl of hamburger, an activity that in itself might have clued a keener observer of socio-economics than I into our status. "Are we rich or poor?" Possibly I had just left a friend's house where I'd caught the scent of a standard of living significantly different from ours. In *The Great Gatsby,* Fitzgerald has Nick Carraway comment on the sound of money in Daisy Buchanan's voice, but class distinctions could just as readily enter through the nose: the antiseptic air of privilege or poverty's stink.

In any event, when I brought the matter up to Mom, she twisted in the kitchen chair and, letting the dinner she was concocting drop back into the bowl, explained, "Well, we aren't rich, that's for sure. We're not poor—I'm not saying that—we're not poor by any means, but we're not rich. We get along well enough, don't you think? You've never wanted for anything, not for anything you really need, have you? Your father works hard, but we get by. We're fine. Not rich and not poor. Normal, you might say. Yes, we're just normal. Why do you ask?"

Dad, meanwhile, was unequivocal about money. Money was the necessity you never talked about. You might risk whispering about an uncle's cancer or, assuming that the children were preoccupied with television, collude over rumors regarding an adultery brewing at the office, but money was never to be mentioned under any circumstances. If at a restaurant my brother or I ever asked about the bill, Dad would say, "Are you paying it?"

"No."

"So it's not your business, is it?"

For that sweet reprieve remembered such wealth brings that then I scorn to change my state with kings. Back then I could afford to be romantic and baffled about finances, which affected me but were not mine. And I tell my daughter much the same thing today when she asks, combining Mom's vacillations with Dad's dismissal.

In truth, I am not much more sophisticated now about money matters than I was when I petitioned my parents decades ago. Stocks, bonds, treasury bills, certificates of deposit, annuities all blear; they represent dire prospects, looming and obscure, like a family history of diabetes. Questions of capital have always seemed to me upper case and out of reach. As for my financial statement, I use the phrase merely to declare whether or not I have to borrow a couple of bucks for lunch, while the only market news I pay much attention to is which store doubles coupons on Wednesdays.

If you know me at all, you know that it's a better bet I'd be enchanted by the inimitable glint of a fresh penny, which is the color of nothing else in nature or the National Mint, or that I'm likelier to be hypnotized by the milling on a dime, than dependably diagnose any more substantial investment. Certainly, I'm father enough to spare my daughter this confession when she asks about money. Being dreamy may be winning in a kid, but it is self-indulgent and embarrassing in an adult. I find it one more wonder that the whole world doesn't wonder more, and I admit that it's sweet to see it when my daughter does. But while I'm touched to discover that she worries the way I worried when I was young and deem it a virtue that she does, I also hope she'll pick up the accounting class one day that I never did.

૪

The trick is to find the flaw inside the diamond and, trickier and deeper still, to find the diamond that lies inside of that.

I am the sort of person who wakes up subdued and always have. Whether I'm responding to some barometric slump that others are not so keenly attuned to, or whether the sadness is my own secretion, I cannot say for sure, and my sense of its source alters from time to time. Suffice to say that although I enjoy myself, albeit less often and more discreetly than the next guy purports to, and although I practice strategies for kickstarting my endorphins when they grow sluggish, the only thing that prevents my depression from being ranked as "clinical" is my refusal to see a psychiatrist regularly enough to certify me so. Over the forty-odd years I've understood that I have lived with variations on the definition ranging from unspecific ("There's something about Art. Something . . . well, quiet about him") to glib ("Yeah, he's probably depressed, as usual") to cynical ("Nothing that fresh air or regular sex wouldn't solve"), I've come to realize that my brand of depression is a fundamental quality, something on the order of the yellow flecks in my blue eyes or my allergy to cats. After a childhood spent avoiding carnivals, birthday parties and other typical summonses to fun because I didn't know how to seize the day's allotment of glee the

338

way other kids did, I have learned how to compensate. With the help of patient friends and steadily improving pharmaceuticals, I have learned how to make the best of the worst of it.

Rules of heredity to the contrary, my daughter seems to have been spared. I do not kid myself that she does not occasionally stumble into gloom or that she inhabits some kind of intrinsic San Diego of unwaveringly balmy inner weather. In the end there are no antonyms that convince either one of us: she is not the opposite of me.

Nevertheless, there is a lightness about her I admire all the more because I cannot emulate it and never offered an example of it for her to follow. She is up for things, with an eagerness for adventure, a flair for flair. She has her moods—or, more precisely, mine—but her moods are not the identifying marks they are for me. Indeed, meeting us together, people have told me that it is hard to believe that she is my daughter. (One of these things doesn't belong with the other, they mean.) They mean it as praise, which is just the way I take it.

Experts in genetics appreciate how species descend and evolve by means of massive trial and error. We repeat our ancestors' inherencies, but with a difference. Our scheming genes notwithstanding, we also depart from the very DNA we carry on. (It is more complicated than that, no doubt, but science was never my strong suit. My daughter, likewise, struggles more with left-brained disciplines than with right.) So it should be no surprise to see my daughter strobe as she seems to do before my eyes. She is at once my analogy and my annulment, my complement and contradiction: my child, in other words, and in these words as well. I watch her play, puzzle, and operate, conspicuously herself. She is rich and poor at once, and precious in both aspects.

In his will a man asks to have his ashes spread over a place where he found fortune or favor. Thus we pretend to enforce in death desire we could not direct or exhaust in life. Thus our longing leaves a stain. Thus, as ever, we sully what we love.

A love for which there is no opposite.

In So Many Words

They keep on / arriving, / wanting names, / wanting // happiness.
—Jorie Graham, "At Luca Signorelli's
Resurrection of the Body"

Gnaw for a moment on this old chestnut. Assuming that a malicious fate were to deposit you and one book intact on a deserted island, what book would you want to rely on to tide you over? You may decide to take refuge in whimsy. Strand me with a boat builder's manual, you might say, or beach me with the *O.E.D.,* since in theory it contains all other books within it, at least some of which you'd have ample time to sort out. But allow me to suggest that in the unlikely event that you find your holdings abridged to a single volume, you could do far worse than opt for the *Ultimate Visual Dictionary.* A peerless compendium of butterflied items, featuring more exploded views than you'll find in the politburo, the *Ultimate Visual Dictionary* pierces atoms and parses planets, vets the molecular structure of cathedrals, carnivores, and car engines, unknits and acknowledges dinosaur skulls, fountain pens, musical instruments, and muscle groups, and girds with words

341

all things esoteric and everyday under the sun, as well as the elemental ensemble of the sun itself.

What a lexical smorgasbord this book lays before us! What a roll call, repast, and hoard! Here are revealed the racecar's diffuser, the mullions separating panes of a Gothic window, the ligature affixed to the mouthpiece of a tenor saxophone, the pallets hooking the pendulum of a mechanical clock, the critical intersection of parrel and jeer on the main mast of a sixteenth-century warship, the Mohorovic discontinuity between the earth's mantle and crust, the medulla at the center of a cross-section of hair. And pretty much any other stuff you might wish to name but can't remember how to.

Would you live deliberately as Thoreau proposed to do? Then you'll need to turn to the right words to deliberate on. Would-be writers would be well advised that, stymied by the blank page, they might unblock themselves by steeping in esoteric dictions. Wax empirical, in other words. Go angling in a given argot for a while—dip into metallurgy, printmaking, carpentry, entomology, skydiving, beer brewing, embalming, or golf—and learn how people dedicated to those concerns do what they do and what words they use while doing them. No plumber reaches for the whatchamacallit; no cobbler calls for the thingamajig; no surgeon in mid-operation relies on a doohickey to save his patient. Nor should we settle for the nebulous if we can help it. The *Ultimate Visual Dictionary* conveniently accommodates this belief by simultaneously honoring and organizing the sprawl.

In So Many Words

On one of his infamous adventures in Swift's novel, Gulliver met the academicians of Lagado, who, frustrated by the elusiveness of language, schlepped all their nouns around in a perpetual, roving context. As a result, they never had to allude beyond arm's length. Then there was the tenth-century grand vizier of Persia, Abdul Kassem, who traveled with his entire library strapped to the backs of camels. When struck with a sudden research question, he would command a runner to rush through the alphabetically ordered caravan to consult the appropriate camel's cargo, then hustle back through the hot sands with the required citation. My suggestion is that outside of fantastic voyages or a pharaoh's resources, the *Ultimate Visual Dictionary* is as close as you are likely to come to satisfying the desire to keep things on hand.

༄

Imagine playing Boswell to Adam. Imagine being amanuensis to his impulsive nominations. Passing wordless herds of animal and all manner of pre-designated matter, you listen to him affix the fateful fricatives and gutturals. He imbeds them with utterances, dubs them with the syllables that are inevitably accurate because Adam deems them so, and you are there. He decants the world into words, instinctively measuring molecules out in apt meanings and amounts, filling bolls, cades, and chaldrons, cloves, fotmals, and gallons, hogsheads, liters, magnums, and nails. He distributes the bushels and quarts, stacks the timbers and quires, parcels out oxgates and roods, pours out the ne-

buchadnezzars and the pipes. Everything cleaves evenly before him like so many quartz crystals; everything
splits cleanly along ideal grains for him to identify. And
you are there, taking all of that newly minted profu-
sion into account. Imagine witnessing the Beginning's
billion signatures upon earth's primordial docket. I
wonder: did Adam have to come up with "portcullis"
before there was even a castle to approach, much less
anything external to Eden yet? Anticipating other cli-
mates, did he invent "sirocco," "cyclone," "tsunami,"
and "simoom" for weather that would one day disrupt
the then-invariable clemency of life on earth? Did we
depend in Genesis on him for prescient coinages for
nose clips, garden hose nozzles, or the guillotine's lu-
nette? What a wonder it must have been for him, and
what a burden, to know we'd eventually need them.

But if the Bible is to be believed, all the enhance-
ments of vocabulary are owed to him. Therefore, ap-
plaud his foresight in stockpiling "intake manifolds"
before there was any engine to take anything in, "food
stamps" millennia before government-sponsored barter had been established, "gunsights" before there was
anything to fire with or upon, much less any reason to
need to. Honor him for "blackjack," "racquetball," and
"colostomy bags"; congratulate him for "escalators,"
"saxophones," "cufflinks," and "condoms"; for "vomit"
and the "missionary position," praise him.

"Is that rude excuse for an animal really a 'rhinoc-
eros'?" you ask Adam. His reply is the same as it always
is: "You'll have to take my word for it."

What a blessing it would have been to watch Adam rectify the environment before there was either insufficiency or sin, not to mention anyone to realize either. In the linguistic vacuum of Paradise, Adam spends days of uninterrupted bliss fashioning perfect attachments, announcing all that's apparent in Eden and everything to come like a butler at the front door of Creation. In his eloquent wake, all things absorb their names the way soil embraces seeds or surfaces take stains. And you are taking it all down, thorough and fastidious, enraptured by the endless particularity of arrival, devising the exhaustive dictionary to cover any actuality and eventuality, the absolute index, sufficient to any vicinity until the shadow of Babel will render it illegible, leading to a diaspora of designation.

Now imagine that after he anoints every evident and prospective noun, he turns his matchless verbal affluence upon you. It is Naming Day in Eden, and Adam is ready to bid your embodiment. He expresses you precisely, cell by cell, much as language itself may be assembled a morpheme at a time. He takes your face in his hands, disclosing your "face" and his "hands" to you, retrofitting your own anonymous visage, conceived in the image of your unnamable Maker, with its "pate" and "follicles," its "glabella," "philtrum," and "jowl." And so you, too, are included in the ritual of pronunciation, fitted with signifiers from sole to crown, endowed with reference, inside and out. Under Adam's gentle jurisdiction you consume a steady diet of consonant clusters like complex carbohydrates in preparation for the long run of the human race. And now you are equipped to go forth, multiplied, and wondering, Did he who named the lamb the "lamb" name thee?

Embraced by language, we can never be entirely abandoned. As in the *Ultimate Visual Dictionary,* so may it be in the Book of Life, where all are vouchsafed and inscribed and, from the largest celestial body to the least component, matter.

Or maybe I have it backward with Adam. Possibly, instead of conferring names upon earth's incipient population, he cajoled them. Plants, animals, and minerals, captivated by the initial glimpse of human enterprise, surrendered their names to him. What if the alphabet had been ubiquitously incubating from the Beginning? Think of the archaeologist brushing clutter and dust away to uncover each fossil—meticulous, loving work—and you might have a feel for Adam's efforts. Better yet, you know the type of person who subscribes to the *New York Times* for the crossword puzzle, then does it in ink? She spreads the paper before her and systematically stitches up the grid like a sewing exercise. She moves sedulously, unflinchingly, from left to right and top to bottom, as though she were not solving a mystery so much as applying an even coat of paint. She will not be defeated by the knotty intersections that do the rest of us in, where, for instance, "River in Upper Volta, *var.*" is joined by "Sanskrit for *sandalwood.*" Whereas even resourceful unpuzzlers must occasionally plug a couple of gaps with best guesses the way wall builders stuff fissures and seams with hearting to resist the weather, she has never known daunt or compromise. That may have been the sort of Adam we're after, in the end, in the Beginning: a champion of determination, the sole, incontrovertible Sherlock deducing in the first burst of universe.

And did Adam intuit a grammar, too, to guide us through our earth's worth of words? And did he foresee what sentences humanity was destined to?

Given the wrathful atmosphere of much of the Old Testament, the procedure may have been more coercive. We may have to consider a grimmer analogy, a harsher scenario, in which every object and entity had to be interrogated like a prisoner of war or like a crime suspect confined to a hard-backed chair and badgered until it squealed. (Soon after the Lord said, "Let there be light," his supreme creature shined it mercilessly in the face of things, pressuring them to name names.) Perhaps Adam had to slap the anteater around a bit before it confessed "anteater" to him; perhaps he had to twist a few twigs of the larch and threaten the fern's family to force "larch" and "fern" out of them. Regardless of all those sentimental manuals for expectant parents suggesting what to name the baby, the method is not for the faint of heart.

But I prefer the more compassionate interpretation, according to which things are inspired to be intelligible. Everything wants to say itself, to announce its essence explicitly, to rise entitled into existence like a fashionable aroma. That would be an Eden to reckon with, with every solid a statement of aims, every hollow a mouth.

☥

Epiphany is solid box office, whatever it may happen to lack in credibility. Is there a skeptic with heart so hard that Cary Grant's realization that Deborah Kerr's legs have deserted her does not make him drop his guard? When Mala Powers's Roxane comes to understand that it's Jose Ferrer's Cyrano who's swayed her, who isn't gratified that the quality of the words he knows and not the quality of the nose he wears wins out? And then there's the sudden culmination of Annie Sullivan's months of effort in *The Miracle Worker,* when the lesson of signification finally breaks through the begrudged capacities of Helen Keller. "W-A-T-E-R: it has a name!" urges Anne Bancroft's Academy Award-winning teacher, as she tries literally to wrestle sense into and out of Patty Duke, her Academy Award-winning charge. When she finally breaks the code—the thrashing fish her teacher makes of her hands in Helen's hands stands for some invisible something she can grasp as well—the girl explodes into a frenzy of exhilarated groping. For the first time, and from now on, she is able to find at her fingertips the miraculous weaving of words and things.

On the other hand, I have noticed that it is possible to undo that tightly woven association. Say any word, like "closet," over and over again, and eventually significance will release its grip, until "closet" holds nothing other than a couple of arbitrary sounds in your ear. I had this experience when reading Robert Pinsky's poem "Shirt" to my class. Ironically, one of Pinsky's motives in this poem is to intensify our sense of the shirt and all the labor, history, sacrifice, and language it comprises. As he partitions our debts, dutifully instructing us to remember the back, the yoke, the yardage, and lapped seams, as well as several possible fabrics and styles, buttons and placket and cuffs, as well as looms, weavers, carders, and spinners, as well as the loader, the docker, the navvy, the sorter, the planter, and the picker responsible—the whole heritage of "shirt," that is, "shirt's" unsung line of succession—he keeps repeating the word "shirt," making a homely mantra out of it. Shirt. Shirt. Shirt. Shirt. Until the colors run and the pattern fades and all that's sewn melts into air, and there is nothing to the shirt but "shirt," that single, incantatory syllable, an achievement utterly unto itself.

When I walk across campus with my botanist friend, Jackson, it's a more intimate, articulate crossing I enjoy. If I am generally relegated to flashcard nominalism, like a kindergartner seeing any tree, flower, and bird as nothing more definitive than "tree," "flower," and "bird," he is rife and heady with reference. For him, the quad is like a frat house or an Elks' Club lodge, where everyone reaches easily, readily out to greet him. Together we stagger through the yammering surround, one of us relatively deaf to it, the other perpetually divining. Familiarity breeds content, as we walk through what for Jackson is wholly focused nature. While I more or less indifferently endure yesterday's scumbled summer or today's autumnal blur, Jackson moves acutely through nature, with its inventory on our passage from the student union to Hearnes Hall ever-ambushing him. I admit that when it comes to the landscape, I'm a forensic bust and, hence, no suitable companion for Jackson. (The closest I've ever come to successfully applying words to the natural environment was back in day camp, when all of us made name tags out of shards of bark by gluing macaroni letters to them.) Ask me to describe the bird that fled the scene or to pick the last pine we passed out of a line-up, and I'd do the cops no good. But while I slog through a thousand scattered leaves and never once think to say "deciduous," while I ignore the billion blades of grass I've broken on my way to class, he salutes leaves he instantly recognizes by their respective vein clusters or serrations, slows to remark upon a half-dozen differentiated mosses, and welcomes each weed in Latin. No local politico has mastered the habit of calling his constituents by name as consistently as Jackson recognizes the flora. By contrast, with more than half of the semester gone, I have trouble coming up with the names of many of my current students. Basically, Jackson always has a quality of buoyancy about him, as if, like Snow White being wafted toward shelter by friendly woodland creatures, he is escorted like a visiting dignitary by every exposed root, spine, and pedicel. I envy but never dream to emulate his rich, specific harvest.

And this field is by no means the only field I find new words flourishing in. In fact, the verbal traffic seems to be getting thicker all the time. On my way to work I hear an advertisement for Verbal Advantage, a pricey yet (so the earnest announcer confides) indispensable cassette program devoted to muscling up my utterances. "More than ever before, communication skills are the key to success. In today's society, people are judged by the words they use—and by those they don't. Increased fluency means increased influence—at work, at home, at social gatherings, anywhere!" With a single "prevarication," I might earn that promotion I've been fretting over. I might break mountains with "majuscule" or at the very least remove blackheads with "bitumen." Or I might pull out "welkin" at a party and watch women go weak at the knees. And if I act now, I can receive a starter's set of fifty words to try out at no cost or obligation. (I can keep them as a gift, regardless of whether or not I commit to the whole program.)

At my office I fire up the computer, and leading the morning's e-mail is my daily offering from Merriam-Webster, which rakes random gems from English's ocean bed and has already this month gifted me with "swivet," "tocsin," "omnibus," "deasil," "compurgator," "alembic," "omphalos," and "tare." I am teased to eagerness over the eventual next edition of the full dictionary, which promises to arrive fresh from the refinery late next year. Overseeing the latest candidates for admission, Merriam-Webster's editorial commission reminds me of nothing so much as the board of a country club. Who will take the chair vacated by the dearly departed "copasetic"? Will "joystick" be granted membership this time around? Will "schlemiehl" be blackballed again for failing to accommodate the dress code? For that matter, what words will be found defective or obsolete and warehoused elsewhere like parts to bygone cars. ("You need 'hardiment,' you say? Yeah, I think we've got one of those in our Buffalo facility. Figure five to seven days for shipping, then another couple of days for installation. Will that work for you?")

But there's no time to ponder this further, because I have a doctor's appointment. Left to my own meager devices in one of the inner exam rooms, and having exhausted the pleasures of swirling the cylinder of tongue depressors and operating the faucet with my elbows, I perch on the edge of the papered table with *Reader's Digest*, which contends, as it does every month, that It Pays to Increase Your Word Power. (No argument there—I have been remiss about what's good for me, a fact I will reflect on later in the day, along with my doctor's admonishments about my blood pressure and cholesterol levels.)

Then it's off to dinner with my daughter. She is excited because her Girl Scout troop gets to go horseback riding, so long as they all master the rudiments of technique and etiquette. They also have to pass a vocabulary test on the parts of a horse and the components of the English and Western saddles. So together over dessert we pore over an anatomical chart, which looks rather disturbingly like a butcher's guide to dividing up the carcass. Elizabeth is barely over four feet tall, and we discover that even if we confine ourselves this evening to what she'll confront from eye-level on down, she has "fetlock," "coronet," "ergot," "hock," "cannon," and "pastern" to master.

Her instructor will hold her horse to no faster than a canter, befitting a novice rider. This will give her time to survey the pasture, I suppose, and to admire the vegetation that we otherwise miss when we zip past it on the interstate. She may come back to me and describe a particularly arresting flower whose blue petals lie tight to the stem and spike straight up like church spires. And I will have to ask Jackson for clarification and hope that he isn't too disappointed in my inability to live up to the landscape, not to mention the demands of fatherhood.

ᶗ

The poets have been embroidering for centuries. They adorn not only conventional magnificence—ritual dousings of the sun into the dappled, rippling horizon every evening, as well as celebrations of deities and seasons, longings for evanescent lusters and perfect loves, requiems to mark the passage of all manner of monarchs and moods—but also humbler encounters, chance sacraments. Sound reveille at Parnassus, and you'll find nothing in nature that hasn't been upholstered by lyricism to some extent. Not a noun's been scanted, it seems; not an atom passes without a wordy entourage murmuring over it. Even heaven's terra incognito, its sublimely subjunctive estate, has been staked out by figuration.

Nor has poetry avoided the void. After we tag each and every star we have laid our eyes or artificial lenses on, we refute emptiness by scribbling on anything we happen upon in the spaces in between. As for death itself, the evidence is undeniable: poetry abhors a vacuum. Aren't all Shakespearean death throes long-winded by definition? Doesn't Milton's elision of Lycidas take two hundred elaborate lines before we're finally rid of him? Even Beckett's desiccated Malone, who does nothing more than die throughout his story, still has wherewithal enough to keep his wordy-gurdy going all along.

"And the moths, the empty moths, stagger against each other, headless, in a confusion of arcing strips of chitin like peeling varnish, like a jumble of buttresses for cathedral domes, like nothing resembling moths, so that I should hesitate to call them moths, except that I have had some experience with the figure Moth reduced to a nub." So Annie Dillard meditates upon the remains that litter the bathroom floor in her remote house on Puget Sound, and in contemplating so grandly refutes the reduction she sees. Whatever death's dominion, then, it seems to have little say over our saying so. Thus even when we are not, we are not in so many words.

And when we depart this wretched state of linguistic longing and disarray, we may be gathered up into an afterlife where every word that followed our fall from grace will be waiting like family—the Platonic vowels, the beatified blends—to welcome us. There we may recover innocence—there, where pure words abide, and dwell adored.

Acknowledgments

The author gratefully acknowledges the following publications, in which some of the essays in this book originally appeared: *Ascent, Bayou, Black Warrior Review, Fiction International, Gingko Tree Review, Iron Horse Literary Review, Many Mountains Moving, Nebraska Review, Oklahoma Review, Pif Magazine*, and *Southeast Review*.